Serial Killers

Serial Killers

Colin and Damon Wilson

Magpie Books, London

Constable & Robinson Ltd
3 The Lanchesters
162 Fulham Palace Road
London W6 9ER
www.constablerobinson.com

Much of the material in this book was published in the UK in 2006 as
The World's Most Evil Murderers by Magpie Books,
an imprint of Constable & Robinson Ltd.

This edition, with additional material, is published by Magpie Books.

Reprinted 2008

ISBN 978-1-84529-793-0

Printed in the EU

PEFC/16-33-111
CATG-PEFC-052
www.pefc.org

Contents

Gilles de Rais

Gilles de Rais was born in 1404, the eldest son of the Baron of Rais (now known as Retz, in the area bordering Brittany called Machecoul). France at the time of his birth had already suffered greatly in what was later to be called the Hundred Years War with England, but worse was to come.

Gilles was orphaned when he was eleven and was afterwards raised by his maternal grandfather. In that same year the English king, Henry V, unexpectedly won a stunning victory at the Battle of Agincourt. French knights charged a well dug-in English battle line and were cut to pieces by the armour-piercing arrows of the English longbowmen. It seems possible that Gilles' father died in the bloody mud at Agincourt, along with a large proportion of the French military aristocracy.

Accurate autobiographical details about the young Gilles de Rais are hard to come by – biographers being fairly rare in the fifteenth century – but we know that his grandfather found it difficult to marry him off when the time came. This was not because Gilles was in any way ugly – not that that mattered much in aristocratic matchmaking. He was actually quiet striking; sporting a dapper beard so black that people swore that in certain lights it looked blueish. This earned Gilles the nickname 'Bluebeard'.

Gilles' early marital misfortunes were entirely a matter of bad luck. Two potential brides dropped dead before marriage alliances could be cemented, but sudden death was not uncommon in disease-ridden Europe at that time. Certainly there is no suspicion that the then teenaged Gilles had anything to do with the deaths. However, it has been suggested by some that the fairy story 'Bluebeard' – in which the eponymous villain marries repeatedly, only to murder his new wives the night after the honeymoon – might be a confused mixing-up of Gilles' story: the dying fiancées, his striking nickname and his later murders.

The third attempt at marriage proved more fortunate. In 1420, de Rais married a wealthy heiress, Catherine de Thouars, and so became one of the richest men in Europe. That said, the courtship did not go entirely smoothly – Catherine had to be kidnapped at one point in order to get the deal settled. But France was in a very chaotic state at that time – with the English 'Goddamn' armies conquering large swathes of the north – so the bandit matchmaking tactics by Gilles' grandfather were probably seen as not entirely inappropriate.

We first see Gilles acting on his own account when he arranged the release of the captured John VI, Duke of Brittany. He did this with such diplomatic aplomb that the Breton parliament granted the young baron a sizeable monetary reward, thus making him even richer. We can also see from this that, even in his early twenties, Gilles de Rais was evidently a smooth talker and a diplomatic courtier. We next hear of him attending the court of the Dauphin Charles, the heir to the French throne.

Gilles was taking a chance by siding with Charles. The Dauphin was a singularly ineffectual man – disowned as a bastard by his own mother and, despite the death of his 'father', unable to get the military and political backing to get himself crowned King of France. In the early 1420s most sensible money was on Charles' destruction and the total conquest of France by England.

Then something extraordinary happened. In 1428, young woman called Joan of Arc – the daughter of a well-off farmer, *not* a lowly peasant as is so often stated – heard voices in her head that she believed to be the messengers of God. The voices told Joan to go to the Dauphin and declare that Heaven was on his side. Charles, bankrupt and terrified, was willing to try anything, so he sent Joan to 'lead' his armies. In fact, capable generals did most of the actual leading, although Joan did prove to be something of a genius in the use of artillery. She also excelled at rallying the flagging morale of the French armies. With her at their head they started a fight-back that was eventually to hurl the English out of France completely. Joan did not live to see this; she was captured by the Burgundians, sold to the English and then burned as a heretic by the Church in 1431.

Not surprisingly, much has been made of the relationship between Gilles de Rais and Joan of Arc: the savage monster and the saintly virgin. But much of this seems to have been wishful thinking by later chroniclers. De Rais certainly knew Joan, and probably fought alongside her in some battles, but he was not her bodyguard, as some have claimed, or one of her key supporters. In fact de Rais is on record as only commanding twenty-five men-at-arms and eleven archers, so he was hardly one of Joan's generals. Even his military title, '*MarËchal*', was largely an honorary designation and was bestowed by Charles VII, at his coronation, more in thanks for Gilles' financial loans than for his martial prowess. After the coronation, despite the fact that the war was still raging, de Rais retired to his many estates, gadding between castles at Machecoul, Malemort, La Suze, Champtoce and Tiffauges.

He lived with immense extravagance: he kept a bodyguard of two hundred knights, a private chapel, and one of the finest manuscript libraries in Europe. This extravagant expenditure soon ate up his huge fortune and forced him to begin to sell his land. When his relatives (and potential heirs) heard of this they obtained an injunction from King Charles to prevent him selling any more land. This order was ignored in semi-autonomous Brittany, where Bishop Malestroit and Duke John VI were eager to acquire Gilles' lands.

Nevertheless, Gilles was still facing bankruptcy so he turned to alchemy to mend his fortunes, seeking the fabled 'Philosopher's Stone' that could turn all base metals to pure gold. He employed one Gilles de Sille, a priest, to conduct more-or-less scientific researches into the possibility; but when he failed, de Rais became prey to a series of charlatans, ending, in 1439, with a defrocked priest, Francesco Prelati of Florence. It was probably Prelati who turned Gilles from the scientific pursuit of the Philosopher's Stone to black magic and invocation of the Devil using the blood of young children.

Over the next six years de Rais is said to have used his position as a baron to secretly kidnap dozens, perhaps hundreds of children, all of whom he tortured and killed. It seems likely that he originally started as a would-be devil worshiper, but in the light of our knowledge of modern serial killer psychology, we can confidently say that he must have soon become addicted to murder. The sheer numbers of children involved, and the cruel methods said to have been used to murder them, do not point to a man whose only interest was the production of magical gold.

De Rais' downfall began with a minor misdemeanour. He sold his estate at Malemort to the Treasurer of Brittany, Geoffroi le Ferron, but then refused admission to Geoffroi's brother, Jean le Ferron, whom he beat and imprisoned. Jean le Ferron was a priest, and Bishop Malestroit seized on this pretext to try to have Gilles declared to a heretic.

Preliminary hearings began on 28 September 1440, and his accusers were so certain of finding him guilty that some of his lands were actually disposed of before the trial began. He was charged with the abuse of a priest, with conjuring demons, and with sexual perversion involving children. Gilles laughed at these charges and declared them too silly to deny. One of the charges declared that 'spurning the natural way of copulation', Gilles had committed sodomy with young boys and girls . . . and that his victims were sometimes alive, sometimes

4

dead, and sometimes even in their death throes when these perversions were committed.

The formal trial opened on 15 October, 1440. It was alleged that dismembered bodies of about fifty children were found in a tower at Machecoul. De Rais was tortured on 19 October, as were his servants and four alleged accomplices. One servant declared that Gilles rubbed his penis against the thighs and bellies of children and, having achieved orgasm, then took pleasure in seeing their heads cut off or in doing this himself. It was also alleged that he also took great pleasure in watching the death throes of children, sometimes sitting on their chests while they were dying and, on one occasion, torturing and killing one child in front of his brother before doing the same to the other.

His own torture had less effect on Gilles than the threat of excommunication which made him break down completely and 'confess everything'. On 26 October 1440 he was strangled (and his body partly burned) together with two of his associates. No final figure was arrived at for the number of children murdered – estimates range between 80 and 200.

But was Gilles de Rais guilty? He himself was up to his neck in debt at the time of his death, but his remaining lands – that he was forbidden to sell – were still worth a fortune. Did his accusers cook up a set of incredible charges against him, with an eye to taking those estates after his death?

Certainly the Catholic Church had shown itself capable of such behaviour before. In 1307, Pope Clement V connived with King Philip IV of France in the destruction of the Order of the Knights Templar. Whether the Templars were really heretics – and if so, to what extent – remains a matter of heated debate, but few deny that one of the main motivations in the crushing of their order – involving the torture and execution of many of them – was to get hold of their tremendous wealth. Was the same trick used on Gilles de Rais?

The answer is probably no. The Church did not, in fact, get its hands on his properties – and were never very likely to do so. It was the Duke of Brittany, John VI, who actually took possession of all de Rais' estates and chattels, because he was Gilles' liege-lord. John VI, it might also be supposed, could have egged the Church on to make false accusations against de Rais, but this does not seem likely.

John VI was a peaceful man in a violent age – he was widely known as 'John the Sage'. As we have seen, he owed de Rais a debt of gratitude for arranging his release from captivity two decades before, and showed that he had not forgotten this debt when he made great efforts to shield de Rais from early attempts at prosecution. It was only when confronted with considerable evidence and witnesses to support the prosecution claims that he withdrew his protection from de Rais. One would have to believe John was a Machiavellian on a par with Shakespeare's villain Iago, to believe he was actually masterminding a grand plot to destroy his innocent friend.

Tempting as it may be to hope that Gilles de Rais did not actually kill tens or hundreds of children in the most disgusting ways imaginable, on the balance of the evidence we must probably accept that he was not only one of history's earliest recorded serial killers, but was also one of the worst serial killers in history.

Martin Dumollard

One of the oddest cases of 'murder addiction' on record took place in the Lyon area of France in the mid-nineteenth century. In May 1861, an attractive twenty-seven-year-old servant girl named Marie Pichon was accosted by a peasant with a deformed upper lip, who asked her the way to the registry office for servants. When the man learned that Marie was looking for work, he offered her a good job at a country house near Montlul. The girl agreed to accompany him there, and they travelled to Montlul by train.

The peasant, who seemed a stolid but decent sort of man, told her that he was the gardener of a certain Madame Girard, and that another servant who was due to arrive the day before had fallen ill, so that Madame was in urgent need of a replacement. At Montlul, the peasant took her box on his shoulder, and told her they would take a short cut across the fields. As night closed in, he stopped to take a breath, and suggested that they should abandon her trunk until morning. Without waiting for her agreement, he dropped it in a ditch, then he plodded on into the darkness. The girl became increasingly nervous at his odd behaviour, and when they came to a hilltop, and there was still no sign of lights, she declared her unwillingness to go any further.

The man then rounded on her suddenly and threw a noose round her neck. She pushed him and they both fell down. Marie was first on her feet, running into the darkness. She

7

crashed through hedges, scratching herself and tearing her clothes, and frequently fell over. But eventually, the footsteps of her pursuer died away, and she almost collapsed with relief when she came to a house. Its owner, who was still unharnessing his horse after a journey, was startled by this bloodstained apparition, but he let her in, and sent for the local constable.

Then she was taken to the police station, where she repeated her story. In spite of her exhaustion, she was taken back over the route she had traced with the murderous peasant. They eventually found the ditch where the man had dropped her trunk – but it had vanished. The news caused a sensation in the Trevoux district – particularly when it was recollected that Marie Pichon was not the first girl to place her trust in a peasant with a deformed lip.

Six years earlier, in 1855, a servant girl named Josephine Charloty had become suspicious as she plodded across the fields behind the squarely built man who was carrying her trunk, and had finally fled and taken refuge in a farmhouse. Another girl, Victorine Perrin, had simply lost her trunk when the man had run off into the trees.

In all, five girls had escaped alive. But others had vanished and never been seen again. In February 1855, a few months before the escape of Josephine Charloty, hunters had found the battered corpse of a young woman hidden in a thicket; she was naked except for her bloodstained shoes and a piece of ribbon. The body was later identified as that of Marie Buday, who had left Lyon with a 'countryman' a few days before she was found.

Another girl, Marie Curt, had turned down the offer of a job from the man with the twisted lip, but recommended a friend named Olympe Alabert; Olympe had then vanished. Now although the police had been aware that a peasant posing as a gardener was abducting and murdering girls, no one seems to have made a determined effort to find him. (The French police force was still in its infancy.) But the case of Marie Pichon

8

was discussed all over the district. And three men in an inn at nearby Dayneux decided that the peasant with the deformed lip sounded like a local gardener known as Raymund, who lived nearby.

Raymund kept himself to himself, spent a great deal of time in Lyon – where he was supposed to work as a porter – and had a lump on his upper lip. His real name, it seemed, was Martin Dumollard. A local justice of the peace agreed that Dumollard certainly sounded as if he might be the wanted man, and issued a search warrant. This search was conducted by the magistrate himself, and it left no doubt that Dumollard was a major suspect. The house was found to contain many women's garments, and some of them were bloodstained. Dumollard was immediately arrested. He strenuously denied knowing anything about missing women, and went on denying it even when confronted by Marie Pichon herself, who identified him as her attacker.

Meanwhile, Dumollard's wife had decided to save her own neck by confessing. She admitted that her husband had brought home Marie Pichon's box, and that he had burned much of its contents in a wood – obviously concerned that if the police tracked him down the box would conclusively prove his guilt. The investigators went to the spot she indicated, and found buried ashes and fragments of books and clothes, which Marie Pichon identified. Martin Dumollard continued to insist stolidly that he knew nothing about any crimes. But his wife Anne admitted that a woman's watch found in their house had been brought home one night four years earlier, with a quantity of bloodstained clothes. Dumollard had told her he had killed a girl in a wood at Mont Main, and was now going to bury her. He left the house with a spade . . . A careful search of the wood revealed a depression that might be a grave. Two feet below the surface, the diggers found a female skeleton. The skull showed she had died from a violent blow on the head. Dumollard continued to deny all knowledge of the crime. But his wife went on to describe another occasion when he had returned home and told her he had killed a girl. This body was also discovered buried in a wood, the Bois de Communes. The dry earth had preserved the flesh, and the position of the body made it clear that the girl had been buried alive and had suffocated while trying to claw her way out of the grave.

She was identified as Marie Eulalie Bursod. In the seven months that followed, it became clear that Martin Dumollard had killed at least six girls (clothes of ten were found in his home), and had unsuccessfully tried to lure another nine to their deaths. On 20 January 1862, he and his wife were tried at the assizes at Bourg (Ain), and he was found guilty and sentenced to death. Anne Dumollard was sentenced to twenty years imprisonment. He was guillotined on 20 March 1862, and his head sent to be examined by phrenologists, who declared that, according to the shape of his skull, Dumollard should have been a man of the finest character.

Why did Dumollard kill? We do not know whether sex played any part in the crimes. But the notion that he murdered purely for profit seemed unlikely. The possessions of a servant girl would fetch very little money on the second-hand market, and it seems relatively certain that such girls would have very little money. So Dumollard's relative prosperity (his house was larger than that of most peasants) can hardly be explained by his crimes. We know little of Dumollard's background except that his parents were tramps who wandered around Italy, and that his father was a murderer who was broken on the wheel. He was undoubtedly miserly, obsessed by money his last words to his wife were to remind her that someone had failed to repay a debt – and it seems just possible that he killed the girls for their meagre possessions.

But the likeliest explanation is that Dumollard became a 'murder addict', and went on killing because it gave him pleasure to lure girls to their death. He had all the characteristics of the modern 'serial killer'.

10

Jack the Ripper

Early in the morning of 31 August 1888, a carter named George Cross was walking along Bucks Row, Whitechapel – in London's East End – when he saw what he thought was a bundle of tarpaulin lying on the pavement. It proved to be a woman with her skirt above her waist. In the local mortuary, it was discovered that she had been disembowelled.

Mary Ann Nicholls was almost certainly the first victim of the sadistic killer who became known as Jack the Ripper. (He provided himself with the nickname in a series of letters that he wrote to the Central News Agency.) Just over a week later, he killed and disembowelled a prostitute named Annie Chapman in a Whitechapel backyard.

On the morning of 30 September, he was interrupted soon after he had cut the throat of a third victim – a woman called Elizabeth Stride – and immediately went and killed and then disembowelled another woman, Catherine Eddowes.

On the morning of 9 November, he committed his last murder indoors, and spent hours dissecting the body of Mary Kelly by the light of a pile of rags burning in the grate. By this time Londoners were in a state of hysteria, and the chief of police was forced to resign. But the Whitechapel murders were at an end. All theories suggesting that the Ripper was a 'gentleman' – an insane doctor, a cricket-playing lawyer, a member of the royal family – are almost certainly wide of the mark. The kind of frustration that produced the Ripper murders is characteristic of someone who lacks other means of self-expression, someone who is illiterate or only semi-literate.

Such a suspect came to the attention of Daniel Farson after he had directed a television programme about Jack the Ripper. He received a letter (signed G.W.B.) from a seventy-seven-year-old man in Melbourne, Australia, who claimed that his father had confessed to being the Ripper.

> My father was a terrible drunkard and night after night he would come home and kick my mother and us kids about, something cruelly. About the year 1902 I was taught boxing and after feeling proficient to hold my own I threatened my father that if he laid a hand on my mother or brothers I would thrash him. He never did after that, but we lived in the same house and never spoke to each other. Later, I emigrated to Australia . . . and my mother asked me to say goodbye to my father. It was then he told me his foul history and why he did these terrible murders, and advised me to change my name because he would confess before he died.

He goes on to explain: 'He did not know what he was doing but his ambition was to get drunk and [he had] an urge to kill every prostitute that accosted him.' Whether or not G.W.B.'s father – whose job was collecting horse-manure – was Jack the Ripper, he is certainly a far more likely suspect than a member of the educated and professional classes. To us, it seems obvious that Jack the Ripper's murders were sex crimes (for example, the impulse that drove him to seek out another victim when he was interrupted while killing Elizabeth Stride). But it was by no means obvious to the Victorians, who preferred to think in terms of religious mania and 'moral insanity'. Sexual murders were a new phenomenon in the 1880s, and the average Victorian still found it puzzling that anyone should want to kill for the sake of sexual satisfaction.

12

The Whitechapel murders changed all this: they produced a deep disquiet, a morbid thrill of horror that made the name of Jack the Ripper a byword all over the world. It was an - instinctive recognition that some strange and frightening change had taken place. In retrospect, we can see that the Ripper murders were a kind of watershed between the century of Victorian values and the age of violence that was to come.

H. H. Holmes

The Chicago murderer H. H. Holmes – real name Herman Webster Mudgett – has some claim to be America's first serial killer. The son of a postmaster, Holmes became a doctor, then a swindler. After a chequered career as a con man, Mudgett moved to Chicago in 1886 – when he was twenty-six – and became the partner of a certain Mrs Holten, who needed an assistant in her drugstore.

Mrs Holten mysteriously vanished, and Holmes – as he now called himself – took over the store. He did so well that he built himself a large house – it was later to become known as 'Murder Castle' – full of hidden passageways and secret rooms; its innovations included chutes down to the basement, whose purpose – it was later realized – was to facilitate the conveyance of bodies to the furnace.

During the World Fair of 1893, many out-of-town guests who came to stay in Holmes's 'castle' disappeared. So did a whole succession of attractive secretaries and mistresses. Holmes was finally betrayed by the train robber Marion Hedgepeth, whom he had met in jail and promised a share in the loot – from a dishonest insurance scheme – in exchange for an introduction to a crooked lawyer. Holmes failed to keep his part of the bargain; Hedgepeth contacted the insurance company, and revealed that the 'accidental' death of a man called Pitezel was actually murder. Holmes's insurance scheme also included killing off Pitezel's wife and five children to cover his tracks, and by the time the police had caught up with him, three of the children were dead, buried under the floorboards of houses rented by Holmes or incinerated in their stoves. The subsequent investigation revealed that Holmes had committed at least twenty-seven murders. He was hanged in May 1895.

Holmes differs from more recent serial killers in that his motives were partly financial – although it seems clear that an intense sexual obsession also played its part in the murders.

Alfred Packer

Alfred G. Packer was a prospector who claimed to know Colorado as well as any man living. He also claimed to know the location of many gold deposits. Both these claims later proved to be untrue, and cost five men their lives.

In the autumn of 1873 Packer, then in his mid-twenties, led the team of nineteen prospectors from Salt Lake City, Utah, to the San Juan country, loaded down with supplies and equipment. The weeks passed and the weary men saw nothing but barren country, eventually arriving close to the snow-capped peaks.

On the point of starvation, they stumbled across an Indian camp, expecting to be butchered. To their surprise the Indians treated them with great hospitality and fed and looked after them. Learning of their hazardous proposed expedition, the Indian leader, Chief Ouray, succeeded in persuading ten of the party to abandon the futile quest. They returned to Salt Lake City; sadder and wiser and, as it turned out, very lucky men.

The rest promised to pay Packer well to continue as their guide, and so they remained at the Indian camp until they were fully recovered, still determined to hunt for gold. All the Indians could do was to supply them with provisions and advise them to follow the course of the Gunnison River.

Alfred Packer was now the undisputed leader of the expedition. Boasting of his knowledge of the area, he led his companions on by telling them that rich seams of gold had recently been discovered near the source of the Rio Grande

17

River. He claimed to be able to guide the party to the area by a much shorter route. However, four of the party insisted on following the Gunnison River, as recommended by the Indians. Packer led the remaining five men, Israel Swan, Frank Miller, George Noon, Shannon Bell and a man named James Humphrey, on his own route.

Of the four men who followed the Gunnison River, two died of starvation before reaching the Los Pinos Agency in February 1874. General Adams was in command of the agency, and saw to it that the two men were nursed back to full health before beginning their trek back to civilization.

In March 1874, General Adams was absent from the agency on business in Denver when a wild-looking man appeared at the agency, begging for food. His face was hideously bloated, but he was in surprisingly good physical condition, everything considered. He gave his name as Packer and explained that his five companions had deserted him while he was ill, leaving him with only a rifle to shoot wild game to survive. He still carried the rifle.

After a ten-day stay at the agency, Packer left, saying that he intended making his way to his brother's home in Pennsylvania. Along the way he stopped in many bars, drinking heavily, and appeared to be in possession of a considerable quantity of money. The conflicting stories he told in those bars about the fate of his companions led to speculation that he had in fact murdered them.

Word of all this reached General Adams, who decided to have Packer tracked down and arrested. He arranged a meeting between Packer and those men who had abandoned the expedition, and it immediately became apparent that most of Packer's story was untrue. General Adams had Packer tightly fettered and taken back to the agency, where he was kept in solitary confinement.

On 2 April 1874, two Indians arrived at the agency, holding what they claimed were strips of 'white man's meat'. They had found it just outside the agency, where the snow had kept it well preserved. It was in fact human flesh, which Packer must have been carrying, and then dumped when he reached safety.

When Packer was shown the flesh he gave a loud groan of despair and fell to the ground. When he had recovered enough, he made the following statement:

When I and five others left Ouray's camp, we estimated that we had sufficient provisions for the long and arduous journey before us, but our food rapidly disappeared and we were soon on the verge of starvation. We dug roots from the ground upon which we subsisted for some days, but as they were not nutritious and as the extreme cold had driven all animals and birds to shelter, the situation became desperate. Strange looks came into the eyes of each of the party and they all became suspicious of each other. One day I went out to gather wood for the fire and when I returned I found that Mr Swan, the oldest man in the party, had been struck on the head and killed, and the remainder of the party were in the act of cutting up the body preparatory to eating it. His money, amounting to $2,000, was divided among the remainder of the party.

This food only lasted a few days and I suggested that Miller be the next victim, because of the large amount of flesh he carried. His skull was split open with a hatchet as he was in the act of picking up a piece of wood. Humphrey and Noon were the next victims. Bell and I then entered into a solemn compact that as we were the only ones left, we would stand by each other whatever befell, and rather than harm each other we would die of starvation.

One day Bell said: 'I can stand it no longer!' and he rushed at me like a famished tiger, at the same time attempting to strike me with his gun. I parried the blow and killed him with a hatchet. I then cut his flesh into strips which I carried with me as I pursued my journey.

19

When I espied the agency from the top of the hill, I threw away the strips I had left, and I confess I did so reluctantly as I had grown fond of human flesh, especially that portion around the breast.

One thing is certain: Parker never wrote nor dictated this statement word for word. The style is not that of an illiterate prospector, but rather that of a military man.

Packer agreed to guide a party to where he had left the murdered men, but during the night, while sleeping out in the open, he assaulted his guard with intent to murder him and escape, but was overpowered. He was taken back to the agency in fetters and was there handed over to the sheriff.

In June 1874, an artist named Reynolds was out sketching in the wilderness when he came across the bodies of five men. Four of them were lying in a row, and the fifth, minus its head, was lying a short distance away. The bodies of Bell, Swan, Humphrey and Noon had rifle bullet wounds in the back of the skull, and when Miller's head was found, it had been crushed by a blow from a rifle butt.

The find made a complete nonsense of Packer's statement. A path led from the bodies to a nearby hut, where blankets and possessions belonging to the murdered men were found, and it was apparent that Packer had lived in that cabin for many days, making frequent trips to the bodies for his supply of meat. Each body had its breast cut away to the ribs.

The sheriff now obtained a warrant charging Packer with five murders, but in the meantime the prisoner had escaped. He was hunted by the authorities but, showing he had more wilderness skill than might have been guessed from his previous expedition, Packer escaped completely.

On 29 January 1883 – some nine years later – General Adams received a letter posted from Cheyenne, Wyoming, in which a Salt Lake City prospector said he had met Packer face to face in that area, going under the name of John Schwartze. It was believed that he was a member of a gang of outlaws.

General Adams alerted the lawmen in Cheyenne, and on 12 March 1883 Sheriff Sharpless of Laramie County arrested Packer and brought him to Lake City, Colorado, to stand trial.

Packer's trial began on 3 April 1883, when he was charged with the murder of Israel Swan in Hinsdale County on 1 March 1874. The prosecution proved that each of the murdered men had been in possession of considerable sums of money, none of which was found on the mutilated bodies. It seemed a clear case of murder for gain.

Packer, in his defence, claimed that he had only killed Bell, and then in self-defence. He told a story of his companions fighting among themselves and of Bell firing at him. This completely contradicted what he had said in his original statement, and the jury did not believe his new account. On 13 April the jury found Packer guilty of murder, and voted for the death penalty. Packer appealed to the Supreme Court and was granted a stay of execution. Meanwhile, he was being lodged in Gunnison Jail to save him from a lynch mob.

In October 1885 the Supreme Court granted him a new trial, and the prosecution decided this time to try him on five charges of manslaughter. Packer was found guilty of each charge and was sentenced to serve eight years for each offence, making a total of forty years.

Sentencing Packer, Judge Melville Gerry said: 'There were only seven Democrats in Hinsdale County, and you ate five of them, you depraved Republican son of a bitch!' It must have been the most unintentionally comic line ever uttered by a judge at any trial.

Packer served seventeen years at hard labour before being released. He proclaimed his innocence throughout all those years. He died on a ranch near Denver on 24 April 1907, aged sixty-five, having been pardoned on 1 January 1901.

Packer had become famous in those years. A song, 'The Man who Ate Democrats', became very popular, and students at Colorado State University named their dining room after him (with a sign above the door suggesting: 'Have a friend for lunch').

Packer, an unlikely folk hero, has been described, rather romantically, as 'a tall man with long, dark, curling hair, dark moustache and goatee, with deep-set grey eyes'. And gradually, over the years, the belief has grown that Packer was innocent after all.

But the evidence, when studied closely, does not support this. Consider the two stories he gave: the first was that his party rejected the advice of an Indian chief and pushed on through heavy snows. He staggered back some weeks later with his story of the entire party killing off one man after another for food, until only Bell and he were left. Then Bell turned on him and Packer killed him in self-defence. Packer never denied necessity-driven cannibalism.

At his trial, ten years later, he told a different story: that Bell had killed all the others while Packer was away hunting. It is notable that in the first version, Packer admitted being involved with the killings – even nominating the first man to be killed for food. In his second statement he was trying to exonerate himself of everything but the self-defence killing of Bell and the cannibalism.

The main physical evidence against Packer at his trial was that he had seemed too fit when he made it to the fort – the Indian Chief, Ouray, who saw him soon after, commented: 'You too damn fat!'

Packer's case was back in the news in July 1989, when a team of scientists went to search Dead Man's Gulch, scene of the murders, in the hope of locating the remains of the victims. The team used sophisticated radar for this purpose. The leader of the expedition, Professor James Starrs, said that he planned to examine the skeletons to see if all the men had died from bullets fired from Packer's gun.

If they had, then both Packer's stories would fall apart. But if one of the bodies bore bullets from a different gun, then that might support his original and probably more accurate statement: that the party had murdered each other, one by one, for food.

The result of the investigation was conclusive. The jury of thirteen experts who dug up the skeletons agreed with the original jury verdict, issuing a statement that said 'Packer was guilty as sin.'

James Starrs, a professor of law and forensic science at Washington State University, said the bones proved 'beyond a shadow of a doubt' that Packer killed all five men.

'It is as plain as a pikestaff that Packer was the one who was on the attack, not Bell,' said Professor Starrs. Wounds on the bones of three of the victims 'were caused with a hatchet-like instrument at a time when these persons were defending themselves from the attack of an aggressor,' he said. The marks suggested that the victims had raised their arms to ward off the blows.

Professor Starrs and his team of experts on archaeology, anthropology, pathology and firearms said that the angle of blade marks on the bones from which the flesh had been taken, including the bones believed to be Bell's, indicated that the cuts were all made by the same person, a clear sign that the lone survivor, Packer, was the killer.

Noting how much meat must have been taken from the dead men, Professor Starrs said that Packer 'was having his flesh fillets morning noon and night'. The professor described Packer as having been 'base, brutish and barbaric'.

But was Alfred Packer a serial killer? In the strict psychological sense the answer is no. Although he murdered more than three people – the minimum quota, as defined by the FBI – he does not seem to have killed them over a prolonged period, as serial killers do, but in a single frenzied attack. More importantly, he does not appear to have become addicted to murder – the true sign of the serial killer. In the nine years he was on the run he almost certainly turned to outlawry, but even given the opportunities that this way of life must have presented to him, there is no evidence that he ever killed and ate anyone else.

The truth is that Packer, in a life-or-death situation, acted as an utterly ruthless survivor. There is no forensic psychological categorisation for that state of mind, as it might, in similar circumstances, include within it a large part of the general population.

Bela Kiss

In 1916, the Hungarian tax authorities noted that it had been a long time since rates had been paid on a house at 17 Rákóczi Street in the village of Cinkota, ten miles north-west of Budapest. It had been empty for two years, and since it seemed impossible to trace the owner, or the man who rented it, the district court of Pest-Pilis decided to sell it. A black-smith named Istvan Molnar purchased it for a modest sum, and moved in with his wife and family. When tidying up the workshop, Molnar came upon a number of sealed oildrums behind a mess of rusty pipes and corrugated iron. They had been solidly welded, and for a few days the blacksmith left them alone. Then his wife asked him what was in the drums – it might, for example, be petrol – and he settled down to removing the top of one of them with various tools. And when Molnar finally raised the lid, he clutched his stomach and rushed to the garden privy. His wife came in to see what had upset him; when she peered into the drum she screamed and fainted. It contained the naked body of a woman, in a crouching position; the practically airless drum had preserved it like canned meat. Six more drums also proved to contain female corpses.

Most of the women were middle-aged; none had ever been beautiful. And the police soon realized they had no way of identifying them. They did not even know the name of the man who placed them there. The previous tenant had gone off to the war in 1914; he had spent little time in the house, and had kept himself to himself, so nobody knew who he was. The police found it difficult even to get a description. They merely had seven unknown victims of an unknown murderer. Professor Balazs Kenyeres, of the police medical laboratory, was of the opinion that the women had been dead for more than two years. But at least he was able to take fingerprints; by 1916, fingerprinting had percolated even to the highly conservative Austro-Hungarian Empire. However, at this stage, fingerprinting was unhelpful, since it only told them that the women had no criminal records. Some three weeks after the discovery, Detective Geza Bialokurszky was placed in charge of the investigation; he was one of the foremost investigators of the Budapest police. He was, in fact, Sir Geza, for he was a nobleman whose family had lost their estates. Now he settled down to the task of identifying the female corpses. If Professor Kenyeres was correct about time of death – and he might easily have been wrong, since few pathologists are asked to determine the age of a canned corpse – the women must have vanished in 1913 or thereabouts.

The Missing Persons' Bureau provided him with a list of about 400 women who had vanished between 1912 and 1914. Eventually, Bialokurszky narrowed these down to fifteen. But these women seemed to have no traceable relatives. Eventually, Bialokurszky found the last employer of a thirty-six-year-old cook namedAnna Novak, who had left her job abruptly in 1911. Her employer was the widow of a Hussar colonel, and she still had Anna's 'servant's book', a kind of identity card that contained a photograph, personal details, and a list of previous employers, as well as their personal comments. The widow assumed that she had simply found a better job or had got married. She still had the woman's trunk in the attic. This offered Bialokurszky the clue he needed so urgently: a sheet from a newspaper, *Pesti Hirlap,* with an advertisement marked in red pencil: 'Widower urgently seeks acquaintance of mature, warm-hearted spinster or widow to help assuage loneliness mutually. Send photo and details, Poste Restante Central P.O. Box 717. Marriage possible and even desirable.'

Now, at last, fingerprinting came into its own. Back at headquarters, the trunk was examined, and a number of prints were found; these matched those of one of the victims. The post office was able to tell Bialokurszky that Box 717 had been rented by a man who had signed for his key in the name of Elemer Nagy, of 14 Kossuth Street, Pestszenterzsebet, a suburb of Budapest. This proved to be an empty plot.

Next, the detective and his team studied the agony column of *Pesti Hirlap* for 1912 and 1913. They found more than twenty requests for 'warm-hearted spinsters' which gave the address of Box 717. This was obviously how the unknown killer of Cinkota had contacted his victims. On one occasion he had paid for the advertisement by postal order, and the post office was able to trace it. (The Austro-Hungarian Empire at least had a super-efficient bureaucracy.)

Elemer Nagy had given an address in Cinkota, where the bodies had been found, but it was not of the house in Rákóczi Street; in fact, it proved to be the address of the undertaker. The killer had a sense of humour. Bialokurszky gave a press conference, and asked the newspapers to publish the signature of 'Elemer Nagy'. This quickly brought a letter from a domestic servant named Rosa Diosi, who was twenty-seven, and admitted that she had been the mistress of the man in question. His real name was Bela Kiss, and she had last heard from him in 1914, when he had written to her from a Serbian prisoner-of-war camp. Bialokurszky had not divulged that he was looking for the Cinkota mass murderer, and Rosa Diosi was shocked and incredulous when he told her. She had met Kiss in 1914; he had beautiful brown eyes, a silky moustache, and a deep, manly voice. Sexually, he had apparently been insatiable . . . Other women contacted the police, and they had identical stories to tell: answering the advertisement, meeting the handsome Kiss, and being quickly invited to become his mistress, with promises of marriage. They were also expected to hand over their life savings, and all had been invited to Cinkota. Some had not gone, some had declined to offer their savings – or had none to offer – and a few had disliked being rushed into sex. Kiss had wasted no further time on them, and simply vanished from their lives.

In July 1914, two years before the discovery of the bodies, Kiss had been conscripted into the Second Regiment of the Third Hungarian Infantry Battalion, and had taken part in the long offensive that led to the fall of Valjevo; but before that city had fallen in November, Kiss had been captured by the Serbs. No one was certain what had become of him after that. But the regiment was able to provide a photograph that showed the soldiers being inspected by the Archduke Joseph; Kiss's face was enlarged, and the detectives at last knew what their quarry looked like. They had also heard that his sexual appetite was awe-inspiring, and this led them to show the photograph in the red-light district around Conti and Magyar Street. Many prostitutes recognized him as a regular customer; all spoke warmly of his generosity and mentioned his sexual prowess. But a waiter who had often served Kiss noticed that the lady with whom he was dining usually paid the bill . . . Now, at last, Bialokurszky was beginning to piece the story together. Pawn tickets found in the Cinkota house revealed that the motive behind the murders was the cash of the victims. But the ultimate motive had been sex, for Kiss promptly spent the cash in the brothels of Budapest and Vienna. The evidence showed that he was, quite literally, a satyr – a man with a raging and boundless appetite for sex. His profession – of plumber and tinsmith – did not enable him to indulge this appetite so he took to murder.

He had received two legacies when he was twenty-three (about 1903) but soon spent them. After this, he had taken to seducing middle-aged women and 'borrowing' their savings. One of these, a cook name Maria Toth, had become a nuisance, and he killed her. After this – like his French contemporary Landru – he had decided that killing women was the easiest way to make a living as well as indulge his sexual appetites.

His favourite reading was true-crime books about con men and adventurers. Bialokurszky's investigations suggested that there had been more than seven victims, and just before Christmas 1916, the garden in the house at Cinkota was dug up; it revealed five more bodies, all of middle-aged women, all naked.

But where was Kiss? The War Office thought that he had died of fever in Serbia. He had been in a field hospital, but when Bialokurszky tracked down one of its nurses, she remembered the deceased as a 'nice boy' with fair hair and blue eyes, which seemed to suggest that Kiss had changed identity with another soldier, possibly someone called Mackavee; but the new 'Mackavee' proved untraceable. And although sightings of Kiss were reported from Budapest in 1919 and even New York as late as 1932 – he was never found.

Henri Désiré Landru

Henri Landru, who was to later be nicknamed 'the modern Bluebeard', was born in Paris in (or around) the year 1869, the son of a fireman at the Vulcain Ironworks. Landru was educated at the Ecole des Freres, Rue de Bretonvillers, and was regarded as a clever boy. He was admitted as sub-deacon at the religious establishment of St Louis en l'Isle. At the age of 16 he took a course at the School of Mechanical Engineering. He served his period as a conscript at St Quentin, and remained in the army for four years, during which time he rose to rank of sergeant. He seduced his cousin, a Mlle Remy, and she bore him a daughter in 1891. In 1893, he married her; this was while he was a quartermaster-sergeant in the 3rd regiment. In 1894, he returned to civilian life.

He then entered the service of a firm where he had to pay a deposit to secure the job; but his employer then disappeared to America with his money. It may have been this experience that made Landru decide to take his 'revenge' in the form of living a life of crime.

In 1900, Landru earned a sentence of two years for fraud; it seems that he tried to withdraw money from the Comptoir d'Escompte, using a false name. He was arrested, and tried (or pretended to try) to commit suicide in prison. However, he survived, served his sentence and doggedly refused to turn over a new, more honest leaf.

In 1904 he was again sentenced to two years; in 1906, to a

further thirteen months; and in 1908, to three years – all for different types of fraud. While in prison serving this latter sentence, he was summoned to Lille to be tried on another charge, and received another three years. It seemed that Landru had inserted a matrimonial advertisement in a Lille newspaper and made the acquaintance of a 40-year-old widow. He handed her his 'deeds', and she handed him a dowry of 15,000 francs, with which he made off. Mme Izore seems to have been his first female victim.

Meanwhile, Madame Landru resolutely stuck by her husband and he, in turn, gave her four children – during the few times when he was out of jail, of course.

Immediately before the 1914 War, the police were searching for Landru for various other offences, and in his absence he was sentenced to four years in prison to be followed by lifelong deportation to New Caledonia – a French colonial island northeast of Australia. This sentence was to be put into effect as soon as Landru could be arrested, and so effectively cut him off from all but fleeting and secretive visits to his wife and family.

It may have been the war that decided Landru to start his career as a murderer. It may have also been the total absence of ties. His wife and children were more-or-less barred to him. His mother had died in 1910. His father, after staying with Landru's wife while Landru was in prison, committed suicide on 28 August 1912 in the Bois de Boulogne, his self-image and reputation shattered by his son's career of crime.

In 1914, Landru made the acquaintance of a widow, Mme Cuchet, age 39, who worked in a lingerie shop in the Rue Monsigny, and had a 16-year-old son. Landru was known to her as M. Diard, an engineer. She and Landru quarrelled then regretting the break, Mme Cuchet begged her parents, sister, and brother-in-law to go with her to 'M. Diard's' house, a villa near Chantilly, to help make things up. He was not in, but in a chest in the house the brother-in-law found many letters from women, and informed Mme Cuchet that he was an impostor.

She refused to listen, preferring to break off all relations with her family. This was to prove a fatal mistake.

She furnished a villa at Vernouillet, and went to live there with 'Diard' and her son, André. Soon afterwards, the mother and son disappeared. This was in January 1915. In the previous June, Landru had opened an account with 5,000 francs at Chantilly; he later claimed that the money was part of an inheritance from his father. Mme Cuchet's gold watch was given as a present to Landru's wife, whom he continued to see secretly.

Landru's next 'fiancée' was Mine Laborde-Line, a native of Buenos Aires, widow of a hotel-keeper. Landru met her at the beginning of June 1915. On 21 June 1915, Mme Laborde-Line sold her furniture, telling the concierge she was going to live with her future husband at Vernouillet. She was later seen at Vernouillet, gathering flowers, but after 26 June she was not seen again. Landru sold her securities and parts of her furniture, and had the rest moved to his garage at Neuilly.

Landru's third victim was a widow, Mme Guillin, whose full name was Marie Angelique Desirée Pelletier, who lived in the Rue Crozatier, Paris. She was 51, and had turned a life annuity into cash, realising 22,000 francs. She met Landru through one of his marriage advertisements, and wrote to him on 1 May 1915. She went out to visit Landru's villa at Vernouillet and returned to Paris delighted. On 2 August she moved to Vernouillet, having given up her apartment in the Rue Crozatier and stored her furniture. On 4 August a removal van transferred all the furniture from Vernouillet to the garage at Neuilly. A few days later, Landru sold bonds belonging to Mme Guillin. In November and December of 1915 he committed various forgeries to get possession of 12,000 francs that Mme Guillin had in the Banque de France, using the name Georges Petit, and claiming to be her brother-in-law. He explained that she was paralysed and had placed her business affairs in his hands.

Now Landru took a villa at Gambais, a village south of

Paris; it was called the Villa Ermitage, and was on the edge of the road, two or three hundred yards from other houses. He rented it from a M. Tric, giving himself the name of Dupont, an engineer of Rouen, and moved in during December 1915. His first victim there was a widow named Mme Heon, nine years Landru's senior, whose son had been killed in the war and whose daughter and best friend had also died recently. Landru evidently took advantage of her need for succour and comfort. In September Landru arranged for her furniture to be sold; she herself disappeared after 8 December. Around that time three of her friends received postcards from Landru, saying that she herself could not write due to illness.

One of Landru's first acts in moving into the Villa Ermitage had been to buy a stove and a quantity of coal. It seems likely that the remains of the late Mme Heon disappeared into this stove, piece by piece.

Landru's next victim was, indirectly, the cause of his ultimate downfall. She was a 45-year-old widow, Mme Collomb, employed as a typist in the Rue Lafayette. She had a nest egg of 10,000 francs and lived with a man named Bernard, who either could nor or would not marry her. She saw Landru's advertisement on 1 May 1915: 'Widower with two children, aged forty-three, with comfortable income, affectionate, serious, and moving in good society, Desires to meet widow with a view to matrimony.'

Mme Collomb replied to the advertisement, giving her age as 29, and soon 'M. Cuchet' (Landru this time adopted the name of his first victim) replied. Mme Collomb was captivated, but although she was only too eager to submit, she and Landru parted for a year – Landru having other fish to fry. When they met again, 'M. Cuchet' took her to Gambais, and agreed reluctantly to meet her family, who all disliked him.

In November 1916 Landru persuaded her to come and live with him in his flat in the Rue Chateaudun. On 24 December her sister came to visit Landru and his 'future wife' at Gambais. After Christmas Day Mme Collomb was seen no more. But a young soldier who claimed he was M. Cuchet's son paid a debt for her on 29 January and took flowers to her sister – flowers with a Nice railway label on them. After that, her family lost all trace of her. They wrote to the mayor at Gambais, asking his help. He put them in touch with the sister of a Mme Buisson, who had also disappeared after visiting the Villa Ermitage. The two families eventually met and compared notes, thus precipitating Landriu's downfall.

This, however, was to come later. Landru's next victim presents one of the most puzzling problems in the case; she was a poor, 19-year-old servant girl, Andrée Babelay, who was crying on a platform in the Metro when Landru asked her what was the matter. This was in January 1917. She had quarrelled with her mother, had no money, and would be out of work the next day. Landru offered her his room in the Rue de Mauberge. On 6 March 1917, Andrée visited her mother to say she intended to get married.

On 29 March she and Landru went out to Gambais; and, like the villain in a comic melodrama, Landru rather broadcast his intentions when he bought a return ticket for himself, but only a single ticket for Andrée. She was not seen after 12 April, although her papers were later found in Landru's possession.

One can only assume that Landru started the liaison with Andrée Babelay with his usual ruthless opportunism. Since she had no money, he probably decided to kill her the moment he became bored with her as a sexual companion. The prosecution at his trial suggested that the girl had discovered something incriminating at the Villa Ermitage that made Landru decide to kill her, but could offer no evidence to prove this. In the light of modern serial killer psychology, it is likely that he had already become addicted to killing, and had intended to murder Andrée from the start.

The next victim was Mme Celestine Buisson, a widow with a small fortune of 10,000 francs, born in 1871. She also started corresponding with Landru in May 1915. She knew Landru for six months, then he disappeared for six months, telling her later that he had been to Tunis on business. In July 1917, at last freed from his other entanglements, Landru began to court her again. He made the acquaintance of her sister and mother, who knew him as Fremyet. Mme Buisson also had a son who lived in Paris. Landru now strove to isolate Mme Buisson from her family, particularly her sister, Mme Lacoste. He persuaded Mme Buisson to change her lodgings in April 1917. In June she ordered a wedding costume from her dressmaker.

On 19 August Landru again took a single and a return ticket to Garencieres, near Gambais, and Mme Buisson was seen no more. The date of her murder was probably 1 September, as on that day Landru's cash increased by 1,000 francs. Later that month Landru took care to settle her affairs, paying for the wedding dress and forging a letter to the concierge of her apartment in which he gave notice. The concierge doubted the signature and asked that Mme Buisson should call and confirm the notice; Landru called instead and explained that Mme Buisson had 'gone south'.

The eighth victim was a Mme Jaume, a religious woman, separated from her husband, who met Landru in the summer of 1917 through a matrimonial agent; she knew him as M. Guillet. In September she paid her first visit to Gambais. She left her house in the Rue de Lyanes on 25 November 1917. Landru purchased a single and return ticket for Gambais. Landru's cash increased by 275 francs (the sum she had on her) and on 30 November he negotiated with the Banque Allaume for the remaining 1,400 francs she possessed.

The ninth victim was a pretty widow of easy morals, a Mme Pascal, 36 years old. Landru had started an affair with her in October 1916 and she quickly became his mistress. She had very little money, and no doubt her case is similar to that of Andrée Babelay. She knew him as M. Forest. On 5 April 1917, she went out to Gambais with Landru – on a single ticket. Her furniture was moved, with the help of Landru's son, and sold.

Landru's last known victim was a Mme Marchadier. She

kept a small lodging house at 330 Rue St Jacques. In 1918, needing money, she corresponded with Landru, who called himself Guillet. She wanted to sell the house for 7,000 francs. Landru had no money at this time, and was forced to borrow money from his wife. He proposed marriage to Mme Marchadier and on 1 January 1919, she wrote, 'I do not ask for anything better than to live in the country.' On 9 January she and Landru went to Gambais, where no doubt Landru's charm finally persuaded her to live with him and sell her possessions. Landru was so short of money on this trip that he took single tickets out, and borrowed his return fare from a M. Vallet, a shoemaker. On returning to Paris, Mme Marchadier sold some of her furniture for 2,000 francs. Then, on the 13th, they returned to Gambais; a bus conductor who saw them travelling from Houdan to Gambais stated that Landru carried two bags of coal. Mme Marchadier's two dogs, of which she was very fond, came with them to Gambais. Mme Marchadier was not seen again.

The result of the meeting between the families of Mme Collomb and Mme Buisson was a police search of the Villa Ermitage, and finally a warrant for Landru's arrest. On 11 April 1919, the day after the warrant was issued, Mme Buisson's sister, Mme Lacoste, was walking down the Rue de Rivoli when she saw Landru with a smart young woman on his arm. She followed him into a shop and heard him order a china dinner service to be sent to his address. She went to the police, who discovered from the shop that Landru was known as Lucien Guillet, an engineer, and that he lived at 76 Rue de Rochechouart. The girl accompanying him was Fernande Segret, 27 years old, an assistant in a furrier's shop. She had been picked up by Landru on a bus and was living with him as his mistress.

Landru was arrested at Rue de Rochechouart on 12 April 1919. In his pocket was found a black covered loose-leaf notebook, which Landru tried unsuccessfully to grab and throw away as the police took him. It contained cryptic notes of all his eleven victims (including Mme Cuchet's son), and was the most important exhibit at the trial.

Landru was taken to Gambais, where a search of the garden revealed only the bodies of three dogs – two of which had presumably belonged to Mme Marchadier. No sign of any of his victims was ever discovered. (This remains the most mysterious aspect of the case – how did he dispose of the bodies so thoroughly?) Landru himself was completely unco-operative. He claimed that the burden of proving him guilty rested on the prosecution, and refused to co-operate in any way in revealing the 'present whereabouts' of his victims, claiming that this was his own business.

This might sound an impossibly optimistic stance by a man on trial for his life, but Landru was no fool and apparently trusted in his own methods of body disposal. Although many small bone splinters were found among the ashes of the stove at Gambais, forensic science at that time was still very primi-tive, and investigators had no conclusive proof that the women had actually been killed. However, the clothes and papers of his victims were found in large quantities.

Landru was tried at Versailles Court from 7 to 30 November 1921 – two-and-a-half years after his arrest. This delay undoubtedly reflected the difficulty of constructing a case against Landru on purely circumstantial evidence. And undoubtedly the French authorities encouraged the press to give a great deal of space to the trial to distract attention from the post-Great War Peace Conference, which was moving in a direction unfavourable to France.

Landru appeared to believe, quite incorrectly, that he could not be convicted 'unless at least one body was found', and his defence consisted entirely of 'stone-walling'. The women had all been merely his business clients, he claimed, and if he knew what had become of them, it was a secret between himself and them. Possibly the jury took pleasure in sentencing him to death out of sheer exasperation with his stubbornness. Like another matrimonial killer, Max Gufler,

Landru kept all his correspondences with potential victims (169 women in all) carefully filed. All were traced except the eleven victims mentioned in his notebook. This alone was enough evidence, if only circumstantial, to put him in the shadow of the guillotine.

In addition to this, witnesses were found who had smelt putrid black smoke pouring from the chimney of the Villa Ermitage. One person had seen Landru throw something into a pond by night; and a youth spoke of fishing in this pond and drawing out a lump of putrid flesh.

The appearance of young Fernande Segret in court caused something of a sensation. She told how she had met Landru on a bus in May 1917, how he had agreed to marry her and she had broken off with a fiancé of her own age, and of how she had eventually agreed to live with Landru. At the time of his arrest the affair with Mlle Segret had been going on for two years, and he may well have been in love with her.

The whole of 28 November was occupied with Maitre Godefroy's speech for the prosecution. The court was, as usual, packed to capacity, so that President Gilbert had to rebuke people who stood up for a better view of Landru, saying, 'You are not in a theatre.' The defence speech of Maitre Moro-Giafferi lasted for two days and was so brilliant that many people declared Landru might yet escape execution.

But the jury found him guilty, although they were persuaded by his advocate to sign a petition for clemency. In spite of this, Landru was guillotined on 23 February 1922.

Although he was undoubtedly a callous and murderous conman, Landru's downfall was not without its dignity. In court, his dry sense of humour frequently caused laughter, as when he remarked that most ladies reckon their age from confirmation, not from their birth (thus knocking a dozen years of their supposed age). One day when a lady in the court could not find a seat, Landru rose to his feet and politely offered her his seat in the dock. And at the end, he refused to be consoled by a priest, telling him to go and save his own soul.

On the other hand, a reading of his trial transcripts can hardly fail to cause irritation; even when the facts against him were overwhelming, he would continue to deny all knowledge with an infuriating persistence. When he was confronted by some fact that he could not explain, he would reply coldly that this was his secret and that French law allowed him the right to remain silent.

He maintained this stubborn defiance all the way to the guillotine.

The Harry Whitecliffe Mystery

According to a book published in France in 1978, one of England's most extraordinary mass murderers committed suicide in a Berlin jail in the middle of the jazz era. His name was Harry Whitecliffe, and he murdered at least forty women. Then why is his name not more widely known – at least among students of crime? Because when he was arrested he was masquerading under the name Lovach Blume, and his suicide concealed his true identity from the authorities.

The full story can be found in a volume called *Nouvelles Histoires Magiques – New Tales of Magic –* by Louis Pauwels and Guy Breton, published by Editions J'ai Lu. In spite of the title – which sounds like fiction – the book is, in fact, a series of studies in the paranormal and bizarre. There are chapters on Nostradamus, Rasputin and Eusapia Palladino, and accounts of such well-known mysteries as the devil's footprints in Devon.

According to the chapter 'The Two Faces of Harry Whitecliffe', there appeared in London in the early 1920s a collection of essays so promising that it sold out in few days; it consisted of a series of marvellous pastiches of Oscar Wilde. But its author, Harry Whitecliffe, apparently preferred to shun publicity; he remained obstinately hidden. Would-be interviewers returned empty-handed. Then, just as people were beginning to suggest that Whitecliffe was a pseudonym for some well-known writer – Bernard Shaw, perhaps, or the young T. S. Eliot – Whitecliffe finally consented to appear. He was a handsome young man of twenty-three, likeable, eccentric and fond of sport. He was also generous; he was said to have ended one convivial evening by casually giving a pretty female beggar £500. He professed to adore flowers, but only provided their stems were not more than twenty centimetres long. He was the kind of person the English love, and was soon a celebrity.

Meanwhile he continued to write: essays, poetry and plays. One of his comedies, *Similia,* had four hundred consecutive performances in London before touring England. It made him a fortune, which he quickly scattered among his friends. By the beginning of 1923, he was one of the 'kings of London society'.

Then, in September of that year, he vanished. He sold all his possessions, and gave his publisher carte blanche to handle his work. But before the end of the year he reappeared in Dresden. The theatre then presented *Similia* with enormous success, the author himself translating it from English into German. It went on to appear in many theatres along the Rhine. He founded a press for publishing modern poetry, and works on modern painting – Dorian Verlag – whose editions are now worth a fortune.

But he was still something of a man of mystery. Every morning he galloped along the banks of the river Elbe until nine o'clock; at ten he went to his office, eating lunch there. At six in the evening, he went to art exhibitions or literary salons, and met friends. At nine, he returned home and no one knew what he did for the rest of the evening. And no one liked to ask him.

One reason for this regular life was that he was in love – the girl was called Wally von Hammerstein, daughter of aristocratic parents, who were favourably impressed with the young writer. Their engagement was to be announced on 4 October 1924.

But on the previous day Whitecliffe disappeared again. He

failed to arrive at his office, and vanished from his flat. The frantic Wally searched Dresden, without success. The police were alerted – discreetly – and pursued diligent inquiries. Their theory was that he had committed suicide. Wally believed he had either met with an accident or been the victim of a crime – he often carried large sums of money. As the weeks dragged by her desperation turned to misery; she talked about entering a convent.

Then she received a letter. It had been found in the cell of a condemned man who had committed suicide in Berlin – he had succeeded in opening his veins with the buckle of his belt. The inscription on the envelope said: "I beg you, monsieur le procureur of the Reich, to forward this letter to its destination without opening it." It was signed: Lovach Blume.

Blume was apparently one of the most horrible of murderers, worse than Jack the Ripper or Peter Kürten, the Düsseldorf sadist. He had admitted to the court that tried him: 'Every ten days I have to kill. I am driven by an irresistible urge, so that until I have killed, I suffer atrociously. But as I disembowel my victims I feel an indescribable pleasure.' Asked about his past, he declared: 'I am a corpse. Why bother about the past of a corpse?'

Blume's victims were prostitutes and homeless girls picked up on the Berlin streets. He would take them to a hotel, and kill them as soon as they were undressed. Then, with a knife like a Malaysian 'kris', with an ivory handle, he would perform horrible mutilations, so awful that even doctors found the sight unbearable. These murders continued over a period of six months, during which the slum quarters of Berlin lived in fear.

Blume was finally arrested by accident, in September 1924. The police thought he was engaged in drug trafficking, and knocked on the door of a hotel room minutes after Blume had entered with a prostitute. Blume had just committed his thirty-first murder in Berlin; he was standing naked by the window, and the woman's body lay at his feet.

He gave no resistance, and admitted freely to his crimes – he could recall only twenty-seven. He declared that he had no fear of death – particularly the way executions were performed in Germany (by decapitation), which he greatly preferred to the English custom of hanging.

This was the man who had committed suicide in his prison cell, and who addressed a long letter to his fiancée, Wally von Hammerstein. He told her that he was certain the devil existed, because he had met him. He was, he explained, a kind of Jekyll and Hyde, an intelligent, talented man who suddenly became cruel and bloodthirsty. He thought of himself as being like victims of demoniacal possession. He had left London after committing nine murders, when he suspected that Scotland Yard was on his trail.

His love for Wally was genuine, he told her, and had caused him to 'die a little'. He had hoped once that she might be able to save him from his demons, but it had proved a vain hope.

Wally fainted as she read the letter. And in 1925 she entered a nunnery and took the name Marie de Douleurs. There she prays for the salvation of a tortured soul.

This is the story, as told by Louis Pauwels – a writer who became famous for his collaboration with Jacques Bergier on a book called *The Morning of the Magicians*. Critics pointed out that that book was full of factual errors, and a number of these can also be found in his article on Whitecliffe. For example, if the date of Blume's arrest is correct – 25 September 1924 – then it took place before Whitecliffe vanished from Dresden, on 3 October 1924. But this, presumably, is a slip of the pen.

Who was Harry Whitecliffe, though? According to Pauwels, he told the Berlin court that his father was German, his mother Danish, and that he was brought up in Australia by an uncle who was a butcher. His uncle lived in Sydney. But in a 'conversation' between Pauwels and his fellow author at the end of one chapter, Pauwels states that Whitecliffe was the son of a great English family. But apart from the three magistrates who opened the

44

suicide letter – ignoring Blume's last wishes – only Wally and her parents knew Whitecliffe's true identity. The judges are dead, so are Wally's parents. Wally is a seventy-five-year-old nun who until now has never told anyone of this drama of her youth. We are left to assume that she has now told the story to Pauwels. This extraordinary tale aroused the curiosity of a well-known French authoress, Françoise d'Eaubonne, who felt that Whitecliffe deserved a book to himself. But her letters to the two authors – Pauwels and Breton – went unanswered. She therefore contacted the British Society of Theatre Research, and so entered into a correspondence with the theatre historian John Kennedy Melling. Melling had never heard of Whitecliffe, or of a play called *Similia*. He decided to begin his researches by contacting Scotland Yard, to ask whether they have any record of an unknown sex killer of the early 1920s. Their reply was negative; there was no series of Ripper-type murders of prostitutes in the early 1920s. He next applied to J.H.H. Gaute, the possessor of the largest crime library in the British Isles; Gaute also could find no trace of such a series of sex crimes in the 1920s. Theatrical reference books contained no mention of Harry Whitecliffe, or of his successful comedy *Similia*. It began to look – as incredible as it sounds – as if Pauwels had simply invented the whole story.

Thelma Holland, Oscar Wilde's daughter-in-law, could find no trace of a volume of parodies of Wilde among the comprehensive collection of her late husband, Vyvyan Holland. But she had a suggestion to make – to address enquiries to the Mitchell Library in Sydney. As an Australian, she felt it was probably Melling's best chance of tracking down Harry Whitecliffe.

Incredibly, this long shot brought positive results: not about Harry Whitecliffe, but about a German murderer called Blume – not Lovach, but Wilhelm Blume. The *Argus* newspaper for 8 August 1922 contained a story headed 'Cultured Murderer', and sub-titled: 'Literary Man's Series of Crimes'. It was dated, 7 August, Berlin.

Wilhelm Blume, a man of wide culture and considerable literary gifts, whose translations of English plays have been produced in Dresden with great success, has confessed to a series of cold-blooded murders, one of which was perpetrated at the Hotel Adlon, the best known Berlin hotel.

The most significant item in the newspaper report is that Blume had founded a publishing house called Dorian Press (Verlag) in Dresden. This is obviously the same Blume who – according to Pauwels – committed suicide in Berlin.

But Wilhelm Blume was not a sex killer. His victims had been postmen, and the motive had been robbery. In Germany postal orders were paid to consignees in their own homes, so postmen often carried fairly large sums of money. Blume had sent himself postal orders, then killed the postmen and robbed them – the exact number is not stated in the *Argus* article. The first time he did this he was interrupted by his landlady while he was strangling the postman with a noose; and he cut her throat. Then he moved on to Dresden, where in due course he attempted to rob another postman. Armed with two revolvers, he waited for the postman in the porch of a house. But the tenant of the house arrived so promptly that he had to flee, shooting one of the postmen. Then his revolvers both misfired, and he was caught.

Apparently he attempted to commit suicide in prison, but failed. He confessed – as the *Argus* states – to several murders, and was presumably executed later in 1922 (although the *Argus* carries no further record). It seems plain, then, that the question "Who was Harry Whitecliffe?" should be reworded, "Who was Wilhelm Blume?"

For Blume and Whitecliffe were obviously the same person. From the information we possess, we can make a tentative reconstruction of the story of Blume–Whitecliffe. He sounds like a typical example of a certain type of killer who is also a conman – other examples are Landru, Petiot, the 'acid bath murderer' Haigh, and the sex-killer Neville Heath. It is an essential part of such a man's personality that he is a fantasist, and that he likes to pose as a success, and to talk casually about past triumphs. (Neville Heath called himself 'Group Captain Rupert Brooke'.) They usually start off as petty swindlers, then gradually become more ambitious and graduate to murder. This is what Blume seems to have done. In the chaos of post-war Berlin he made a quick fortune by murdering and robbing postmen. Perhaps his last coup made him a fortune beyond his expectations, or perhaps the Berlin postal authorities were now on the alert for the killer. Blume decided it was time to make an attempt to live a respectable life, and to put his literary fantasies into operation. He moved to Dresden, calling himself Harry Whitecliffe, and set up Dorian Verlag. He became a successful translator of English plays, and may have helped to finance their production in Dresden and in theatres along the Rhine. Since he was posing as an upper-class Englishman, and must have occasionally run into other Englishmen in Dresden, we may assume that his English was perfect, and that his story of being brought up in Australia was probably true. Since he also spoke perfect German, it is also a fair assumption that he was, as he told the court, the son of a German father and a Danish mother.

He fell in love with an upper-class girl and told her a romantic story that was typical of the inveterate daydreamer: that he was the son of a 'great English family', that he had become an overnight literary success in London as a result of his pastiches of Oscar Wilde, but had at first preferred to shun the limelight (this is the true Walter Mitty touch) until increasing success made this impossible. His wealth was the result of a successful play, *Similia*. (The similarity of the title to *Salome* is obvious, and we may infer that Blume was an ardent admirer of Wilde.) But in order to avoid too much publicity – after all, victims of previous swindles might expose him – he lived the quiet, regular life of a crook in hiding.

And just as all seemed to be going so well – just as success, respectability and a happy marriage seemed so close – he once again ran out of money. There was only one solution: a brief return to a life of crime. One or two robberies of postmen could replenish his bank account and secure his future . . . But this time it went disastrously wrong. Harry Whitecliffe was exposed as the swindler and murderer Wilhelm Blume. He made no attempt to deny it, and confessed to his previous murders; his world had collapsed in ruins. He was sent back to Berlin, where the murders were committed, and he attempted suicide in his cell.

Soon after, he died by the guillotine. And in Dresden the true story of Wilhelm Blume was quickly embroidered into a horrifying tale of a Jekyll and Hyde mass murderer, whose early career in London was confused with Jack the Ripper . . .

Do any records of Wilhelm Blume still exist? It seems doubtful – the fire-bombing of Dresden destroyed most of the civic records, and the people who knew him more than sixty years ago must now all be dead. Yet Pauwels has obviously come across some garbled and wildly inaccurate account of Blume's career as Harry Whitecliffe. It would be interesting to know where he obtained his information; but neither Françoise d'Eaubonne nor John Kennedy Melling has been successful in persuading him to respond to letters.

Fritz Haarmann

Where sex crime is concerned, the first World War seems to have been a kind of watershed. Now, suddenly, the twentieth century entered the 'age of sex crime'. And – perhaps predictably – the country in which this first became apparent was Germany where, after 1918, the miseries and deprivations of inflation and food shortage made a maximum impact.

Hanover in Saxony was one of the cities that was most badly hit. It was in Hanover that Haarmann committed one of the most amazing series of crimes in modern times.

Haarmann was born in Hanover on 25 October 1879; he was the sixth child of an ill-matched couple; a morose locomotive stoker known as 'Sulky Olle' and his invalid wife, seven years his senior. Fritz was his mother's pet and hated his father. He liked playing with dolls, and disliked games. At sixteen he was sent to a military school (for NCOs) at Neuf-Breisach, but soon released when he showed signs of epileptic fits. He went to work in his father's cigar factory but was lazy and inefficient. He was soon accused of indecent behaviour with small children and sent to an asylum for observation; he escaped after six months. He then took to petty crime, as well as indecent assaults on minors. He also had a brief sexually normal period about 1900, when he seduced a girl to whom he was engaged and then deserted her to join the Jäger regiment.The baby was stillborn.

He served satisfactorily until 1903, then returned to

Hanover, where his father tried to have him certified insane again – without success. He served several sentences in jail for burglary, pocket-picking and confidence trickery. His father tried getting him to do respectable work, setting him up as the keeper of a fish and chip shop. Fritz promptly stole all the money he could lay his hands on.

In 1914 he was sentenced to five years in jail for theft from a warehouse. Released in 1918, he joined a smuggling ring, and soon became prosperous. With his headquarters at 27 Cellarstrasse, he conducted business as a smuggler, thief and police spy. (This latter activity guaranteed that his smuggling should not be too closely scrutinized.) Many refugee trains came into Hanover; Haarmann picked up youths and offered them a night's lodging. One of the first of these was seventeen-year-old Friedel Rothe. The lad's worried parents found that he had been friendly with 'detective' Haarmann; the police searched his room, but found nothing. (Haarmann later admitted that the boy's head lay wrapped in a newspaper behind his stove at the time.)

But they caught Haarmann *in flagrante delicto* with another boy, and he received nine months in jail for indecency. Back in Hanover in September 1919, he changed his lodging to the Neuestrasse. He met another homosexual, Hans Grans, a pimp and petty thief, and the two formed an alliance. They used to meet in a café that catered for all kinds of perverts, the Café Kröpcke. Their method was always the same; they enticed a youth from the railway station back to Haarmann's room; Haarmann killed him (according to his own account, by biting his throat), and the boy's body was dismembered and sold as meat through Haarmann's usual channels for smuggled meat. His clothes were sold, and the useless (i.e. uneatable) portions were thrown into the Leine. At the trial, a list of twenty-eight victims was offered, their ages ranging between thirteen and twenty. One boy was killed only because Grans took a fancy to his trousers. Only one victim, a lad named Keimes, was found, strangled in the canal.

There was a curious incident in connection with this case; Haarmann called on the missing youth's parents as a 'detective' and assured them he would restore their son in three days; he then went to the police and denounced Grans as the murderer! Grans was in prison at the time, so nothing came of the charge. Haarmann had some narrow escapes; some of his meat was taken to the police because the buyer thought it was human flesh; the police analyst pronounced it pork! On another occasion, a neighbour stopped to talk to him on the stairs when some paper blew off the bucket he was carrying; it was revealed to contain blood. But Haarmann's trade as a meat smuggler kept him from suspicion. In May 1924, a skull was discovered on the banks of the river, and some weeks later, another one. People continued to report the disappearance of their sons, and Haarmann was definitely suspected; but months went by and Haarmann continued to kill. Two detectives from Berlin watched him, and he was arrested for indecency. His lodgings were searched and many articles of clothing taken away. His landlady's son was found to be wearing a coat belonging to one of the missing boys. And boys playing near the river discovered more bones, including a sack stuffed with them. A police pathologist declared they represented the remains of at least twenty-seven bodies.

Haarmann decided to confess. His trial began at the Hanover Assizes on 4 December 1924. It lasted fourteen days and 130 witnesses were called. The public prosecutor was Oberstaatsanwalt Dr Wilde, assisted by Dr Wagenschiefer; the defence was conducted by Justizrat Philipp Benfey and Rechtsanwalt Oz Lotzen. Haarmann was allowed remarkable freedom; he was usually gay and irresponsible, frequently interrupting the proceedings. At one point he demanded indignantly why there were so many women in court; the judge answered apologetically that he had no power to keep them out. When a woman witness was too distraught to give her evidence about her son with clarity, Haarmann got bored and asked to be allowed to smoke a cigar; permission was immediately granted.

He persisted to the end in his explanation of how he had killed his victims – biting them through the throat. Some boys he denied killing – for example, a boy named Hermann Wolf, whose photograph showed an ugly and ill-dressed youth; like Oscar Wilde, Haarmann declared that the boy was far too ugly to interest him. Haarmann was sentenced to death by decapitation; Grans to twelve years in jail.

Peter Kürten, the 'Düsseldorf Vampire'

In the year 1913 another notorious sex killer committed his first murder. On a summer morning, a ten-year-old girl named Christine Klein was found murdered in her bed in a tavern in Köln-Mülheim, on the Rhine. The tavern was kept by her father, Peter Klein, and suspicion immediately fell on his brother Otto.

On the previous evening, Otto Klein had asked his brother for a loan and been refused; in a violent rage, he had threatened to do something his brother 'would remember', police found a handkerchief with the initials 'P.K.', and it seemed conceivable that Otto Klein had borrowed it from his brother Peter. Suspicion of Otto was deepened by the fact that the murder seemed otherwise motiveless; the child had been throttled unconscious, then her throat had been cut with a sharp knife. There were signs of some sexual molestation, but not of rape, and again, it seemed possible that Otto Klein had penetrated the child's genitals with his fingers in order to provide an apparent motive.

He was charged with Christine Klein's murder, but the jury, although partly convinced of his guilt, felt that the evidence was not sufficiently strong, and he was acquitted.

Sixteen years later, in Düsseldorf, a series of murders and sexual atrocities made the police aware that an extremely dangerous sexual pervert was roaming the streets. These began on 9 February 1929, when the body of an eight-year-old girl,

Rosa Ohliger, was found under a hedge. She had been stabbed thirteen times, and an attempt had been made to burn the body with petrol. The murderer had also stabbed her in the vagina – the weapon was later identified as a pair of scissors – and seminal stains on the knickers indicated that he had experienced emission.

Six days earlier, a woman named Kuhn had been overtaken by a man who grabbed her by the lapels and stabbed her repeatedly and rapidly. She fell down and screamed, and the man ran away. Frau Kuhn survived the attack with twenty-four stab wounds, but was in hospital for many months. Five days after the murder of Rosa Ohliger, a forty-five-year-old mechanic named Scheer was found stabbed to death on a road in Flingern; he had twenty stab wounds, including several in the head.

Soon after this, two women were attacked by a man with a noose, and described the man as an idiot with a hare lip. An idiot named Stausberg was arrested, and confessed not only to the attacks but to the murders. He was confined in a mental home, and for the next six months there were no more attacks.

But in August they began again. Two women and a man were stabbed as they walked home at night, none of them fatally. But on 24 August two children were found dead on an allotment in Düsseldorf; both had been strangled, then had their throats cut. Gertrude Hamacher was five, Louise Lenzen fourteen. That same afternoon a servant girl named Gertrude Schulte was accosted by a man who tried to persuade her to have sexual intercourse; when she said 'I'd rather die', he answered: 'Die then,' and stabbed her.

But she survived, and was able to give a good description of her assailant, who proved to be a pleasant-looking, nondescript man of about forty. The murders and attacks went on, throwing the whole area into a panic comparable to that caused by Jack the Ripper.

A servant girl named Ida Reuter was battered to death with a hammer and raped in September; in October, another servant, Elizabeth Dorrier, was battered to death. A woman out for a walk was asked by a man whether she was not afraid to be out alone, and knocked unconscious with a hammer; later the same evening, a prostitute was attacked with a hammer.

On 7 November, five-year-old Gertrude Albermann disappeared; two days later, the communist newspaper *Freedom* received a letter stating that the child's body would be found near a factory wall, and enclosing a map. It also described the whereabouts of another body in the Pappendelle meadows. Gertrude Albermann's body was found where the letter had described, amidst bricks and rubble; she had been strangled and stabbed thirty-five times. A large party of men digging on the Rhine meadows eventually discovered the naked body of a servant girl, Maria Hahn, who had disappeared in the previous August; she had also been stabbed.

By the end of 1929, the 'Düsseldorf murderer' was known all over the world, and the manhunt reached enormous proportions. But the attacks had ceased. The capture of the killer happened almost by chance.

On 19 May 1930, a certain Frau Brugmann opened a letter that had been delivered to her accidentally; it was actually addressed to a Frau Bruckner, whose name had been misspelled. It was from a twenty-year-old domestic servant named Maria Budlick (or Butlies), and she described an alarming adventure she had met with two days earlier.

Maria had travelled from Cologne to Düsseldorf in search of work, and on the train had fallen into conversation with Frau Bruckner, who had given the girl her address and offered to help her find accommodation. That same evening, Maria Budlick had been waiting at the Düsseldorf railway station, hoping to meet Frau Bruckner, when she was accosted by a man who offered to help her find a bed for the night. He led her through the crowded streets and into a park. The girl was becoming alarmed, and was relieved when a kindly looking man intervened and asked her companion where he was taking her. Within a few moments, her former companion had slunk off, and the kindly man offered to take the girl back to his room in the Mettmänner Strasse. There she decided his intentions were also dishonourable, and asked to be taken to a hostel. The man agreed; but when they reached a lonely spot, he kissed her roughly and asked for sex.

The frightened girl agreed; the man tugged down her knickers, and they had sex standing up. After this, the man led her back to the tram stop, and left her. She eventually found a lodging for the night with some nuns, and the next day wrote about her encounter to Frau Bruckner. Frau Brugmann, who opened the letter, decided to take it to the police. And Chief Inspector Gennat, who was in charge of the murder case, sought out Maria Budlick, and asked her if she thought she could lead him to the address where the man had taken her. It seemed a remote chance that the man was the Düsseldorf murderer, but Gennat was desperate.

Maria remembered that the street was called Mettmänner Strasse, but had no idea of the address. It took her a long time and considerable hesitation before she led Gennat into the hallway of No. 71, and said she thought this was the place. The landlady let her into the room, which was empty, and she recognized it as the one she had been in a week earlier. As they were going downstairs, she met the man who had raped her. He went pale when he saw her, and walked out of the house. But the landlady was able to tell her his name. It was Peter Kürten.

Kürten, it seemed, lived with his wife in a top room in the house. He was known to be frequently unfaithful to her. But neighbours seemed to feel that he was a pleasant, likeable man. Children took to him instinctively.

On 24 May 1930, a raw-boned middle-aged woman went to the police station and told them that her husband was the Düsseldorf murderer. Frau Kürten had been fetched home from work by detectives on the day Maria Budlick had been to the room in Mettmänner Strasse, but her husband was nowhere to be found. Frau Kürten knew that he had been in jail on many occasions, usually for burglary, sometimes for sexual offences.

Now, she felt, he was likely to be imprisoned for a long time. The thought of a lonely and penniless old age made her desperate, and when her husband finally reappeared, she asked him frantically what he had been doing. When he told her that he was the Düsseldorf killer, she thought he was joking. But finally he convinced her. Her reaction was to suggest a suicide pact. But Kürten had a better idea. There was a large reward offered for the capture of the sadist; if his wife could claim that, she could have a comfortable old age. They argued for many hours; she still wanted to kill herself. But eventually, she was persuaded. And on the afternoon of 24 May, Kürten met his wife outside the St Rochus church, and four policemen rushed at him waving revolvers. Kürten smiled reassuringly and told them not to be afraid. Then he was taken into police custody.

In prison, Kürten spoke frankly about his career of murder with the police psychiatrist, Professor Karl Berg. He had been born in Köln-Mülheim in 1883, son of a drunkard who often forced his wife to have sexual intercourse in the same bedroom as the children; after an attempt to rape one of his daughters, the father was imprisoned, and Frau Kürten obtained a separation and married again.

Even as a child Kürten was oversexed, and tried to have intercourse with the sister his father had attacked. At the age of eight he became friendly with a local dog-catcher, who taught him how to masturbate the dogs; the dog-catcher also ill-treated them in the child's presence. At the age of nine, Kürten pushed a schoolfellow off a raft, and when another boy dived in, managed to push his head under, so that both were drowned.

At the age of thirteen he began to practise bestiality with sheep, pigs, and goats, but discovered that he had his most powerful sensation when he stabbed a sheep as he had intercourse, and began to do it with increasing frequency.

57

At sixteen he stole money and ran away from home; soon after, he received the first of seventeen prison sentences that occupied twenty-four years of his life. And during long periods of solitary confinement for insubordination he indulged in endless sadistic daydreams, which 'fixed' his tendency to associate sexual excitement with blood.

In 1913, he had entered the tavern in Köln-Mülheim and murdered the ten-year-old girl as she lay in bed; he had experienced orgasm as he cut her throat. The handkerchief with the initials P. K. belonged, of course, to Peter Kürten.

And so Kürten's career continued – periods in jail, and brief periods of freedom during which he committed sexual attacks on women, sometimes stabbing them, sometimes strangling them. If he experienced orgasm as he squeezed a girl's throat, he immediately became courteous and apologetic, explaining, 'That's what love's about.'

The psychiatrist Karl Berg was impressed by his intelligence and frankness, and later wrote a classic book on the case. Kürten told him candidly that he looked with longing at the white throat of the stenographer who took down his confession, and longed to strangle her. He also confided to Berg that his greatest wish was to hear his own blood gushing into the basket as his head was cut off. He ate an enormous last meal before he was guillotined on 2 July 1931.

Carl Panzram

In 1970, an American publisher brought out a volume called *Killer, A Journal of Murder*, and made the world suddenly aware of one of the most dangerous serial killers of the first half of the twentieth century.

His name was Carl Panzram, and the book was his autobiography, written more than forty years earlier. It was regarded as too horrifying to publish at the time, but when it finally appeared, it was hailed as a revelation of the inner workings of the mind of a serial killer. However, Panzram belongs to a rare species that criminologists label 'the resentment killer'. Far more common – particularly in the last decades of the twentieth century – is the travelling serial killer, the man who moves restlessly from place to place. In a country as large as America, this makes him particularly difficult to catch, since communication between police forces in different states is often less efficient than it should be.

Earle Nelson, the 'Gorilla Murderer', is generally regarded as the first example of the 'travelling serial killer'.

Panzram was born in June 1891, on a small farm in Minnesota, in the American Midwest. His father had deserted the family when Carl was a child, leaving his mother to care for a family of six. When Carl came home from school in the afternoon he was immediately put to working in the fields. 'My portion of pay consisted of plenty of work and a sound beating every time I'd done anything that displeased anyone who was older and stronger . . .'

When he was eleven, Carl burgled the house of a well-to-do neighbour and was sent to reform school. He was a rebellious boy, and was often violently beaten. Because he was a highly 'dominant' personality, the beatings only deepened the desire to avenge the injustice on 'society'. He would have agreed with the painter Gauguin who said: 'Life being what it is, one dreams of revenge.'

Travelling around the country on freight trains, the young Panzram was sexually violated by four hoboes. The experience suggested a new method of expressing his aggression: 'Whenever I met [a hobo] who wasn't too rusty looking I would make him raise his hands and drop his pants. I wasn't very particular either. I rode them old and young, tall and short, white and black.'

When a brakesman caught Panzram and two other hoboes in a railway truck Panzram drew his revolver and raped the man, then forced the other two hoboes to do the same at gunpoint. It was his way of telling 'authority' what he thought of it.

Panzram lived by burglary, mugging and robbing churches. He spent a great deal of time in prison, but became a skilled escapist. But he had his own peculiar sense of loyalty. After breaking jail in Salem, Oregon, he broke in again to try to rescue a safe blower named Cal Jordan; he was caught and got thirty days. 'The thanks I got from old Cal was that he thought I was in love with him and he tried to mount me, but I wasn't broke to ride and he was, so I rode him. At that time he was about fifty years old and I was twenty or twenty-one, but I was strong and he was weak.'

In various prisons, he became known as one of the toughest troublemakers ever encountered. What drove him to his most violent frenzies was a sense of injustice. In Oregon he was offered a minimal sentence if he would reveal the whereabouts of the stolen goods; Panzram kept his side of the bargain but was sentenced to seven years. He managed to escape from his cell and wreck the jail, burning furniture and mattresses. They beat him up and sent him to the toughest prison in the state. There he promptly threw the contents of a chamberpot in a guard's face; he was beaten unconscious and chained to the door of a dark cell for thirty days, where he screamed defiance. He aided another prisoner to escape, and in the hunt the warden was shot dead.

The new warden was tougher than ever. Panzram burned down the prison workshop and later a flax mill. Given a job in the kitchen, he went berserk with an axe. He incited the other prisoners to revolt, and the atmosphere became so tense that guards would not venture into the yard.

Finally, the warden was dismissed. The new warden, a man named Murphy, was an idealist who believed that prisoners would respond to kindness. When Panzram was caught trying to escape, Murphy sent for him and told him that, according to reports, he was 'the meanest and most cowardly degenerate that they had ever seen'. When Panzram agreed, Murphy astonished him by telling him that he would let him walk out of the jail if he would swear to return in time for supper. Panzram agreed – with no intention of keeping his word; but when supper time came, something made him go back.

Gradually, Murphy increased his freedom, and that of the other prisoners. But one night Panzram got drunk with a pretty nurse and decided to abscond. Recaptured after a gun battle, he was thrown into the punishment cell, and Murphy's humanitarian regime came to an abrupt end. This experience seems to have been something of a turning point. So far, Panzram had been against the world, but not against himself.

His betrayal of Murphy's trust seems to have set up a reaction of self-hatred. He escaped from prison again, stole a yacht, and began his career of murder. He would offer sailors a job and take them to the stolen yacht; there he would rob them, commit sodomy, and throw their bodies into the sea. 'They are there yet, ten of 'em.'

Then he went to West Africa to work for an oil company, where he soon lost his job for committing sodomy on the table waiter. The US consul declined to help him and he sat down in a park 'to think things over'. 'While I was sitting there, a little nigger boy about eleven or twelve years came bumming around. He was looking for something. He found it too. I took him out to a gravel pit a quarter of a mile from the main camp . . . I left him there, but first I committed sodomy on him and then killed him. His brains were coming out of his ears when I left him and he will never be any deader. Then I went to town, bought a ticket on the Belgian steamer to Lobito Bay down the coast. There I hired a canoe and six niggers and went out hunting in the bay and backwaters. I was looking for crocodiles. I found them, plenty. They were all hungry. I fed them. I shot all six of those niggers and dumped 'em in. The crocks done the rest. I stole their canoe and went back to town, tied the canoe to a dock, and that night someone stole the canoe from me.'

Back in America he raped and killed three more boys, bringing his murders up to twenty. After five years of rape, robbery and arson, Panzram was caught as he robbed the express office in Larchmont, New York and sent to one of America's toughest prisons, Dannemora. 'I hated everybody I saw.' And again more defiance, more beatings. Like a stubborn child, he had decided to turn his life into a competition to see whether he could take more beatings than society could hand out. In Dannemora he leapt from a high gallery, fracturing a leg, and walked for the rest of his life with a limp.

He spent his days brooding on schemes of revenge against the whole human race: how to blow up a railway tunnel with a train in it, how to poison a whole city by putting arsenic into the water supply, even how to cause a war between England and America by blowing up a British battleship in American waters. It was during this period in jail that Panzram met a young Jewish guard named Henry Lesser. Lesser was a shy man who enjoyed prison work because it conferred automatic status, which eased his inferiority complex. Lesser was struck by Panzram's curious immobility, a quality of cold detachment.

When he asked him: 'What's your racket?' Panzram replied with a curious smile: 'What I do is reform people.' After brooding on this, Lesser went back to ask him how he did it; Panzram replied that the only way to reform people is to kill them. He described himself as 'the man who goes around doing good'. He meant that life is so vile that to kill someone is to do them a favour. When a loosened bar was discovered in his cell, Panzram received yet another brutal beating – perhaps the hundredth of his life. In the basement of the jail he was subjected to a torture that in medieval times was known as the strappado. His hands were tied behind his back; then a rope was passed over a beam and he was heaved up by the wrists so that his shoulder sockets bore the full weight of his body.

Twelve hours later, when the doctor checked his heart, Panzram shrieked and blasphemed, cursing his mother for bringing him into the world and declaring that he would kill every human being. He was allowed to lie on the floor of his cell all day, but when he cursed a guard, four guards knocked him unconscious with a blackjack and again suspended him from a beam. Lesser was so shocked by this treatment that he sent Panzram a dollar by a 'trusty'.

At first, Panzram thought it was a joke. When he realized that it was a gesture of sympathy, his eyes filled with tears. He told Lesser that if he could get him paper and a pencil, he would write him his life story. This is how Panzram's autobiography came to be written. When Lesser read the opening pages, he was struck by the remarkable literacy and keen intelligence. Panzram made no excuses for himself:

If any man was a habitual criminal, I am one. In my life time I have broken every law that was ever made by God and man. If either had made any more, I should very cheerfully have broken them also. The mere fact that I have done these things is quite sufficient for the average person. Very few people even consider it worthwhile to wonder why I am what I am and do what I do. All that they think is necessary to do is to catch me, try me, convict me and send me to prison for a few years, make life miserable for me while in prison and turn me loose again . . . If someone had a young tiger cub in a cage and then mistreated it until it got savage and bloodthirsty and then turned it loose to prey on the rest of the world . . . there would be a hell of a roar . . . But if some people do the same thing to other people, then the world is surprised, shocked and offended because they get robbed, raped and killed. They done it to me and then don't like it when I give them the same dose they gave me. (From *Killer, A Journal of Murder,* edited by Thomas E. Gaddis and James O. Long, Macmillan, 1970.)

Panzram's confession is an attempt to justify himself to one other human being. Where others were concerned, he remained as savagely intractable as ever. At his trial he told the jury: 'While you were trying me here, I was trying all of you too. I've found you guilty. Some of you, I've already executed. If I live, I'll execute some more of you. I hate the whole human race.' The judge sentenced him to twenty-five years.

Transferred to Leavenworth penitentiary, Panzram murdered the foreman of the working party with an iron bar and was sentenced to death. Meanwhile, Lesser had been showing the autobiography to various literary men, including H. L. Mencken, who were impressed.

But when Panzram heard there was a movement to get him reprieved, he protested violently: 'I would not reform if the front gate was opened right now and I was given a million dollars when I stepped out. I have no desire to do good or become good.'

And in a letter to Henry Lesser he showed a wry self-knowledge: 'I could not reform if I wanted to. It has taken me all my life so far, thirty-eight years of it, to reach my present state of mind. In that time I have acquired some habits. It took me a lifetime to form these habits, and I believe it would take more than another lifetime to break myself of these same habits even if I wanted to . . . what gets me is how in the heck any man of your intelligence and ability, knowing as much about me as you do, can still be friendly towards a thing like me when I even despise and detest my own self.'

When he stepped onto the scaffold on the morning of 11 September 1930, the hangman asked him if he had anything to say. 'Yes, hurry it up, you hoosier bastard. I could hang a dozen men while you're fooling around.'

Earle Nelson

On 24 February 1926, a man named Richard Newman went to call on his aunt, who advertised rooms to let in San Francisco; he found the naked body of the sixty-year-old woman in an upstairs toilet. She had been strangled with her pearl necklace, then repeatedly raped.

Clara Newman was the first of twenty-two victims of a man who became known as 'the Gorilla Murderer'. The killer made a habit of calling at houses with a 'Room to Let' notice in the window; if the landlady was alone, he strangled and raped her.

His victims included a fourteen-year-old girl and an eight-month-old baby. And as he travelled around from San Francisco to San Jose, from Portland, Oregon to Council Bluffs, Iowa, from Philadelphia to Buffalo, from Detroit to Chicago, the police found him as elusive as the French police had found Joseph Vacher thirty years earlier. Their problem was simply that the women who could identify 'the Dark Strangler' (as the newspapers had christened him) were dead, and they had no idea of what he looked like.

But when the Portland police had the idea of asking newspapers to publish descriptions of jewellery that had been stolen from some of the strangler's victims, three old ladies in a South Portland lodging house recalled that they had bought a few items of jewellery from a pleasant young man who had stayed with them for a few days. They decided purely as a precaution to take it to the police.

It proved to belong to a Seattle landlady, Mrs Florence Monks, who had been strangled and raped on 24 November 1926. And the old ladies were able to tell the police that the Dark Strangler was a short, blue-eyed young man with a round face and slightly simian mouth and jaw. He was quietly spoken, and claimed to be deeply religious.

On 8 June 1927, the strangler crossed the Canadian border, and rented a room in Winnipeg from a Mrs Catherine Hill. He stayed for three nights. But on 9 June a couple named Cowan, who lived in the house, reported that their fourteen-year-old daughter Lola had vanished. That same evening, a man named William Patterson returned home to find his wife absent. After making supper and putting the children to bed, he rang the police. Then he dropped on his knees beside the bed to pray; as he did so, he saw his wife's hand sticking out. Her naked body lay under the bed.

The Winnipeg police recognized the *modus operandi* of the Gorilla Murderer. A check on boarding-house landladies brought them to Mrs Hill's establishment. She assured them that she had taken in no suspicious characters recently – her last lodger had been a Roger Wilson, who had been carrying a Bible and been highly religious. When she told them that Roger Wilson was short, with piercing blue eyes and a dark complexion, they asked to see the room he had stayed in. They were greeted by the stench of decay. The body of Lola Cowan lay under the bed, mutilated as if by Jack the Ripper. The murderer had slept with it in his room for three days. From the Patterson household, the strangler had taken some of the husband's clothes, leaving his own behind. But he changed these at a second-hand shop, leaving behind a fountain pen belonging to Patterson, and paying in $10 bills stolen from his house. So the police now not only had a good description of the killer, but the clothes he was wearing, including corduroy trousers and a plaid shirt.

The next sighting came from Regina, 200 miles west; a landlady heard the screams of a pretty girl who worked for the telephone company, and interrupted the man who had been trying to throttle her; he ran away. The police guessed that he might be heading back towards the American border, which would take him across prairie country with few towns; there was a good chance that a lone hitch-hiker would be noticed.

Descriptions of the wanted man were sent out to all police stations and post offices. Five days later, two constables saw a man wearing corduroys and a plaid shirt walking down a road near Killarney, twelve miles from the border. He gave his name as Virgil Wilson and said he was a farmworker; he seemed quite unperturbed when the police told him they were looking for a mass murderer, and would have to take him in on suspicion. His behaviour was so unalarmed they were convinced he was innocent. But when they telephoned the Winnipeg chief of police, and described Virgil Wilson, he told them that the man was undoubtedly 'Roger Wilson', the Dark Strangler. They hurried back to the jail – to find that their prisoner had picked the lock of his handcuffs and escaped. Detectives were rushed to the town by aeroplane, and posses spread out over the area. 'Wilson' had slept in a barn close to the jail, and the next morning broke into a house and stole a change of clothing. The first man he spoke to that morning noticed his dishevelled appearance and asked if he had spent the night in the open; the man admitted that he had.

When told that police were on their way to Killarney by train to look for the strangler, he ran away towards the railway. At that moment a police car appeared; after a short chase, the fugitive was captured. He was identified as Earle Leonard Nelson, born in Philadelphia in 1897; his mother had died of venereal disease contracted from his father. At the age of ten, Nelson was knocked down by a streetcar and was unconscious with concussion for six days. From then on, he experienced violent periodic headaches. He began to make a habit of peering through the keyhole of his cousin Rachel's bedroom when she was getting undressed. At twenty-one he was arrested for trying to rape a girl in a basement. Sent to a penal farm, he soon escaped, and was recaptured peering in through the window of his cousin as she undressed for bed.

A marriage was unsuccessful; when his wife had a nervous breakdown, Nelson visited her in hospital and tried to rape her in bed. Nothing is known of Nelson's whereabouts for the next three years, until the evening in February 1926, when he knocked on the door of Mrs Clara Newman in San Francisco and asked if he could see the room she had to let . . .

The Case of the Croydon Poisonings

The London suburb of Croydon has always been a quiet and respectable area – one in which scandals tend to be of a domestic rather criminal nature. Yet, in the early months of 1929, this peaceful backwater was discovered to be the scene of what was to become one of the most notorious cases of mass poisoning in British legal history.

In April 1928, Edmund Creighton Duff was living with his wife Grace and their three children at 16 South Park Road, Croydon. At fifty-nine, Duff, a retired British Resident in the civil service of Northern Nigeria and veteran of the Boer War, was supplementing his modest pension by working at a City firm of paper manufacturers and indulging in the odd financial investment. He was a jovial and well-liked man – nicknamed "Major Duff" by his friends – who gave the impression of exceptional fitness and robust constitution.

Thus, while enjoying a spring fishing trip, he was disturbed to find he was running a fever. He returned home early and complained of it to his wife, but she paid it little heed; he had a tendency to overreact on the rare occasions he felt under the weather. Despite the fever he ate a supper of chicken and vegetables and washed it down with bottled beer. Shortly afterwards he complained of severe stomach-ache and, on his way to bed, of leg cramps. During the night his condition worsened and a physician, Dr John Binning, was called to attend him. Binning diagnosed colic, but as Duff worsened he

71

realized it was something far more dangerous. He and his partner, Dr Robert Elwell, fought hard to keep their patient alive, but at 11.20 p.m. on the evening after his return from his fishing trip, Edmund Duff died in agony.

The two doctors were at a loss to explain their patient's death and so were legally unable to sign the death certificate; in such circumstances an inquest is automatically carried out. Despite the fact that Duff had exhibited all the major symptoms of arsenic poisoning, neither doctor was inclined to follow this suggestion to its logical conclusion. They were both friends of the Duffs – Dr Elwell especially, who liked to half-jokingly flirt with Grace Duff – and understandably dismissed the possibility of murder.

The pathologist who performed the autopsy, Dr Robert Bronte, reported to the coroner's inquest that the body showed no sign of the ingestion of arsenic. He attributed the death to a heart attack brought on by sunstroke sustained on the fishing trip. In the light of subsequent events this autopsy report was rather amazing to say the least; Dr Bronte had made a misjudgement of staggering proportions. If he had conducted the autopsy more thoroughly a murder inquiry would have ensued and, quite possibly, two lives would have been saved. When Sir Bernard Spilsbury performed a second inquest, he found that Bronte had left most of the intestines unexamined, and that he had accidentally put back into Duff's body some of the organs from a woman on whom he had been performing an inquest the same day.

Duff's funeral was, of course, attended by his wife's family; her mother, the rather imperious Mrs Violet Emilia Sidney, her younger sister Miss Vera Sidney – unmarried and at forty, a boisterous good-natured woman and the apple of her mother's eye – and her brother Thomas Sidney, a professional entertainer.

Although not noticeably well-to-do the Sidneys were an upper-class family and highly respected in the local community. They were a close-knit, not to say clannish family, and

Edmund had always been treated as a bit of an outsider. In fact, there had been some friction between Edmund Duff and the Sidneys. Mrs Sidney had felt Duff to be rather too lower class and underpaid for her daughter – especially after he lost £5,000 of Grace's money on a bad investment. The abrasively humorous Tom Sidney considered Edmund too stuffy and often made jokes at his expense. It was also suggested, after the discovery of the murders, that Duff had had an affair with Tom's attractive American wife, Margaret. Even so, the idea of any foul play involved in his death had, as yet, occurred to nobody. On 11 February 1929, almost a year after the death, Vera Sidney – Grace's younger sister – complained of feeling off-colour.

This in itself was unusual since she generally refused to give in to sicknesses and thought little of those that did. In fact she was not the only person in Violet Sidney's house who felt ill that day. The maid, Kate Noakes, and the family cat were also ill. The connecting factor was the soup all three had eaten at lunchtime.

Vera rallied a couple of days later, as did the maid and cat, but then made the mistake of taking the soup again for lunch, this time joined by her Aunt Gwen. Both became ill, but only Vera was seriously affected. Again Doctors Binning and Elwell were called. This time they were unwilling to take any chances and brought in a stomach specialist. He diagnosed intestinal influenza.

Vera died in great pain on 15 February, four days after she was first taken ill. Again, the possibility of murder was still not considered by the family physicians despite the fact that she had displayed virtually the same symptoms of arsenic poisoning as had Edmund Duff.

Violet Sidney was shattered by her daughter's death and her family feared that the old lady might die of the shock. Doctor Elwell prescribed her a strengthening tonic to be taking before meals and she started to slowly recover. Then, on 5 March 1929, she took her tonic, ate her lunch and became very ill. In

73

her lucid moments she insisted that she had been poisoned. The tonic had tasted oddly gritty and bitter and she was convinced that something had been added to it. The already weakened, seventy-year-old lady died within hours, once again displaying the symptoms of arsenic poisoning.

This time even Elwell and Binning could not ignore the evidence and refused to sign the death certificate. Even so, Violet Sidney had been laid to rest by the time the Home Office decided to make enquiries; so she had to be disinterred, along with her daughter and later her son-in-law, to be re-examined.

This time the autopsies were carried out by Dr Bernard Spilsbury, a brilliant pathologist who did much to advance the field of forensic science. His more expert examination found the bodies to contain up to five grains of arsenic each; more than enough to cause death. At last the murders were out.

The poisonings received much media coverage and people up and down the country followed the reports of the three inquests with avid interest. It seemed clear to most observers that a member of the family or somebody close to it was probably responsible. The chances of an outsider, for whatever reason, being able to administer poison surreptitiously was next to nil.

Edmund Duff, it was reported, had quite probably been poisoned on his return from the fishing trip; most likely administered in his bottled beer. Vera had almost certainly been fed the arsenic in her soup; Violet Sidney never partook of soup and the maid had ineffectually been told she could not have any (let alone give it to the cat). Finally forensic examination indeed found heavy traces of arsenic in Violet's tonic bottle. The likeliest source of the arsenic was deduced to be weedkiller, freely available and present in the houses of all the male participants. Police conducted a large and exhaustive investigation and the Coroner's Court questioned all possible suspects with great care, but in the end the case came to nothing The evidence was too scanty to implicate any one

74

person or persons of committing the murders and no solid motive could be attached to any of them.

In the end, the three people considered most likely to have been the murdered were Tom Sidney, Grace Duff and, rather weirdly, Violet Sidney, the poisoned mother. Violet was accused by some of hating Edmund Duff and of somehow getting into his pantry and doctoring a bottle of his beer. Then a year later, mad with guilt, she was said to have poisoned her much-loved daughter to punish herself. Finally she committed suicide, revealing as she died that the poison had been in her tonic.

It is probably quite safe to reject this theory completely. Violet was not fond of Duff, but had never shown any sign of virulently hating him. All agreed that her shock and grief over the death of Vera were genuine and finally she had seemed both amazed and affronted when proclaiming that she had been poisoned.

Tom Sidney had some financial motive for killing his sister and mother; he stood to gain about £8,000 from their wills, but at the time of the murders he was doing quite well himself and his finances were on a comfortable upturn. An anonymous letter was sent to the coroner at the time of the inquests claiming that Duff was seeing Tom's wife, but no other evidence was ever found to suggest that he had a reason to kill his stuffy brother-in-law.

The most likely candidate, in fact, was Grace Duff. Outwardly a bright and cheerful woman, she was known by close acquaintances to have dark mood swings and to have resented her husband's overly brutal amorous advances (she complained that he left her covered in bruises). Edmund had been away working in Africa for much of their married life and his retirement and permanent return might have upset the balance of her life. She was highly protective of her children and Edmund's dodgy financial deals threatened the future of the whole family. She may have wanted him out of the way so that she might marry Dr Elwell, her flirtatious family physician. It is even possible that she killed him for sleeping with her brother's wife.

Her financial state was improved by her husband's death; in fact she gained enough from his life insurance to buy the house they had previously only rented. Even so, she was still far from being comfortably off; £8,000 might have seemed very tempting and having committed one murder others might have seemed less difficult.

Tom Sidney claimed to have no doubt that Grace was the murderer, and apparently neither did Scotland Yard. He later said that the police suggested that he move as far from Grace as possible, so he took his family to the USA. But we only have his word that this was the case; in the States he was also somewhat safer from British justice if new evidence were to be uncovered. It had also come to light that Violet's estranged husband, the father of Grace, Tom and Vera, had had an illegitimate son who was said to have resented his father's previous family. There is still no definite proof to connect Grace with the poisonings and in the end she remains merely the most likely of several suspects.

The Cleveland Torso Killer

On a warm September afternoon in 1935, two boys on their way home from school walked along a dusty, sooty gully called Kingsbury Run, in the heart of Cleveland, Ohio. On a weed-covered slope known as Jackass Hill, one challenged the other to a race, and they hurtled 60 feet down the slope to the bottom.

Sixteen-year-old James Wagner was the winner, and as he halted, panting, he noticed something white in the bushes a few yards away. A closer look revealed that it was a naked body, and that it was headless.

The police who arrived soon after found the body of a young white male clad only in black socks; the genitals had also been removed. The body lay on its back, with the legs stretched out and the arms placed neatly by the sides, as if laid out for a funeral. Thirty feet away, the policemen found another body, lying in the same position; it was of an older man, and had also been decapitated and emasculated.

Hair sticking out of the ground revealed one of the heads a few yards away, and the second was found nearby. The genitals were also found lying nearby, as if thrown away by the killer. One curious feature of the case was that there was no blood on the ground or on the bodies, which were quite clean. It looked as if they had been killed and beheaded elsewhere, then carefully washed when they had ceased to bleed.

77

Medical examination made the case more baffling than ever. The older corpse was badly decomposed, and the skin discoloured; the pathologists discovered that this was due to some chemical substance, as if the killer had tried to preserve the body. The older victim had been dead about two weeks. The younger man had only been dead three days. His finger-prints enabled the police to identify him as twenty-eight-year-old Edward Andrassy, who had a minor police record for carrying concealed weapons. He lived near Kingsbury Run and had a reputation as a drunken brawler.

But the most chilling discovery was that Andrassy had been killed by decapitation. Rope marks on his wrists revealed that he had been tied and had struggled violently. The killer had apparently cut off his head with a knife. The skill with which the operation had been performed suggested a butcher – or possibly a surgeon.

It proved impossible to identify the older man. But the identification of Andrassy led the police to hope that it should not be too difficult to trace his killer. He had spent his nights gambling and drinking in a slum part of town and was known as a pimp.

But further investigation also revealed that he had male lovers. Lead after lead looked marvellously promising. The husband of a married woman with whom he had had an affair had sworn to kill him. But the man was able to prove his innocence. So were various shady characters who might have borne a grudge.

Lengthy police investigation led to a dead end – as it did in another ten cases of the killer who became known as 'the Mad Butcher of Kingsbury Run'.

Four months later, on a raw January Sunday, the howling of a dog finally led a black woman resident of East Twentieth Street – not far from Kingsbury Run – to go and investigate. She found the chained animal trying to get at a basket near a factory wall.

Minutes later, she told a neighbour that the basket contained 'hams'. But the neighbour soon recognized the 'hams' as parts of a human arm. A burlap bag proved to contain the lower half of a female torso. The head was missing, as were the left arm and lower parts of both legs. But fingerprints again enabled the police to trace the victim, who had a record for soliciting. She proved to be a forty-one-year-old prostitute named Florence Polillo, a squat, double-chinned woman who was well known in the bars of the neighbourhood.

Again, there were plenty of leads, and again, all of them petered out. Two weeks later, the left arm and lower leg were found in a vacant lot. The head was never recovered. The murder of Flo Polillo raised an unwelcome question. The first two murders had convinced the police that they were looking for a homosexual sadist; this latest crime made it look as if this killer was quite simply a sadist – like Peter Kürten, the Düsseldorf killer, executed in 1931; he had killed men, women and children indifferently, and he was not remotely homosexual. And now the pathologist recalled that, a year before the first double murder, the torso of an unknown woman had been found on the edge of Lake Erie. It began to look as if the Mad Butcher was quite simply a sadist.

At least the Cleveland public felt they had one thing in their favour. Since the double killing, the famous Eliot Ness had been appointed Cleveland's Director of Public Safety. Ness and his "Untouchables" had cleared up Chicago's Prohibition rackets, then, in 1934, Ness had moved to Cleveland to fight its gangsters. With Ness in charge, the Head Hunter of Kingsbury Run – another press sobriquet – would find himself becoming the hunted.

But it was soon clear to Ness that hunting a sadistic pervert is nothing like hunting professional gangsters. The killer struck at random, and unless he was careless enough to leave behind a clue – like a fingerprint – then the only hope of catching him was in the act. And Ness soon became convinced that the Mad Butcher took great pleasure in feeling that he was several steps ahead of the police.

The Head Hunter waited until the summer before killing again, then lived up to his name by leaving the head of a young man, wrapped in a pair of trousers, under a bridge in Kingsbury Run; again, two boys found it, on 22 June 1936. The body was found a quarter of a mile away, and it was obvious from the blood that he had died where he lay. And medical evidence showed that he had died from decapitation – it was not clear how the killer had prevented him from struggling while he did it. The victim was about twenty-five, and heavily tattooed. His fingerprints were not in police files. Three weeks later, a young female hiker discovered another decapitated body in a gully; the head lay nearby. The decomposition made it clear that this man had been killed before the previously discovered victim.

The last 'Butchery' of 1936 was of another man of about thirty, found in Kingsbury Run; the body had been cut in two, and emasculated. A hat found nearby led to a partial identification: a housewife recalled giving it to a young tramp. Not far away there was a 'hobo camp' where down-and-outs slept; this was obviously where the Butcher had found his latest victim.

The fact that Cleveland had been the scene of a Republican Convention and was now the site of a 'Great Expo', led to even more frantic police activity and much press criticism. The murders were reported all over the world and, in Nazi Germany and Fascist Italy, were cited as proof of the decadence of the New World.

As month after month went by with no further grisly discoveries, Clevelanders hoped they had heard the last of the Mad Butcher. But in February 1937, that hope was dashed when the killer left the body of a young woman in a chopped-up pile on the shores of Lake Erie. She was never identified. The eighth victim, a young black woman, was identified from her teeth as Mrs Rose Wallace, forty; only the skeleton remained, and it looked as if she may have been killed in the previous year.

Victim number nine was male and had been dismembered; when he was fished out of the river, the head was missing, and was never found. This time the killer had gone even further in his mutilations – like Jack the Ripper, it was impossible to identify the victim. Two men seen in a boat were thought to be the Butcher with an accomplice, but this suggestion that there might be two Butchers led nowhere.

The Butcher now seems to have taken a rest until nine months later. Then the lower part of a leg was pulled out of the river.

Three weeks later, two burlap bags in the river proved to contain more body fragments, which enabled the pathologist to announce that the victim was female, a brunette of about twenty-five. She was never identified.

The killer was to strike twice more. More than a year after the last discovery, in August 1938, the dismembered torso of a woman was found on a dump on the lakefront, and a search of the area revealed the bones of a second victim, a male. A quilt in which the remains of this twelfth victim were wrapped was identified as having been given to a junk man. Neither body could be identified.

One thing was now obvious: the Butcher was selecting his victims from vagrants and down-and-outs. Ness decided to take the only kind of action that seemed left to him: two days after the last find, police raided the 'shantytown' near Kingsbury Run, arrested hundreds of vagrants, and burned it down. Whether or not by coincidence, the murders now ceased.

The suspects. Two of the Ness's most efficient of the manhunters, Detectives Merylo and Zalewski, had spent a great deal of time searching for the killer's 'laboratory'. At one point they thought they had found it – but, like all leads, this one faded away.

Next the investigators discovered that Flo Polillo and Rose Wallace – victim number eight – had frequented the same saloon, and that Andrassy – number two – had been a 'regular' there too. They also learned of a middle-aged man called Frank who carried knives and threatened people with them when drunk. When they learned that this man – Frank Dolezal – had also been living with Flo Polillo, they felt they had finally identified the killer. Dolezal was arrested, and police discovered a brown substance like dried blood in the cracks of his bathroom floor. Knives with dried bloodstains on them provided further incriminating evidence. Under intensive questioning, Dolezal – a bleary-eyed, unkempt man – confessed to the murder of Flo Polillo. Newspapers announced the capture of the Butcher. Then things began to go wrong. The 'dried blood' in the bathroom proved not to be blood after all. Dolezal's 'confession' proved to be full of errors about the corpse and method of disposal. And when, in August 1939, Dolezal hanged himself in jail, the autopsy revealed that he had two cracked ribs, and suggested that his confession had been obtained by force.

Yet Ness himself claimed that he knew the solution to the murders. He reasoned that the killer was a man who had a house of his own in which to dismember the bodies, and a car in which to transport them. So he was not a down-and-out. The skill of the mutilations suggested medical training. The fact that some of the victims had been strong men suggested that the Butcher had to be big and powerful – a conclusion supported by a size-twelve footprint near one of the bodies.

Ness sent three of his top agents, Virginia Allen, Barney Davis and Jim Manski, to make enquiries among the upper levels of Cleveland society. Virginia was a sophisticated girl with contacts among Cleveland socialites. And it was she who learned about a man who sounded like the ideal suspect. Years later, in his bestselling memoirs, Ness was to call him 'Gaylord Sundheim' – a big man from a well-to-do family, who had a history of psychiatric problems. He had also studied medicine. When the three 'Untouchables' called on him, he leered sarcastically at Virginia and closed the door in their faces. Ness invited him – pressingly – to lunch, and he came under protest.

When Ness finally told him he suspected him of being the Butcher – hoping that shock tactics might trigger a confession – 'Sundheim' sneered: 'Prove it.'

Soon after this, 'Sundheim' had himself committed to a mental institution. Ness knew he was now 'untouchable', for even if Ness could prove his guilt, he could plead insanity.

During the next two years Ness received a series of jeering postcards, some signed 'Your paranoid nemesis'. They ceased abruptly when 'Sundheim' died in the mental institution.

Was 'Sundheim' the Butcher? Probably. But not certainly. In Pittsburgh in 1940, three decapitated bodies were found in old boxcars (railway coaches). Members of Ness's team went to investigate, but no clue to the treble murder was ever discovered.

The case remains unsolved.

Gordon Cummins,
the 'Blackout Ripper'

Sex crimes invariably increase during wartime. This is partly because the anarchic social atmosphere produces a loss of inhibition, partly because so many soldiers have been deprived of their usual sexual outlet. Nevertheless, the rate of sex crime in England during the second World War remained low, while the murder rate actually fell.

One of the few cases to excite widespread attention occurred during the 'blackouts' of 1942. Between 9 and 15 February, four women were murdered in London. Evelyn Hamilton, a forty-year-old schoolteacher, was found strangled in an air raid shelter; Evelyn Oatley, an ex-revue actress, was found naked on her bed, her throat cut and her belly mutilated with a tin opener; Margaret Lower was strangled with a silk stocking and mutilated with a razor blade, and Doris Jouannet was killed in an identical manner. The killer's bloody fingerprints were found on the tin opener and on a mirror in Evelyn Oatley's flat. A few days later a young airman dragged a woman into a doorway near Piccadilly and throttled her into unconsciousness, but a passer-by overheard the scuffle and went to investigate. The airman ran away, dropping his gasmask case with his service number stencilled on it. Immediately afterwards, he accompanied a prostitute to her flat in Paddington and began to throttle her; her screams and struggles again frightened him away.

From the gas-mask case the man was identified as twenty-eight-year-old Gordon Cummins, from north London, and he was arrested as soon as he returned to his billet. The finger-print evidence identified him as the 'blackout ripper', and he was hanged in June 1942. Sir Bernard Spilsbury, who had performed the postmortem on Evelyn Oatley, also performed one on Cummins.

Dr Marcel Petiot

Doctor Marcel Petiot was perhaps the most iconic serial killer of his day. A conman, egotist and sadist, his murderous career seemed almost to ape those greatest mass murderers of the period: the Nazis.

Petoit was born in Auxerre in 1897, the son of a minor official in the French Post Office. He showed some criminal tendencies at school, regularly stealing from classmates. But he began his real criminal career by robbing letterboxes. In 1917 he was conscripted into the army and stole drugs from a casualty clearing station and sold them at black-market prices to morphine addicts in the nearby town of Dijon. Petiot was eventually discharged from the army on psychological grounds, along with a military pension.

The pension doubtless helped him to be able to afford to go on to study medicine. There can be no doubt of his remarkable mental abilities; he spent part of his three years of study in an asylum, and the rest at home with his mother. She later declared that she never saw him study. Nevertheless, Petiot qualified as a doctor in 1921.

He practised medicine in Villeneuve, and in 1928 became mayor. While still a bachelor he employed an unusually attractive housekeeper. But when she became noticeably pregnant, she suddenly disappeared. She was never seen again.

Petiot married and had one son. Even as mayor he seems to have retained his tendency for petty crime, and was in trouble with the police for robbing his electric meter. He was also convicted of thefts from a municipal store, and sent to prison; this appears to be the reason that he ceased to be mayor in 1930. Nevertheless, he continued to be well liked by his fellow townsmen.

It was also in 1930 that one of his patients, Madame Debauve, was robbed and killed. Gossip named Petiot as her killer, but when his chief accuser – whom Petiot happened to be treating for rheumatism – died suddenly, the gossip petered out. Petiot signed the death certificate, blaming natural causes. Another woman, who accused him of encouraging her daughter's drug addiction – which he was supposed to be curing – also disappeared. In 1945 an inquiry was made into these deaths and disappearances, but it was found that his police dossier had also disappeared from Villeneuve.

While visiting Paris he was convicted of theft of a book from a shop, but was finally discharged on condition he submit to psychiatric treatment. Then, at the beginning of the Second World War, he was convicted of drug trafficking and was stated in the court records to be an addict himself; but he managed to get off with only a small fine to pay.

Meanwhile the world was going to war. In May 1940 the Germans invaded France. After six weeks of savage fighting, and after suffering 130,000 soldiers killed in action, France surrendered to Nazi occupation in July 1940. Almost immediately French Jews and other 'undesirables' started to be rounded up and sent east to German concentration camps and, for very many of them, death. A lot of people suddenly needed to get out of France as quickly and quietly as possible. Dr Petiot evidently realised this; and decided to take advantage of them.

It seems probable that Petiot acquired his house in the Rue Lesueur with the express purpose of committing of multiple murders. A builder made certain alterations to the structure, completing them in September 1941; they included a strange, windowless triangular cellar, and an outside wall that was increased in height to prevent neighbours from being able to see into the courtyard. The upper part of the house was not to be used. Other, more sinister constructions were made by Dr Petiot himself in secret. Petiot also had a flat and small consulting room at 66 Rue Caumartin, where his wife and son lived.

A detailed list of Petiot's victims is not known, but it seems reasonably certain that the first 'refugee victim' was a Polish furrier named Joachim Gusbinov, a neighbour of Petiot's in the Rue Caumartin. He sold his fur business and withdrew two million francs from his bank. Then, in January 1942, he called on Petiot at Rue Lesueur, and was never seen again. Another early victim was a colleague of Petiot's, Dr Paul Braunberger; there was also a whole family, the Knellers.

Petiot's method seemed to be to employ four men to find his victims. These agents lounged around cafes and bars on the lookout for men and women who wanted to escape abroad. Petiot's employees had no idea of the ultimate fate of his 'customers,' and might well have felt that they were helping to save people from the Nazi occupation.

The murders continued throughout 1942, until May 1943. Then, ironically, Petiot was himself arrested by the Gestapo under suspicion of helping 'saboteurs' to escape from France. His arrest was preceded by a sad incident; the Gestapo blackmailed a Jewish man into calling on Petiot to inquire about escaping. When the man disappeared, the Germans assumed that he had taken advantage of Petiot's escape facilities. In fact, the Germans had accidentally sent yet another Jew to his death.

Although all Gestapo records were later destroyed by the retreating Germans, it seems likely that Dr Petiot eventually confessed that he was not helping but killing people attempting to flee from the Nazis. His interrogators were therefore placed in an odd position – did they shoot him as a mass murderer or give him a medal for so enthusiastically embracing the Nazi ideology? In the end they took the middle route and, in December 1943, released him without charge or comment. Petiot continued his career of murdering Jews and Frenchmen who wanted to escape – this time without fear of Nazi intervention.

On Saturday 11 March 1944 Petiot's neighbour in the Rue Lesueur, M. Jacques Marcais, was sickened by the greasy black smoke that poured from his neighbour's house, and complained to the police. Two policemen called, and found a card pinned to the door that directed inquiries to Rue Caumartin. They telephoned Petiot, who replied that he would be over immediately. But in the meantime the smoke from the chimney so enraged the police sergeant that he called the fire brigade.

The chimney was on fire thanks, in part, to all the vapourised human fat that had previously passed through it. When the firemen forced an entry, they found the offending stove in the cellar. They also found the remains of twenty-seven bodies lying around the cellar, most of them partly dismembered. As the police crowded through the house, Petiot entered and calmly walked around introducing himself as the owner of the house.

When the police sergeant told him that he would have to arrest him, Petiot showed his unpleasant streak of genius once again. He took the policeman aside and quietly informed him that what he had discovered was the secret execution chamber of the French Resistance; the bodies were those of pro-Nazis, collaborators and other traitors, he assured him. This was a risk, of course, because if the sergeant had himself been a pro-Nazi it would have guaranteed Petiot's arrest. But most Frenchmen were pro-Resistance, so the risk was not so great. The sergeant let the doctor go.

Petiot returned to the Rue Caumartin, packed some suitcases, and fled with his wife Georgette and 17-year-old son. The police investigation continued in Auxerre and the radio shop of Petiot's brother, where it was soon established that Petiot had spent a night on leaving Paris. Petiot's wife was also found in

Auxerre, but she appeared to be ignorant of her husband's grisly hobby. The Gestapo joined the quisling French authorities in hunting the murderer, but had as little luck.

Investigation of the house on the Rue Lesueur showed just how Petiot had killed his victims. The triangular-shaped cellar was a home-made gas chamber. The doctor would get his victims to enter – doubtless claiming that it was a safe place to hide from the Germans until transport out of the country could be arranged. He then sealed the ceiling hatch from the outside and gassed them. Much of the 'empty' upstairs of the house was filled with the belongings of his victims, including 47 empty suitcases. Further investigation suggested that he had sold many portable valuables, like jewellery, on the black market, gaining perhaps a million francs as a result.

But financial gain was clearly not the doctor's main reason for killing men, women and children. He had built a periscope into his gas chamber, allowing him to watch his victim's death agonies.

In June 1944 came D-Day, and on 24 August Paris was liberated. Doctor Petiot remained at large. The newspapers devoted a great deal of space to him, and there were many conflicting reports – of his body being recovered from two different rivers, of his being a doctor in a German concentration camp, and several other such groundless speculations. Some people believed what his wife Georgette had suggested, that Petiot was working for the Resistance. But many newspapers stated their belief that he had actually been working for the Gestapo.

In October, Petiot made a major mistake: he wrote to the newspaper *Resistance* declaring that he had been 'framed' by the Gestapo, who had made his house a dumping ground for corpses while he was in prison. He stated that the Gestapo's purpose in hunting him, and in making such a fuss about the murders, was to distract attention from Russian victories on the Eastern Front. Petiot then foolishly stated that he was still a signed-up officer in the Resistance.

It was already known that he had never joined the Resistance under his own name, but what about under a false name in order to create a false identity? The handwriting of the letter was checked against that of all officers who were enrolled in the Free French forces in Paris. Finally, it was found that it corresponded exactly with that of a 'Captain Henri Valery', serving at Reuilly; he had been a member of the Free French forces for exactly six weeks before disappearing. 'Valery' might have been the name that Petiot was using. In fact, the false name led to Petiot's whereabouts.

He was arrested on 2 November 1944, as he left the Metro station at St Mande Tourelle on the eastern outskirts of Paris. It turned out that he had been hiding in a flat in the Rue Faubourg St Denis, and had grown a beard. Because of a habit of standing at the open window with a hairy, bare chest, he became known locally as 'Tarzan', and a complaint had even been made to the police about his semi-nudism. The man who had been sheltering Petiot was a house painter, Georges Redoute, who knew Petiot. Petiot had told Reodoute that his home had been destroyed in an air raid and his wife killed, though, in view of the tremendous publicity that followed the hunt for Petiot, it is hard to see how Redoute continued to believe this during the seven months Petiot stayed with him.

Petiot was interrogated at the Quai des Orfevres. It was discovered that he had entered the army on 27 September, and had been given the task of making prisoners talk. His secretary, 25-year-old Mlle Cecile Dylma, described him as a gentle man who had some curious sadistic traits.

Petiot declared that the twenty-seven bodies found in his cellar were mostly of German soldiers. He admitted that he had killed sixty-three people, but declared he had been working for the Resistance, and had also helped many patriotic Frenchmen to escape. He even named several famous Resistance leaders as his colleagues. All too fortuitously for Petiot, these leaders were all dead.

His trial opened after seventeen months of investigation, on

18 March 1946 and lasted for three weeks. It took place at the Seine Assize Court. M. Pierre Duval was the Public Prosecutor, while a brilliant lawyer, René Floriot, defended. The long, sad procession of relatives of the victims threaded through the courtroom. A Resistance officer was called to prove that Petiot was completely ignorant of many matters of which he claimed inside knowledge. In his own evidence to the court Petiot put up a spirited defence, but came across as arrogant and egotistical.

On the fifth day of the trial the entire court went to Rue Lesueur and looked at the murder room, and at the periscope through which he had watched his victims die, and at the cellar on the other side of the courtyard which Petiot had filled with quicklime 'for whitewashing'. And at the grease-blackened stove that had eventually given him away.

At 9.30 p.m. on 4 April 1946, the jury of seven members and three judges retired; at midnight, they were back, with a verdict of guilty for twenty-four of the twenty-seven murders. It was a scene of such uproar in the court that Judge Leser could not initially make himself heard; when Petiot finally made out the verdict, he bellowed with rage and fought with his guards.

His appeal was rejected and he was guillotined on the morning of 26 May 1946. The number and identities of Doctor Petiot's victims are unknown. Petiot himself admitted 63 murders (claiming that they had all been 'enemies of France') but the true figure is probably higher. We do know that he killed entire families at the same time – just as the SS did in the extermination camps.

Christie, the
'Monster of Notting Hill'

John Reginald Halliday Christie, whose crimes created a sensation in post-war London, belonged to another typical class of serial killer: the necrophile. (Henry Lee Lucas and Jeffrey Dahmer are later examples.)

On 24 March 1953, a Jamaican tenant of 10 Rillington Place was sounding the walls in the kitchen on the ground floor, previously occupied by Christie. One wall sounded hollow and the Jamaican pulled off a corner of wallpaper. He discovered that the paper covered a cupboard, one corner of which was missing. He was able to peer into the cupboard with the help of a torch and saw the naked back of a woman.

Hastily summoned policemen discovered that the cupboard contained three female bodies. The first was naked except for a brassiere and suspender belt; the other two were wrapped in blankets secured with electric wire. There was very little smell, which was due to atmospheric conditions causing dehydration. (Some of the more sensational accounts of the case state inaccurately that the tenant was led to the discovery by the smell of decomposition.) Floorboards in the front room appeared to have been disturbed, and they were taken up to reveal a fourth body, also wrapped in a blanket. Christie had left on 20 March, sub-letting to a Mr and Mrs Reilly, who had paid him £7 13s. in advance. The Reillys had been turned out almost immediately by the owner, a Jamaican, Charles

Brown, since Christie had no right to sub-let, and had, in fact, left owing rent.

The back garden was dug up and revealed human bones, the skeletons of two more bodies. A human femur was being used to prop up the fence. It was now remembered that in 1949, two other bodies – those of Mrs Evans and her baby daughter Geraldine – had been discovered at the same address. Both had been strangled, and the husband, Timothy Evans, was hanged for the double murder.

Evans was a near-mental defective, and it seemed conceivable that the murders for which he was hanged were the work of the man who had killed the women in the downstairs flat. On 31 March, Christie was recognized by PC Ledger on the embankment near Putney Bridge and was taken to Putney Bridge police station. In the week since the discovery of the bodies, the hue and cry had been extraordinary, and newspapers ran pictures of the back garden of 10 Rillington Place and endless speculations about the murders and whether the murderer would commit another sex crime before his arrest. (Mr Alexei Surkov, the secretary of the Soviet League of Writers, happened to be in England at the time, and later commented with irony on the press furore.) Christie made a statement admitting to the murders of the four women in the house. In it he claimed that his wife had been getting into an increasingly nervous condition because of attacks from the coloured people in the house, and that on the morning of 14 December 1952, he had been awakened by his wife's convulsive movements; she was having some kind of a fit; Christie 'could not bear to see her', and strangled her with a stocking. His account of the other three murders – Rita Nelson, aged twenty-five, Kathleen Maloney, aged twenty-six, Hectorina McLennan, aged twenty-six, described quarrels with the women (who were prostitutes) during the course of which Christie strangled them.

Later, he also confessed to the murders of the two women in the garden. One was an Austrian girl, Ruth Fuerst, whom

Christie claimed he had murdered during sexual intercourse; and Muriel Eady, a fellow employee at the Ultra Radio factory in Park Royal where Christie had worked in late 1944. A tobacco tin containing four lots of pubic hair was also found in the house. There were many curious features in the murders. Carbon monoxide was found in the blood of the three women in the cupboard, although not in Mrs Christie's. The three had semen in the vagina; none was wearing knickers, but all had a piece of white material between the legs in the form of a diaper. This has never been satisfactorily explained.

Christie admitted at his trial that his method of murder had been to invite women to his house and to get them partly drunk. They were persuaded to sit in a deckchair with a canopy, and a gas pipe was placed near the floor and turned on. When the girl lost consciousness from coal-gas poisoning, Christie would strangle her and then rape her. But since the women were prostitutes, it would hardly seem necessary to render them unconscious to have sexual intercourse.

One theory to explain this has been advanced by Dr Francis Camps, the pathologist who examined the bodies. He suggests that Christie had reached a stage of sexual incapability where the woman needed to be unconscious before he could possess her. (In Halifax, as a young man, Christie had earned from some girl the derogatory nicknames 'Can't Do It Christie' and 'Reggie-No-Dick'.)

The body of Rita Nelson was found to be six months pregnant. Christie was tried only for the murder of his wife; his trial opened at the Central Committee Court on Monday, 22 June 1953, before Mr Justice Finnemore; the Attorney-General, Sir Lionel Heald, led for the Crown; Mr Derek Curtis Bennett QC defended. Christie's case history, as it emerged at his trial, was as follows: he was fifty-five years old at the time of his arrest. He was born in Chester Street, Boothstown, Yorkshire, in April 1898, son of Ernest Christie, a carpet designer. The father was a harsh man who treated his seven children with Victorian sternness and offered no affection. Christie was a weak child, myopic, introverted, and jeered at by his fellow pupils as a 'cissy'. He had many minor illnesses in his childhood – possibly to compensate for lack of attention. He was in trouble with the police for trivial offences, and was beaten by his father whenever this occurred. At the age of fifteen (this would be in about 1913) he left school and got a post as a clerk to the Halifax Borough Police. Petty pilfering lost him the job. He then worked in his father's carpet factory; when he was dismissed from there for petty theft, his father threw him out of the house.

Christie was a chronic hypochondriac, a man who enjoyed being ill and talking about his past illnesses. (His first confession starts with an account of his poor health.) In 1915 he suffered from pneumonia. He then went to war, and was mustard-gassed and blown up. He claimed that he was blind for five months and lost his voice for three and a half years. The loss of voice was the psychological effect of hysteria, for there was no physical abnormality to account for it. His voice returned spontaneously at a time of emotional excitement.

Christie claimed that one of the most important events in his childhood was seeing his grandfather's body when he was eight. In 1920, Christie met his wife Ethel, and they were married in the same year. They had no children. Christie claimed he had no sexual relations with his wife for about two years – which, if true, supports the view of his sexual inadequacy and the inferiority neurosis that afflicted his relations with women.

In 1923 he quarrelled with his wife and they separated; he also lost his voice for three months. Details of the life of the Christies between the two wars are not available, except that he was knocked down by a car which did not stop, in 1934, and sustained injuries to the head, the knee and collarbone. (Christie seems to have been one of those unfortunate people who are born unlucky.)

And when he worked for the post office, it was found that

he was stealing money and postal orders from letters; for this he received seven months in prison. His longest term of employment was with a transport firm; this lasted for five years.

Duncan Webb, who was not the most reliable of crime writers, declared that Christie claimed to be a rich man when he married his wife, and that he joined the Conservative Association (presumably in Halifax) and tried to play the man about town. On separating from his wife in 1923 (after a second term in prison for false pretences), he came to London, and lodged in Brixton and Battersea. He struck a woman over the head with a cricket bat and went to jail again. His wife was induced to visit him, and started to live with him again when he came out.

In 1939, Christie joined the War Reserve Police, and became known as an officious constable who enjoyed showing his authority and 'running in' people for minor blackout offences. His wife often went to visit her family in Sheffield, and it was during one of her visits there that Christie brought Ruth Fuerst back to the house and strangled her. Although in his second confession he mentions strangling her during the act of intercourse, it is almost certain that he somehow persuaded her to inhale gas – perhaps from the square jar of Friar's Balsam, which he covered with a towel, claiming that it was a cure for nose and throat infections; while the victim's head was hidden under the towel, Christie inserted a tube leading from the gas tap. It may be that he only wanted to render the girl unconscious in order to have sexual intercourse, and decided to kill her later to cover up the assault.

In his confession he told of hiding Ruth Fuerst's body under the floorboards when his wife returned with her brother. The next day, when they were out, he moved the body to the wash-house and later buried it in the back garden under cover of darkness. At his trial, Christie declared that he was not sure whether Ruth Fuerst was his first victim. However, unless he had some other place in which to dispose of bodies, it seems probable that his 'vagueness' was intended to impress the jury that his mind was wandering.

In December 1943, Christie was released from the War Reserve and went to work at Ultra Radio. Here he became friendly with Muriel Eady, who often came to visit the Christies. On one occasion she came alone when Christie's wife was on holiday, and complained of catarrh. She buried her face in Christie's jar of Friar's Balsam, and later ended, like Ruth Fuerst, buried in the tiny garden. Whether the Evans murders were committed by Christie or by Timothy Evans will now never be known, but it seems almost certain that Christie committed them. In his third confession from Brixton prison, he declares that in August 1949, Timothy Evans and his young wife (who lived above the Christies) quarrelled violently about a blonde woman. Christie claimed that he found Mrs Evans lying on the floor in front of the gas fire, having attempted suicide, and that he gave her a cup of tea. The next day he found her there once again, and she asked his help in killing herself, offering to let him have sexual inter-course. He strangled her with a stocking, and (in view of the later cases) probably had intercourse with her.

When Timothy Evans came home, Christie told him that his wife had gassed herself and that no doubt Evans would be suspected of her murder. What happened then is not certain. It is possible that Evans then murdered the baby, Geraldine, who was later found with her mother in the wash-house. Within a few days he sold his furniture and disappeared.

But he then walked into the Merthyr Tydfil police station and claimed that he had killed his wife and put her body down a drain. The bodies were discovered in the wash-house, and Evans was charged with murder. At one point he claimed that Christie was the murderer, but when told that the child's body had also been found, he withdrew this allegation. Evans was of low mentality and illiterate; it is impossible to know what went on in his mind before his execution, or whether he murdered his daughter.

What is most surprising is that he did not inform on Christie when he found that his wife was strangled; this makes it seem possible that he had murdered his daughter, and saw no point in involving Christie too.

In December 1952 came the murder of his wife. The motive for this is not clear, although it may well have been a desire to have the house to himself for further murders. Whether or not this was his intention, Christie killed again a few weeks later. Rita Nelson had last been seen alive on 2 January 1953. Hers was the second body in the cupboard. Christie claimed she had accosted him and demanded money, finally forcing herself into his house and starting a fight. What seems more likely is that she came back to the house by his invitation and was gassed as she sat in the deckchair.

The next victim was Kathleen Maloney, last seen alive on 12 January 1953. Again, Christie claims she started a fight, but this seems unlikely.

Christie had no money at this time, and sold his furniture for £11 and his wife's wedding ring. He had written to his wife's bank in Sheffield, forging her signature, and asked for her money to be sent. (He had also sent a postcard to his wife's sister before Christmas claiming that she had rheumatism in her fingers and could not write.) Some time in February, Christie claims that he met a couple who told him they had nowhere to stay. The man was out of work. They came and stayed with Christie for a few days, and then left. Later, the woman – Hectorina McLennan – returned alone, and was murdered by Christie around 3 March.

After this, Christie claims he lost his memory and wandered around London (subsequent to 20 March, when he left Rillington Place), sleeping in a working men's hostel part of the time. When caught, he was unshaven and shabby, with no money. The defence was of insanity, but the jury rejected it, following several medical opinions that Christie was sane, and he was sentenced to death and executed on 15 July 1953.

Melvin Rees

From Martin Dumollard onwards, most serial killers have been curiously stupid – Carl Panzram was one of the few exceptions. But in the second half of the twentieth century, criminologists became aware of a new phenomenon – the 'high IQ' killer. Dumollard killed for money; Earle Nelson and Christie killed for sex. But the 'high IQ' killer cannot be classified so simply. He has often read books on criminology and psychology, and he may argue lucidly in favour of a life of crime. The 'Moors murderer' Ian Brady was of this type; so was the Muswell Hill murderer Dennis Nilsen and the 'Hillside Strangler' Kenneth Bianchi. The emergence of the 'high IQ' killer dates from the 1960s. But Brady and Manson were pre-dated by an American case from the late 1950s.

On Sunday, 11 January 1959 an old blue Chevrolet forced another car off a lonely country road in Virginia, and a tall, thin young man with staring eyes advanced on it waving a revolver. He ordered the Jackson family – consisting of Carrol Jackson, his wife Mildred, and their two children, Susan, aged five, and a baby, Janet – into the boot of his car, and sped off. Carrol Jackson was later found dead in a ditch; underneath him lay Janet, who had also been shot. Two months later, the bodies of Mildred Jackson and Susan were uncovered in Maryland; Mildred Jackson had been strangled with a stocking and Susan battered to death. Two years earlier, in June 1957, a man with staring eyes had approached a courting couple in a car – an army sergeant and a woman named Margaret Harold – and asked for a lift. On the way he pulled out a gun and demanded money; when Margaret Harold said: 'Don't give it to him,' he shot her in the back of the head. The sergeant flung open the door and ran.

When police found the car, they also found the body of Margaret Harold lying across the front seat without her dress; a police spokesman described the killer as 'a sexual degenerate'. Near the scene of the crime the police discovered a deserted shack full of pornographic pictures. Five months after the murders of the Jackson family, in May 1959, the police received an anonymous tip-off that the murderer was a jazz musician named Melvin Rees; but police were unable to trace Rees. Early the following year, a salesman named Glenn Moser went to the police, acknowledged that he was the author of the anonymous tip-off, and told them that he now had the suspect's address: Melvin Rees was working in a music shop in Memphis, Arkansas. Rees was arrested there, and soon after he was identified by the army sergeant as the man who had shot Margaret Harold. A search of the home of Rees's parents uncovered the revolver with which Carrol Jackson had been shot, and a diary describing the abduction of the Jacksons and their murder. 'Caught on a lonely road . . . Drove to a select area and killed the husband and baby. Now the mother and daughter were all mine.' He described forcing Mildred Jackson to perform oral sex, and then raping her repeatedly; the child was also apparently raped. (Full details have never been released.) He concluded: 'I was her master.'

The diary also described the sex murders of four more girls in Maryland. Rees was executed in 1961. Violent sex murders were common enough by the late 1950s, what makes this one unique for its period was Rees's 'Sadeian' attitude of self-justification. On the night before the Jackson killings, Rees had been on a 'benzedrine kick', and in the course of a rambling argument had told Moser: 'You can't say it's wrong to kill. Only individual standards make it right or wrong.' He had also explained that he wanted to experience everything: love, hate, life, death . . . When, after the murders, Moser asked him outright whether he was the killer, Rees disdained to lie; he simply refused to answer, leaving Moser to draw the self-evident conclusion. Rees was an 'intellectual' who, like Moors murderer Ian Brady in the following decade, made the decision to rape and kill on the grounds that 'everything is lawful'. He may therefore be regarded as one of the first examples of the curious modern phenomenon, the 'high IQ killer'. His sexual fantasies involved sadism (Mildred Jackson's death had been long and agonizing) and power. In that sense, his crimes anticipate those of the serial killer who was to emerge two decades later. Unfortunately we know nothing of Rees's background, or what turned him into a serial killer. Yet on the basis of other cases, we can state with a fair degree of confidence that parental affection was lacking in childhood, and that he was a lonely introverted child who was not much liked by his schoolmates. It is difficult, if not impossible, to find a case of a serial killer of whom this is not true.

Werner Boost, the Düsseldorf 'Doubles Killer'

In Düsseldorf, West Germany, 7 January 1953 was a cold, snowy night. Shortly before midnight, a fair-haired young man, who was bleeding from a head wound, staggered into the police station and said that his friend had just been murdered. The 'friend', it seemed, was a distinguished lawyer named Dr Lothar Servé. The officer on duty immediately telephoned Kriminal Hauptkommissar Mattias Eynck, chief of the North Rhineland murder squad, who hurried down to the station. The young man had identified himself as Adolf Hullecremer, a nineteen-year-old student, and explained that he and Dr Servé had been sitting in the car 'discussing business', and looking at the lights on the river, when both doors of the car had been jerked open by two men in handkerchief masks. One of the men began to swear, then shot Servé in the head. As Hullecremer begged for his life, the second man whispered that if he wished to stay alive, he should 'sham dead'. He then hit Hullecremer on the head with a pistol. As he lost consciousness, Hullecremer heard him say: 'He won't wake again.'

When the men had gone, he made off as fast as he could. After Hullecremer's head had been bandaged, he said he felt well enough to take the police and the doctor back to the car. It was parked in a grove of trees on the edge of the river, its engine still running. Across the rear seat lay the

107

body of a man of about fifty, bleeding from a wound in the temple. The doctor pronounced him dead. The motive was clearly robbery – the dead man's wallet was missing. Eynck concluded that the robbers were 'stick-up men' who had chosen this spot because it was known as a 'lovers' lane'. The fact that the two men had been in the rear seat when attacked suggested a homosexual relationship. Forensic examination revealed no fingerprints on the car, and falling snow had obliterated any footprints or tyre tracks.

The murder inquiry had reached an impasse when, a few weeks later, a tramp found a .32 calibre pistol – of Belgian make in the woods, and forensic tests showed it to be the murder weapon. Photographs of its bullets were sent to all police stations, and the Magdeburg police – in former East Germany – contacted Eynck to say that the same gun had been used in a murder a few years earlier in a town called Hadersleben. Two East Germans attempting to flee to the former West had been shot with the same weapon. This seemed to suggest that the murderer was himself an East German refugee who had moved to Düsseldorf. But there the trail went cold – thousands of East Germans had fled the communist regime to the large cities of West Germany since the war.

Almost three years later, in October 1955, Eynck found himself wondering whether the doubles killer had struck again. A young couple had vanished after an evening date. The man was twenty-six-year-old Friedhelm Behre, a baker, and his fiancée was twenty-three-year-old Thea Kurmann. They had spent the evening of 31 October in a 'bohemian' restaurant called the Café Czikos, in the old quarter of Düsseldorf, and had driven off soon after midnight in Behre's blue Ford. The next day, worried relatives reported them missing. But there was no sign of the couple or of the blue car. Four weeks later, a contractor standing by a half-dredged gravel pit near Düsseldorf was throwing stones at a metal object when he realized that it was the top of a blue car. He

108

called some of his men, and they heaved it ashore. In the back seat lay two decomposing corpses. They proved to be those of the missing couple, the girl still dressed in her red satin evening dress, which had been torn and pulled up. The medical report revealed that Friedhelm Behre had been shot through the head at close range. The girl had been garrotted, possibly by a man's tie, after being raped. It looked as if the killer had wrenched open the rear door as the couple were petting, shot the man, then dragged the girl out. After rape, her body was thrown into the back seat, and the car driven to the gravel pit, where it was pushed into the water.

To Eynck, this sounded ominously like the Servé murder. Again, there were no fingerprints – suggesting that the killer had worn gloves. The bullet had disappeared. It had gone right through the victim's skull, but it should have been somewhere in the car. Its absence suggested that the murderer had removed it to prevent the identification of the gun. The murder caused panic among Düsseldorf's young lovers, and over the Christmas period the usual lay-bys were deserted. Meanwhile, Chief Inspector Botte, in charge of the investigation, quickly found that he had run out of clues.

Three months later, on the morning of 8 February 1956, a businessman named Julius Dreyfuss reported that his Mercedes car was missing – together with its chauffeur, a young man named Peter Falkenberg. The chauffeur had failed to arrive to pick up his employer. It seemed possible that Falkenberg had driven away to sell the expensive car. But an hour or so later a woman reported that a black car was parked in front of her house with its headlights on. It proved to be the missing Mercedes. And there was a great deal of blood inside – both in the front and the rear seats. At about the same time a woman had reported that her daughter, twenty-three-year-old Hildegard Wassing, had failed to return home after a date. A few days before, Hildegard and a friend had met a young man named Peter at a dance; he had told them he was a chauffeur. Hildegard had agreed to go out with him the following Tuesday, 7 February, and her brother had noticed that he was driving a black Mercedes.

To Eynck, it sounded as if Peter Falkenberg and Hildegard Wassing had fallen victim to the 'car murderer'. The next morning, a gardener was cycling to work near the small village of Lank-Ilverich, near Düsseldorf, when he saw the remains of a burning haystack some distance from the path. He strolled over to look – and then rushed for the nearest telephone as he saw the remains of two corpses among the burned hay. Eynck arrived soon after, and noticed the smell of petrol. Both bodies were badly charred, but rain had prevented the fire from totally incinerating them. Forensic examination revealed that the man – identified from dental charts as Peter Falkenberg – had been shot through the head. Hildegard Wassing had been raped and then strangled – the rope was still sunk in the burned flesh. Thousands of Düsseldorf residents were questioned, but, once again, there were no obvious leads. The car killer was evidently a man who took great care to leave no clues.

Then a detective named Bohm came upon a possible suspect. In the small town of Buderich, not far from the burned haystack, he was told of a young man named Erich von der Leyen, who had once attacked some children with a manure fork, and was regarded as a 'loner' by his neighbours. He was originally from East Germany, and now lived in lodgings in a place called Veert. Von der Leyen worked as a travelling salesman for agricultural machinery, so his logbook should have shown precisely where he was when the couple were murdered. But the entry for 7 February had been made later, and the travelling times for drives seemed implausible. Moreover, there were red spots on the front seat covers. These were sent for forensic examination, and were reported to be human bloodstains. Erich von der Leyen was placed under arrest. Stains on his trousers also proved to be blood. Von der Leyen insisted that he had no idea where the stains came from – the only way he could account for them was to recall that his

110

girlfriend's dachsund had been in his car when it was on heat. That sounded unlikely. The police asked another forensic expert to examine the bloodstains on the trousers, and see if he could determine their age. Under the microscope, he saw epithelial cell evidence that it *was* menstrual blood. The stains on the car seat were retested, and the laboratory admitted with embarrassment that these were also of menstrual blood – and, moreover, from a dog. The police had to release von der Leyen, and to apologize for the intense interrogations he had endured.

Soon after this, on the evening of 6 June 1956, a forest ranger named Erich Spath was walking through woods near Meererbusch, not far from the burned haystack site, when he saw a man lurking in the undergrowth, and peering from behind a tree at a car in which a courting couple were petting. The man was so absorbed that he did not hear the ranger. Then Spath saw him draw a revolver from his pocket and creep towards the car. Spath placed his rifle to his shoulder and crept up behind the young man. 'Drop it!' The man turned round, then threw away his gun and ran. Spath chased him and soon caught up with him, crouching in a hollow. Half an hour later, the car with the courting couple – and also containing the ranger and his captive – pulled up in front of Düsseldorf's main police station. The suspect – who was dark and good-looking – had accompanied them without protest and without apparent concern, as if his conscience was clear. And when they stood in the office of Kriminal Hauptkommissar Mattias Eynck, Spath understood why. The young man – who gave his name as Werner Boost – explained that he had merely been doing a little target practice in the woods, and had thought *he* was being attacked. He obviously felt that no one could disprove his story and that therefore the police would be unable to hold him. 'Is your gun licensed?' asked Eynck. 'Well . . . no. It's a war trophy.' 'In that case, I am charging you with possessing an illegal weapon.' The gun was found in the undergrowth where Boost had thrown it. Nearby was a motorcycle, which proved to have been stolen. Boost was also charged with its theft. A magistrate promptly sentenced him to six months in jail, which gave Eynck the time he needed to investigate the suspect.

At first the trail seemed to be leading nowhere. The pistol had not been used in any known crime; Boost was, as he said, an electrical engineer who worked in a factory, and who was regarded as a highly intelligent and efficient worker; he had been married for six years, had two children, and was a good husband and provider. His wife, Hanna, told Eynck that he spent most of his evenings at home, working in his own laboratory or reading – he was an obsessive reader. Occasionally, she admitted, he became restless and went out until the early hours of the morning. She led Eynck down to the basement laboratory. There he discovered various ingredients for explosives, as well as some deadly poison. He also found a quantity of morphine.

Back in the flat, Eynck noticed a letter postmarked Hadersleben. He recalled that the Belgian pistol, which had been found within a few hundred yards of Boost's flat, had been used in a double murder in Hadersleben, near Magdeburg. 'Do you know someone in Hadersleben?' he asked. Hanna Boost told him that it was her home town, and that she had married her husband there.

'How did you both escape from East Germany?'

'Werner knew a safe route through the woods.'

But she insisted that, as far as she knew, her husband had never owned a gun. Now, at last, the case was beginning to look more promising. Back in his office, Eynck looked through the latest batch of information about Boost, which had come from a town called Helmstedt, which had been taken over by the Russians in 1945. And at about this period, there had been a great many murders – about fifty in all – of people trying to escape from the Russian to the British zone. Werner Boost had been in Helmstedt at the time. Then he had moved to Hadersleben, and the murders had ceased. But the two would-be émigrés had been shot in Hadersleben while trying to escape . . . There was another interesting item – a notebook which had been found in the saddle of Boost's stolen motorcycle. And it contained an entry: 'Sunday 3 June. Lorbach in need of another shot. Must attend to it.' Eynck sent for Boost and questioned him about the item. Boost said smoothly: 'Frank Lorbach is a friend of mine, and we go shooting together. On that day, he just couldn't hit the bull's eye, so I made a note to give him another shot.' Eynck did not believe a word of it. He asked Boost about his days in Helmstedt, and whether he had ever helped refugees to escape. Boost admitted that he had, and said he was proud of it. 'And did you ever shoot them?' Boost looked horrified. 'Of course not!'

Eynck now sent out one of his detectives to try to locate Franz Lorbach. This was not difficult. Lorbach proved to be a man of twenty-three with dark curly hair, whose good-looking face lacked the strength of Werner Boost's. He was a locksmith, and insisted that he only had the most casual acquaintance with Boost. Eynck knew that he was lying. He also noticed Lorbach's dilated pupils, and surmised that he was a drug addict, and that Boost was his supplier. He was certain that, when his craving became strong enough, Lorbach would talk. He held him in custody for questioning.

Meanwhile, Boost and Lorbach were placed in a police line-up, wearing handkerchief masks over the lower half of their faces. Adolf Hullecremer, the student who had been with Dr Servé when he was shot, was able to identify Boost as Servé's assailant. He said he recognized the eyes. But he failed to identify Lorbach. After a day or two in custody, Lorbach began to show symptoms of withdrawal from drugs. And one day, as Eynck was questioning Boost again – and getting nowhere – he received a phone call saying that Lorbach wanted to talk to him.

Lorbach was pale, his eyes were watery, and his nose twitched like a rabbit's. 'I want to tell you the truth. Werner

113

Boost is a monster. It *was* he who killed Dr Servé, and I was his accomplice.' Lorbach admitted that it was a love of poaching that had drawn the two of them together in 1952. They often went shooting in the woods. But Boost seemed to have a maniacal hatred of courting couples. 'These sex horrors are the curse of Germany.' So they would often creep up on couples who were making love in cars and rob them. Then, he said, Boost had an idea for rendering them unconscious. He had concocted some mixture which he forced them to drink. Then he and Lorbach would rape the unconscious girls. 'Some of them were very lovely. I feel ashamed – my wife is going to have a baby. But it was Boost who made me do it. I had to do it. He kept me supplied with morphine, which he obtained from the chemist who sold him chemicals.' He insisted that he had taken part only in the attack on Servé and Hullecremer. Boost had been indignant to see two men in a car together, and had ordered him to kill the young man. But Lorbach had not the stomach for it. Instead, he had whispered to him to pretend to be dead. Lorbach's failure to shoot Hullecremer enraged Boost – he made Lorbach kneel in the snow, and said: 'I ought to kill you too . . .'

Lorbach led the police to a place at the edge of the forest, where Boost kept his loot concealed. In a buried chest, they found watches, rings and jewellery. There were also bottles of poison, some knives, and a roll of cord which proved to be identical to that which had been used to strangle Hildegard Wassing. Lorbach also disclosed that Boost had ordered Lorbach to kill his wife, Hanna Boost, if he was arrested. There was a phial of cyanide hidden behind a pipe in his flat, and Lorbach was to slip it into her drink, so that she could not incriminate her husband. Eynck found the phial exactly where Lorbach had said it was. Lorbach also confirmed that he and Boost had been involved in an earlier attempt at crime, a year before the murder of Dr Servé. The two men had placed a heavy plank studded with long nails across the road, to force motorists to stop. But the first car to come along had

114

contained four men – too many for them to tackle – and it had driven on to the verge and around the plank. Two more cars also contained too many passengers. Then a security van came, and a man with a gun removed the plank. After that, police arrived – evidently alerted by one of the cars – and Boost and Lorbach had to flee.

In fact, as long ago as 1953, Eynck had suspected that Dr Servé's murderer was responsible for this earlier attempt. Lorbach also detailed Boost's plans to rob a post office by knocking everyone unconscious with poison gas, and to kidnap and murder a child of a rich industrialist for ransom.

On 11 December 1956, Boost was charged with the murders of Dr Servé, Friedhelm Behre, Thea Kurmann, Peter Falkenberg and Hildegard Wassing. But when Lorbach, the main prosecution witness, suffered a nervous breakdown due to drug problems, the trial had to be postponed. Meanwhile, Boost was extradited to Magdeburg for questioning about the murder of the couple at Hadersleben. But he stonewalled his questioners as he had tried to stonewall the Düsseldorf police, and was finally returned to Eynck's jurisdiction with no additional charges against him.

Boost's trial began in the courthouse at Düsseldorf on 3 November 1961, before Judge Hans Naecke, two associate magistrates, Dr Warda and Dr Schmidt, and a six-man jury. Boost maintained his total innocence, and his lawyer, Dr Koehler, lost no time in pointing out that the testimony of a drug addict like Franz Lorbach was hardly reliable. Lorbach himself was a poor witness, who mumbled and became confused. But he was able to tell one story that strengthened the case against Boost.

Lorbach confessed that Boost had blackmailed him – by threatening withdrawal of his drug supply – into taking part in another attack on a couple. They had held up two lovers in the woods. Boost had tried to kill the man, but the gun had misfired. The girl had run away screaming, and Boost had ordered Lorbach to catch her. Lorbach had done so – but then whispered to her to lie low for a while. When he returned, Boost had knocked the man unconscious – but Lorbach had warned him there was a car coming, and they had roared away on Boost's motorbike.

Eynck told the court that he had traced this couple, and that they had confirmed the story in every detail. They were not married – at least not to one another – which is why they had failed to report the incident. But Eynck was able to offer their deposition in evidence. Boost's lawyer counter-attacked by pointing out that there had recently been a murder of a couple in a car near Cologne, and that Boost was obviously not guilty of this crime. After a month of listening to this and similar evidence, the six jurors decided that the evidence that Boost had murdered the two couples was insufficient. But they found him guilty of murdering Dr Servé. He was sentenced to life imprisonment, and Lorbach to three years, as his accomplice – much of which he had already served. Boost's sentence was exactly the same as if he had been found guilty on all charges.

Henri Lee Lucas and Ottis Toole

Henry Lee Lucas might be regarded as the American equivalent of Pedro Alonzo Lopez, at least as far as the number of his victims is concerned: he confessed to three hundred and sixty murders. That said, however, most investigators now believe that Lucas was both a serial killer and a habitual liar who was addicted to making false confessions. So the actual number of his victims will probably never be known.

Born in 1937 in Blacksburg, Virginia, Lucas was the son of a prostitute and a railway worker who had lost both legs in an accident. His mother seems to have detested the child and treated him with sadistic cruelty, once causing brain damage when she struck him on the head with a piece of wood. His teacher, who often gave him hot meals, described him as one of the most impoverished and desperate hill children she had ever met. An accident led to the loss of one eye, so that he had to have it replaced with a glass one.

By the age of fifteen he had become a juvenile delinquent, and was sent to a reformatory for breaking and entering. 'I started stealing as soon as I could run fast.' He had also by this time committed his first murder, attempting to rape a seventeen-year-old girl at a bus stop and strangling her when she resisted.

In January 1960, he murdered his mother during the course of a quarrel. He told arresting police officers that, at the time, he was unaware that he was responsible for his mother's

117

death, putting her sudden collapse down to a heart attack. Since she was actually slashed to death with a knife, the reader may judge Lucas' ability at self-deception.

He was sentenced to forty years in prison, where he made several suicide attempts. He was recommended for parole after ten years. In fact, he seems to have felt secure in prison and wanted to stay there; when paroled, he told the board that he would kill again. On the day he left prison, he kept his word, raping and killing a woman in Jackson. The murder remained unsolved until he eventually confessed to it years later.

There followed an unsuccessful marriage, which lasted only a short time. In Carbondale, Pennsylvania, he met another drifter, Ottis Toole, a homosexual who fantasised about cannibalism. The two teamed up and, according to Lucas's biographer Max Call, 'left a bloody trail through Michigan, Ohio, Indiana, Illinois and Wisconsin'.

The pair went about their murder spree with a cavalier abandon. Call claims that they kept the head of one murder victim in the trunk of their car for two days. 'I was bitter at the world,' Lucas later said. 'I hated everything. Killing someone is just like walking outdoors. If I wanted a victim I'd just go to get one.'

Ottis Toole's parents liked Lucas enough to appoint him the guardian of their two youngest children, Frieda Powell, nine, and her younger brother Frank. A year or two later, Frieda – who hated her name and insisted on being called 'Becky' – left her Florida home with Lucas and her brother Ottis, and became Lucas's mistress. She was present during a number of his killings, and even helped to bury the bodies. (Lucas claimed that it was his care in disposing of the bodies that prevented the law from catching up with him for so long.)

When Becky was thirteen she was caught and sent to a juvenile detention centre in Florida; with the help of Lucas and her brother she escaped, and the three of them went on another killing spree. Lucas later claimed that he was also then a contract killer for an organisation called 'Hand of Death', but this part of his story is, to say the least, unverified. He also told his captors that he had personally murdered the corrupt union boss Jimmy Hoffa, and had hand-delivered the cyanide that the cult leader, the Reverend Jim Jones, used to kill over 900 of his followers at the Guyanan settlement called Jonestown in 1978. There is no evidence – or indeed any logical reason – to back either fantastic claim. His evidently free-running imagination has led many to discount most, but by no means all, of Lucas' murderous pretensions.

What is certain is that in 1982 he was paid to look after an eighty-eight-year-old woman named Kate – 'Granny' – Rich, and that he eventually murdered her. Before then, he and Becky had become members of a fundamentalist sect called House of Prayer in Stoneberg, Texas, and lived and worked there for several weeks. Under the influence of the religious teaching, Becky decided she wanted to go back to Florida and finish her sentence in the reformatory. Lucas wanted her to stay, but finally agreed. On the way to Florida they stopped to make love in a field, then they quarrelled, and, when Becky suddenly slapped his face, Lucas stabbed her to death. He then dismembered her body and buried it.

It might seem surprising that for a man who had by that time killed dozens (by his own claims, hundreds) of people, this one extra betrayal and murder would have a shattering effect; but that is not to take into account the fragile humanity and emotional instability that seem to lurk in even the most monstrous serial killer. Lucas deliberately had no feelings, other than negative and sexual, for most of his victims. He blanked any natural empathy for them, much as a diner makes a point of not regretting the premature death of the chicken he is eating. But Lucas had actually loved Becky, and her death struck him under his emotional armour. As far as Lucas was concerned, the murder of his lover was the beginning of the end.

Back in Texas at the House of Prayer, he took Kate Rich for

a long drive and both drank cans of beer. A quarrel developed, or Lucas became angry at her questions about Becky; so he stabbed her to death, raped her corpse, and hid it in a culvert.

Lucas was the chief suspect in Granny Rich's disappearance, but there was no evidence against him. In June 1983 his friend Reuben Moore, head of the House of Prayer, reported to the police that Lucas owned a gun, a felony for an ex-convict. He was arrested and in prison underwent a religious conversion that led him to confess to murdering Becky and Kate Rich. He then also confessed to a total of three-hundred-and-sixty murders.

Naturally the police used every available lead to confirm Lucas' claims, and soon found convincing evidence that he had committed a number of his professed kills. These included the rape and murder of the woman in Jackson, of a West Virginia police officer, and of an unknown female hitch-hiker known simply as 'orange socks' because that was all she was wearing when police found her body and because that was all Lucas could remember about her (apart from relished details of her murder).

Since the legal definition of a serial killer is one who kills at least three persons over a protracted period of time with no direct reason to do so, Lucas was officially designated a serial killer. He was eventually sentenced to death for eleven murders; his accomplice Ottis Toole also received a death sentence.

Sheriff Jim Boutwell of Williamson County, Texas, who came to know Lucas well in prison, noted in 1985: 'Henry Lee Lucas is helping write a new chapter in the history of law enforcement . . . Henry's confessions, and the subsequent investigations, have exposed the mobility of crime in the United States.' In fact, it was the Lucas case more than any other that made America aware of the existence of the mobile serial killer.

Lucas' confession showed him to be what A.E.Van Vogt called a 'Right Man' – a ruthless egotist who is moved to

120

violence by even the smallest humiliation or evidence of disrespect; such men feel that they are always right and everyone else is wrong. From the first murder, at the age of fifteen, Lucas killed those who resisted him. Lucas was a high-dominance, highly sexed male, with an extremely low bursting-point. 'Sex is one of my downfalls. I get sex any way I can get it. If I have to force somebody to do it, I do. If I don't, I don't. I rape them; I've done that. I've killed animals to have sex with them . . .' He also admitted that he had skinned animals alive during his teens.

Asked about the problems of interrogating Lucas, Sheriff Boutwell replied: 'You don't interrogate him . . . You talk with him just as a conversation. The good/bad guy role that officers traditionally use with suspects wouldn't work with him ... If at any time you indicate you disbelieve him . . . you'll ruin your credibility with him.' Boutwell describes a case in which a police officer had driven three thousand miles to interview Lucas and, even though he had been warned against it, called Lucas a liar within the first two minutes. His journey was wasted; Lucas immediately refused to hold any further conversation.

This is, of course, the behaviour of a Right Man, a man who refuses, in any circumstances, to admit that he could be wrong or a liar. Boutwell also commented on Lucas's high I.Q. and remarked that successfully interrogating him depended on an appeal to his ego. Lucas was allowed all kinds of privileges – as much coffee as he liked (he was a coffee addict) and endless cigarettes. Asked by the interviewer whether this was not 'babying' him, Boutwell again emphasised that this was the only way to get Lucas to co-operate – to take care that he felt he was not just an ordinary prisoner.

The murder of Becky Powell seems to have been a watershed for Lucas. It is obvious – from his confession – that he loved her in a way he had never loved anyone else; she was at once his wife, mistress and daughter, the only person who had ever accepted him without criticism, who regarded him as a kind of god – the kind of ego-balm that the Right Man craves above all else. Yet, because of that fatal tendency to explode under pressure, he killed her. Now he was not only on his own, but deprived of his one reason for living. The murder of Granny Rich – one of the few people who had treated him with kindness – may have been a masochistic gesture of defiance and despair, like shaking his fist at the sky.

That said, although Lucas was certainly a prolific serial killer, he was also a prolific liar and he seems to have thoroughly taken advantage of Sheriff Boutwell's evident trust. As seen above, some of Lucas' claims were fantastic to say the least, and one may suspect that Lucas would have claimed to have been the assassin of President John F. Kennedy, if he had not then been in jail for matricide at the time of the Dallas shooting.

The Texas authorities quickly set up a 'Lucas Task Force' and flew the killer from state to state to meet with local law-enforcement officials who had unsolved murders on their books. Again and again Lucas gave convincing details of cases and eventually the Lucas Task Force claimed to have 'cleared up' 213 previously unsolved murders. It is for this reason that some crime books still list Lucas as the most prolific serial killer on record but, unfortunately, those books are wrong.

It seems now that Lucas made up many – some say most – of his confessions. The authorities would give him details of a case before he met local law officers. This was doubtless done with the best of intentions – they believed that he had killed several hundred people and therefore was unlikely to remember key details of each murder. So they gave Lucas the files on each case to 'jog his memory'. If, in fact, Lucas had had nothing to do with the murder case he was being shown, he would nevertheless concoct a story, based on the file he had been given. Since local police were not told that he had read their own files on the case, they would usually be convinced that he had knowledge that only the killer could have known.

And thus yet another murder would have been 'cleared up' and added to Lucas' roster.

Lucas later retracted most of his 'confessions.' His reasons for originally giving them seem to have been three-fold. Firstly, as we have seen from Sheriff Boutwell's own statement above, Lucas was given special privileges because the authorities so valued his stream of confessions. Secondly, Lucas took a malicious pleasure in misleading everyone. And thirdly, he had the typical antisocial serial killer egotism that made him want to be known as the most prolific murderer in the world.

Subsequent investigation of Lucas' movements over the years of his killing spree has shown conclusively that he could not have committed a large number of the murders originally ascribed to him. But because the authorities indulged in this bogus 'clearing up' of unsolved cases, many murder investigations were closed down, leaving the real killers free. Since a number of these are likely to have killed again because they were not originally apprehended, it could be thought that the over-enthusiasm (and some might say incompetence) of the Lucas Task Force ultimately cost an unknown number of people their lives.

The fact is that nobody can be sure just who, or how many people Lucas and Toole killed. The waters were so muddied by the Lucas Task Force, that we will probably never know. Neither Toole nor Lucas can help either. Ottis Toole died in prison of cirrhosis of the liver in 1996. Lucas escaped execution when then Texas Governor George W. Bush surprised just about everyone by commuting his death sentence to life imprisonment – surprised because Governor Bush had previously, and subsequently, been a keen advocate of the death penalty. But then Henry Lee Lucas died of heart failure in 2001 – almost certainly brought on by all the extra coffee and cigarettes he had been given by the authorities over the years.

Estimates at the number killed by Lucas and Toole are now

comparatively 'low'. Indeed, Texas Ranger Phil Ryan – who was involved in the case – is on record as believing that 'at most . . . 15 murders' can be pinned to the pair. That would mean that 198 of the cases 'cleared up' by the Lucas Task Force, were actually closed prematurely.

Lucien Staniak, the 'Red Spider'

For criminologists, one of the most frustrating things about the Iron Curtain was that it was virtually impossible to learn whether its police were facing the same types of crimes as in the West. But in the late 1960s, accounts of the 'Red Spider' case made it clear that communist regimes also spawned serial killers. In July 1964, the communist regime in Poland was getting prepared to celebrate the twentieth anniversary of the liberation of Warsaw by Russian troops; a great parade was due to take place in Warsaw on the 22nd. On 4 July the editor of *Przeglad Polityczny,* the Polish equivalent of *Pravda,* received an anonymous letter in spidery red handwriting: 'There is no happiness without tears, no life without death. Beware! I am going to make you cry.'

Marian Starzynski thought the anonymous writer had him in mind, and requested police protection. But on the day of the big parade, a seventeen-year-old blonde, Danka Maciejowitz, failed to arrive home from a parade organized by the School of Choreography and Folklore in Olsztyn, 160 miles north of Warsaw. The next day, a gardener in the Olsztyn Park of Polish Heroes discovered the girl's body in some shrubbery. She had been stripped naked and raped, and the lower part of her body was covered with Jack-the-Ripper-type mutilations. And the following day, the 24th, another red ink letter was delivered to *Kulisy,* a Warsaw newspaper: 'I picked a juicy flower in Olsztyn and I shall do it again somewhere else, for there is no holiday without a funeral.'

Analysis of the ink showed that it had been made by dissolving red art paint in turpentine. On 16 January 1965 the Warsaw newspaper *Zycie Warsawy* published the picture of a pretty sixteen-year-old girl, Aniuta Kaliniak, who had been chosen to lead a parade of students in another celebration rally the following day. She left her home in Praga, an eastern suburb of Warsaw, and crossed the River Vistula to reach the parade. Later, she thumbed a lift from a lorry driver, who dropped her close to her home at a crossroads. (The fact that a sixteen-year-old girl would thumb a lift like this indicates that the level of sex crime in Poland must be a great deal lower than in England or the US.)

The day after the parade, her body was found in a basement in a leather factory opposite her home. The killer had removed a grating to get in. The crime had obviously been carefully planned. He had waited in the shadows of the wall, and cut off her cry with a wire noose dropped over her head. In the basement, he had raped her, and left a six-inch spike sticking in her sexual organs (an echo of the Boston Strangler). While the search went on another red ink letter advised the police where to look for her body.

Olsztyn and Warsaw are 160 miles apart; this modern Ripper differed from his predecessor in not sticking to the same area. Moreover, like Klaus Gosmann, he was a man with a strong dramatic sense: the selection of national holidays for his crimes, the letter philosophizing about life and death. The Red Spider – as he had come to be known, from his spidery writing – chose All Saints Day, 1 November, for his next murder, and Poznan, 124 miles west of Warsaw, as the site.

A young, blonde hotel receptionist, Janka Popielski, was on her way to look for a lift to a nearby village, where she meant to meet her boyfriend. Since it was a holiday, the freight terminal was almost deserted. Her killer pressed a chloroform-soaked bandage over her nose and mouth. Then he removed her skirt, stockings and panties, and raped her behind a packing shed. After this, he killed her with a screwdriver. The mutilations were so thorough and revolting that the authorities suppressed all details. The Red Spider differed from many sex killers in apparently being totally uninterested in the upper half of his victims. Janka was stuffed into a packing case, where she was discovered an hour later.

The police swooped on all trains and buses leaving Poznan, looking for a man with bloodstained clothes; but they failed to find one. The next day, the Poznan newspaper *Courier Zachodni* received one of the now notorious letters in red ink, containing a quotation from Stefan Zeromsky's national epic *Popioly* (1928): 'Only tears of sorrow can wash out the stain of shame; only pangs of suffering can blot out the fires of lust.' May Day 1966 was both a communist and a national holiday. Marysia Galazka, seventeen, went out to look for her cat in the quiet suburb of Zoliborz, in northern Warsaw. When she did not return, her father went out to look for her. He found her lying in the typical rape position, with her entrails forming an abstract pattern over her thighs, in a tool shed behind the house. Medical evidence revealed that the killer had raped her before disembowelling her. Major Ciznek, of the Warsaw homicide squad, was in charge of the case, and he made a series of deductions. The first was that the Red Spider was unlikely to confine himself to his well-publicized murders on national holidays. Such killers seek victims when their sexual desire is at maximum tension, not according to some preconceived timetable. Ciznek examined evidence of some thirteen other murders that had taken place since the first one in April 1964, one each in Lublin, Radom, Kielce, Lodz, Bialystock, Lomza, two in Bydgoszcz, five in the Poznan district. All places were easily reached by railway; the *modus operandi* was always the same. Every major district of Poland within 240 miles of Warsaw was covered. Ciznek stuck pins in a map and examined the result. It looked as if Warsaw might be the home of the killer, since the murders took place all round it. But one thing was

127

noticeable. The murders extended much further south than north, and there were also more of them to the south. It rather looked as if the killer had gone to Bialystock, Lomza and Olsztyn as a token gesture of extending his boundaries. Assuming, then, that the killer lived somewhere south of Warsaw, where would this be most likely to be? There were five murders in the Poznan district, to the west of Warsaw. Poznan is, of course, easily reached from Warsaw. But where in the south could it be reached from just as easily? Cracow was an obvious choice. So was Katowice, twenty miles or so from Cracow. This town was also at the centre of a network of railway lines.

On Christmas Eve 1966, Cracow was suddenly ruled out as a possibility. Three servicemen getting on a train between Cracow and Warsaw looked into a reserved compartment and found the half-naked and mutilated corpse of a girl on the floor. The leather miniskirt had been slashed to pieces; so had her abdomen and thighs. The servicemen notified the guard, and a message was quickly sent to Warsaw, who instructed the train driver to go straight through to Warsaw, non-stop, in case the killer managed to escape at one of the intervening stations.

A careful check of passengers at Warsaw revealed no one stained with blood or in any way suspicious. But the police were able to locate the latest letter from the killer, dropped into the post slot of the mail van on top of all the others. It merely said: 'I have done it again,' and was addressed to *Zycie Warsawy*.

It looked as if the Red Spider had got off the train in Cracow, after killing the girl, and dropped the letter into the slot. The girl was identified as Janina Kozielska, of Cracow. And the police recalled something else: another girl named Kozielska had been murdered in Warsaw in 1964. This proved to be Janina's sister Aniela. For Ciznek, this ruled out Cracow as the possible home of the killer. For he would be likely to avoid his home territory. Moreover, there surely had to be some connection between the murders of two sisters . . . The compartment on the Cracow–Warsaw train had been booked over the telephone by a man who said his name was Stanislav

128

Kozielski, and that his wife would pick up the tickets. Janina had paid 1,422 zloty for them – about twenty-five pounds. Janina had come to the train alone and been shown to her compartment by the ticket inspector. She said that her husband would be joining her shortly. The inspector had also checked a man's ticket a few moments later, but could not recall the man. It was fairly clear, then, that the Red Spider knew the girl well enough to persuade her to travel with him as his wife, and had probably paid for the ticket. He had murdered her in ten minutes or so, and then hurried off the train. Ciznek questioned the dead girl's family. They could not suggest who might have killed their daughter, but they mentioned that she sometimes worked as a model – as her sister had. She worked at the School of Plastic Arts and at a club called the Art Lovers Club. Ciznek recollected that the red ink was made of artist's paint dissolved in turpentine and water; this looked like a lead.

The Art Lovers Club proved to have 118 members. For an Iron Curtain country, its principles were remarkably liberal; many of its members painted abstract, tachiste and pop-art pictures. Most of them were respectable professional men – doctors, dentists, officials, newspapermen. And one of them came from Katowice. His name was Lucian Staniak and he was a twenty-six-year-old translator who worked for the official Polish publishing house. Staniak's business caused him to travel a great deal – in fact, he had bought an *ulgowy bilet*, a train ticket that enabled him to travel anywhere in Poland. Ciznek asked if he could see Staniak's locker. It confirmed his increasing hope that he had found the killer. It was full of knives – used for painting, the club manager explained. Staniak daubed the paint on with a knife blade. He liked to use red paint. And one of his paintings, called *The Circle of Life*, showed a flower being eaten by a cow, the cow being eaten by a wolf, the wolf being shot by a hunter, the hunter being killed by a car driven by a woman, and the woman lying with her stomach ripped open in a field, with flowers sprouting from her body.

Ciznek now knew he had his man, and he telephoned the Katowice police. They went to Staniak's address at 117 Aleje Wyzwolenia, but found no one at home. In fact, Staniak was out committing another murder – his last. It was a mere month after the train murder – 31 January 1967 – but he was impatient at the total lack of publicity given to the previous murder. So he took Bozhena Raczkiewicz, an eighteen-year-old student from the Lodz Institute of Cinematographic Arts, to a shelter built at the railway station for the use of stranded overnight travellers, and there stunned her with a vodka bottle. In accordance with his method when in a hurry, he cut off her skirt and panties with his knife. He had killed her in a few minutes between six o'clock and twenty-five past. The neck of the broken bottle had a clear fingerprint on it.

Staniak was picked up at dawn the next day; he had spent the night getting drunk. His fingerprints matched those on the bottle. He was a good-looking young man of twenty-six. And when he realized that there was no chance of escape, he confessed fully to twenty murders. He told the police that his parents and sister had been crossing an icy road when they were hit by a skidding car, being driven too fast by the young wife of a Polish air force pilot. The girl had been acquitted of careless driving. Staniak had seen the picture of his first victim in a newspaper, and thought she looked like the wife of the pilot; this was his motive for killing her. He had decided against killing the wife of the pilot because it would be traced back to him. Sentenced to death for six of the murders – the six described here – Staniak was later reprieved and sent to the Katowice asylum for the criminally insane.

Ian Brady and Myra Hindley,
the 'Moors Murderers'

Compared to America, or even Germany, France and Italy, Great Britain has had few cases of serial murder. In fact, compared to America, England's murder rate is absurdly low. Until well into the 1960s it was a mere 150 a year, compared to America's 10,000. (America's population is about three times that of England.) By the 1990s England's murder rate has risen to around 700 a year; America's was 23,000. (Los Angeles alone has more murders per year than the whole of Great Britain.) It seems odd, then, that in spite of its low murder rate, Britain has produced three of the most horrific cases of serial murder of the twentieth century. The first of these has become known simply as the Moors Murder Case.

Between July 1963 and October 1965, Ian Brady and his mistress Myra Hindley collaborated on five child murders. They were finally arrested because they tried to involve Myra's brother-in-law, David Smith, in one of the murders, and he went to the police. Ian Brady, who was twenty-seven at the time of his arrest, was a typical social misfit.

The illegitimate son of a Glasgow waitress, he was brought up in a slum area of Clydeside. Until the age of eleven he seems to have been a good student; then he was sent to a 'posh' school, together with a number of other rehoused slum boys, and began to develop a resentment towards the better-off pupils.

From then on he took to petty crime; his first appearance in court was at the age of thirteen, on a charge of housebreaking. He had served four years on probation for more burglaries when he moved to Manchester to live with his mother and a new stepfather in 1954. As a result of another theft he was sentenced to a year in Borstal.

Back in Manchester, he went back on the dole. It was a dull life in a small house, and he seems to have been glad to get a job as a stock clerk at Millwards, a chemical firm, when he was twenty-one. It was at this point that he became fascinated by the Nazis and began collecting books about them. They fed his fantasies of power. So did his discovery of the ideas of the Marquis de Sade, with his philosophy of total selfishness and his daydreams of torture.

It becomes clear in retrospect that Brady always had a streak of sadism. A childhood friend later described how he had dropped a cat into a deep hole in a graveyard and sealed it up with a stone. When the friend moved the stone to check on his story, the cat escaped.

For Brady, the Nazis represented salvation from mediocrity and boredom, while de Sade justified his feeling that most people are contemptible. Brady particularly liked the idea that society is corrupt, and that God is a lie invented by priests to keep the poor in a state of subjugation. Stifled by ennui, seething with resentment, Brady was like a bomb that is ready to explode by the time he was twenty-three.

It was at this time that a new typist came to work in the office. Eighteen-year-old Myra Hindley was a normal girl from a normal family background, a Catholic convert who loved animals and children, and favoured blonde hairstyles and bright lipstick. She had been engaged, but had broken it off because she found the boy immature. Brady had the sullen look of a delinquent Elvis Presley, and within weeks, Myra was in love. Brady ignored her, probably regarding her as a typical working-class moron. Her diary records: 'I hope he loves me and will marry me some day.'

132

When he burst into profanity after losing a bet she was deeply shocked. It was almost a year later, at the firm's Christmas party in 1961, that he offered to walk her home, and asked her out that evening. When he took her home, she declined to allow him into the house – she lived with her grandmother – but a week later, after another evening out, she surrendered her virginity on her gran's settee. After that, he spent every Saturday night with her. Myra found her lover marvellously exciting and sophisticated. He wore black shirts, read 'intellectual' books, and was learning German. He introduced her to German wine, and she travelled as a pillion passenger on his motorbike. He talked to her about the Nazis, and liked to call her Myra Hess (a combination of a famous pianist and Hitler's deputy).

He also introduced her to the ideas of the Marquis de Sade, and set out converting her to atheism, pointing out the discrepancies in the gospels – it did not take long to demolish her faith. He also talked to her a great deal about his favourite novel, *Compulsion* by Meyer Levin, a fictionalized account of the Leopold and Loeb murder case. It was in July 1963 – according to her later confession – that he first began to talk to her about committing 'the perfect murder', and suggesting that she should help him. In her 'confession' (to Chief Superintendent Peter Topping) she alleges that Brady blackmailed her by threatening to harm her grandmother, and by showing her some pornographic photographs of her that he had taken on an occasion when he had slipped a drug into her wine. The photographs certainly exist – thirty of them – some showing them engaged in sexual intercourse and wearing hoods. (These were taken with a time-lapse camera.) Emlyn Williams, who saw them, states that some show keen pleasure on their faces, which would seem to dispose of Myra's claim that they were taken when she was unconscious. Whether or not she was telling the truth about blackmail, it seems clear that Brady could have persuaded her to do anything anyway. In her confession to Chief Inspector Peter Topping (published in 1989 in his book *Topping*), she described how, on 12 July 1963, she and Brady set out on their first 'murder hunt'. By now Myra Hindley owned a dilapidated van. She was sent ahead in the van, with Brady following behind on his motorbike. Her job was to pick up a girl and offer her a lift. The first child they saw was Myra's next-door neighbour, so she drove past her. The second was sixteen-year-old Pauline Reade, who was on her way to a dance. Myra offered her a lift, and she accepted. In the van, Myra explained that she was on her way to Saddleworth Moor to look for a glove she had lost at a picnic. If Pauline would like to come and help her search, she would give her a pile of records in the back of the van. Pauline was delighted to accept. Once on the moor, Brady arrived on his motorbike, and was introduced as Myra's boyfriend. Then Brady and Pauline went off to look for the glove. (Since it was July it was still daylight.) By the time Brady returned to the car, it was dark. He led Myra to the spot where Pauline Reade's body was lying. Her throat had been cut, and her clothes were in disarray; Myra accepted that Brady had raped her. That, after all, had been the whole point of the murder. Together they buried the body, using a spade they had brought with them. Brady told her that at one point Pauline was struggling so much that he had thought of calling for her to hold the girl's hands – clearly, he had no doubt that she would co-operate. On the way home, they passed Pauline's mother and brother, apparently searching for her. Back at home, Brady burned his bloodstained shoes and trousers. In an open letter to the press in January 1990, Brady was to contradict Myra Hindley's account; he insisted that injuries to the nose and forehead of Pauline Reade had been inflicted by her, and that she had also committed some form of lesbian assault on Pauline Reade. According to Brady, Myra participated actively and willingly in the murders.

Five months later, Brady was ready for another murder. On Saturday, 23 November 1963 they hired a car – the van had been sold – and drove to nearby Ashton market. There, according to Myra, Brady got into conversation with a twelve-year-old boy, John Kilbride, and told him that, 'If Jack would help them look for a missing glove, he would give him a bottle of sherry he had won in the raffle'. Because Myra was present, John Kilbride accompanied them without suspicion. They drove up to Saddleworth Moor, and the boy unsuspectingly accompanied Brady into the darkness. Myra Hindley claims that she drove around for a while, and that when she came back and flashed her lights, Brady came out of the darkness and told her that he had already buried the body. He also mentioned taking the boy's trousers down and giving him a slap on the buttocks. In fact, Myra said, she was fairly certain that he had raped John Kilbride. He had explained that he had strangled him because the knife he had was too blunt to cut his throat.

In June the following year – in 1964 – Brady told her he was 'ready to do another one'. (Like all serial killers he had a 'cooling-off period' – in this case about six months.) According to Myra, he told her that committing a murder gave him a feeling of power. By now they had their own car, a Mini. On 16 June 1964 she stopped her car and asked a twelve-year-old boy, Keith Bennett, if he would help her load some boxes from an off-licence; like John Kilbride, Keith Bennett climbed in unsuspectingly. The murder was almost a carbon copy of the previous one; Keith Bennett was strangled and buried on Saddleworth Moor. Brady admitted this time that he had raped him, and added: 'What does it matter?' Keith Bennett's body has never been found.

On Boxing Day 1965, Brady and Hindley picked up a ten-year-old girl, Lesley Ann Downey, at a fairground at Ancoats. Myra Hindley had taken her grandmother to visit an uncle. They took the child back to the house; and Brady switched on a tape recorder. Myra claims she was in the kitchen with the dogs when she heard the child screaming. Brady was ordering her to take off her coat and squeezing her by the back of the neck. Then Brady set up the camera and a bright light. The child was ordered to undress, and Brady then made her assume various pornographic poses while he filmed her. At this point, Myra claims she was ordered to go and run a bath; she stayed in the bathroom until the water became cold. When she went back into the bedroom, Lesley had been strangled, and there was blood on her thighs – from which Myra realized that she had been raped. At eight o'clock that evening they took the body up to Saddleworth Moor and buried it.

In his open letter to the press in January 1990, Ian Brady denied that Myra had played no active part in the murder of Lesley Ann Downey. 'She insisted upon killing Lesley Ann Downey with her own hands, using a two-foot length of silk cord, which she later used to enjoy toying with in public, in the secret knowledge of what it had been used for.'

In October 1965, Brady decided it was time for another murder. He had also decided that he needed another partner in crime, and that Myra's seventeen-year-old brother-in-law, David Smith, was the obvious choice. Smith had already been in trouble with the law. He seemed unable to hold down a job. His wife was pregnant for the second time, and they had just been given an eviction notice. So Smith listened with interest when Brady suggested a hold-up at an Electricity Board showroom.

On 6 October Smith came to the house hoping to borrow some money, but they were all broke. Brady suggested: 'We'll have to roll a queer.' An hour later, Brady picked up a seventeen-year-old homosexual, Edward Evans, and invited him back to the house in Hattersley. Back at the flat, Myra went off to fetch David Smith. They had only just returned when there was a crash from the living room. Brady was rolling on the floor, grappling with Evans. Then he seized an axe and struck him repeatedly: 'Everywhere was one complete pool of blood.' When Evans lay still, Brady strangled him. Then he handed the bloodstained hatchet to Smith, saying, 'Feel the weight of that.' His motive was obviously to get Smith's fingerprints on the haft.

Together, they mopped up the blood and wrapped up the body in polythene. Then Smith went home, promising to return the next day to help dispose of the body. But Brady had miscalculated. Smith might feel in theory that 'people are like maggots, small, blind and worthless', but the fact of murder was too much for him. When he arrived home he was violently sick and told his wife what had happened. Together they decided to phone the police, creeping downstairs armed with a screwdriver and carving knife in case Brady was waiting for them. The following morning, a man dressed as a baker's roundsman knocked at Brady's door, and when Myra opened it, identified himself as a police officer. Evans's body was found in the spare bedroom. Forensic examination revealed dog hair on his underclothes – the hair of Myra Hindley's dog indicating that he and Brady had engaged in sex, probably while Myra was fetching David Smith. Hidden in the spine of a prayer book police found a cloakroom ticket, which led them to Manchester Central Station. In two suitcases they discovered pornographic photos, tapes and books on sex and torture; the photographs included those of Lesley Ann Downey, with a tape recording of her voice pleading for mercy.

A twelve-year-old girl, Patricia Hodges, who had occasionally accompanied Brady and Hindley to the moors, took the police to Hollin Brown Knoll, and there the body of Lesley Ann Downey was dug up.

John Kilbride's grave was located through a photograph that showed Hindley crouching on it with a dog. Pauline Reade's body was not found until 1987, as a result of Myra Hindley's confession to Topping. Brady helped in the search on the moor and, as we know, the body of Keith Bennett has never been recovered. Brady's defence was that Evans had been killed unintentionally, in the course of a struggle, when he and Smith tried to rob him. Lesley Ann Downey, he claimed, had been brought to the house by Smith to pose for pornographic pictures, for which she had been paid ten shillings. (His original story was that she had been brought to the house by two men.) After the session, she left the house with Smith. He flatly denied knowing anything about any of the other murders, but the tape recording of Lesley Ann Downey's screams and pleas for mercy made it clear that Brady and Hindley were responsible for her death. Both were sentenced to life imprisonment.

John Wayne Gacy

On 11 December 1978 Elizabeth Piest drove to the Nisson Pharmacy in Des Plaines, Illinois, to pick up her fifteen-year-old son Robert; it was her birthday and she intended to have a party. It was nine in the evening when she arrived, and the boy asked her to wait a few minutes while he went to see a man about a summer job that would pay $5 an hour. By 9.30 p.m. Robert had still not returned. She drove home to tell her husband and at 11.30 p.m. they rang the police to report his disappearance. The police investigated at the drug store, and noticed that the inside had been renovated recently; they inquired about the contractor, and were told that his name was Gacy, and that he could have been the man who had offered Robert Piest the job.

The police already knew about Gacy. On 21 March, a 27-year-old Chicagoan, Jeffrey Rignall, had got into conversation with a fat man who drove a sleek Oldsmobile, and accepted an invitation to smoke a joint in the car. The man had clapped a chloroform-soaked rag over Rignall's face, driven him to a house, and there spent several hours raping him and flogging him with whips. Rignall woke up in the dawn by the lake in Lincoln Park. In hospital, it was discovered that he was bleeding from the anus, and that the chloroform that had been repeatedly administered had permanently damaged his liver.

The police said they were unable to help, since he knew so little about his molester, so Rignall hired a car and spent days sitting near motorway entrances looking for the black

Oldsmobile. Eventually, his patience paid off; he saw the Oldsmobile, followed it, and noted the number. It proved to belong to John Wayne Gacy. But in spite of issuing a warrant for Gacy's arrest, the police still delayed. It was mid-July before they more-or-less accidentally arrested Gacy on a misdemeanour charge, but the abduction case was not pursued very rigorously; the police felt that since Rignall had been chloroformed so much of the time, he might well be mistaken in his identification. And Mr Gacy, who denied everything, was a respected member of the community – one might almost guess that the police did not want to believe that he might be a dangerous abductor and rapist.

Yet even a cursory check of Gacy's police records would have showed that he had been sentenced to ten years in a 'correctional institution' in Waterloo, Iowa, ten years previously. The charges included handcuffing an employee and trying to sodomize him, paying a youth to perform fellatio on him, and then hiring someone to beat up the same youth when he gave evidence against Gacy. At that period, Gacy had been married and managing a fried chicken business; he had then also appeared to be a decent member of the community. He had been paroled after only eighteen months – described as a model prisoner – and placed on probation in Chicago. In 1971 he had been arrested for picking up a teenager and trying to force him to engage in sex. The boy failed to appear in court and the case was dismissed. Another man had accused Gacy of trying to force him to have sex at gunpoint in his house, and had even boasted that he had already killed somebody.

Eventually the police called at Gacy's house at 8213 West Summerdale Avenue, Des Plaines, and questioned him further about Robert Piest. As they talked they noticed an odd, unpleasant odour in the house. Finally, tracking the smell, they raised a trapdoor leading to a crawl space under the house. There was a heavy odour of decaying flesh, and the beam of the torch picked up bodies and human bones.

At the police station, Gacy admitted that he had killed

thirty-two male teenagers – in the course of raping them – and said that twenty-seven of these had been buried or disposed of in or around his house; the remaining five – including Robert Piest – had been disposed of in other ways; Piest had been dumped in the Des Plaines River.

Seven bodies were found in the crawl space under the house, and various parts of others. In another crawl space in another part of the house, bodies were found covered with quicklime in trenches that had been dug for them. Eight more were quickly unearthed. Gacy's house was demolished in the search for more corpses; eventually, the remains of twenty-eight were discovered – Gacy had lost count by one. When he had run out of burial space around his house, he had started dumping bodies in the river.

John Gacy had been born on 17 March 1942 in Chicago; his mother was Danish, his father Polish. When he was eleven he was struck on the head by a swing, and had blackouts from then on; at sixteen, the cause was diagnosed as a blood clot on the brain, which was dissolved by medication. He then developed heart trouble, possibly as a result of the treatment for the blood clot.

In spite of this he went to business college, became a shoe salesman, and married a co-worker whose parents owned a fried chicken business in Waterloo, Iowa. Gacy became a member of the Junior Chamber of Commerce. He was known as an affable man who badly wanted to be liked, and who tried to buy popularity with generosity. He was also known as a liar and a boaster – in short, a thoroughly weak character. What was not realised was that he had a secret homosexual life in which he was becoming increasingly predatory.

His married life came to an end with his imprisonment for attempted homosexual rape: his wife divorced him, taking their son and a daughter with her. In prison, Gacy worked hard, avoided other homosexuals, and obtained parole. In 1972 he married a second time, and started in business as a building contractor. But his wife found his violent tempers a

141

strain. His sexual performance was also infrequent. And then there was the peculiar odour that hung about the house.

In 1976 they divorced. Gacy continued indefatigably to try to rise in the world and to impress people: when he became involved with the local Democrats, he had cards printed identifying himself as a precinct police captain – an out-and-out lie. In 1978 he was photographed shaking hands with President Jimmy Carter's wife.

He used the building business to contact young males. One of these was John Butkovich, who vanished on 1 August 1975; he may have been the first victim. He had quarrelled with Gacy about pay; Gacy was notoriously mean, and refused to pay his employees for travelling time to the jobs. It was probably John Butkovich's body that caused the unpleasant smell in the house during the last year of Gacy's second marriage. Greg Godzik came to work for Gacy in 1976; on 11 December he vanished. A few weeks later, on 20 January 1977, a friend of Godzik's, John Szyc, also vanished.

There were many others. Billy Carrol disappeared on 10 June 1976, and in the previous month, three other boys, Randall Reffett, Samuel Stapleton and Michael Bonnin also vanished. Rick Johnston was dropped off by his mother at a rock concert on 6 August, and never seen again. Once Gacy was separated from his wife, there was nothing to stop him inviting young men to his house. Some of these – like a young male prostitute named Jaimie – were handcuffed and violently sodomized, but allowed to go – with payment. The boys who resisted were killed. A nine-year-old boy who was known as a procurer was driven off in the black Oldsmobile, and vanished. The Oldsmobile became familiar in the Newtown district of Chicago, where homosexuals could be picked up in bars or on the pavement. And the disappearances continued, until the killing of the thirty-third victim, Robert Piest, finally brought police with a search warrant to the house.

In 1980 Gacy was sentenced to death, and was executed in May 1994, still insisting on his innocence.

Ed Kemper

Edmund Emil Kemper, born on 18 December 1948, began to show signs of severe psychological disturbance as a small child. His mother and father separated when he was seven; he seems to have been one of those children who badly needed a male role-model, and later became an obsessive fan of John Wayne movies. He had been a boy scout, and was taught to shoot and handle a knife at summer camp. He claimed that his mother ridiculed him, and grew up with a highly ambivalent attitude towards her. A morbid child, he played games with his sister in which she led him to die in the gas chamber, and he once cut the hands and feet off her doll.

At thirteen he cut the family cat into pieces – animal cruelty is classic sign of potential violent tendencies in later life. He also had sadistic fantasies which included killing his mother, and often went into her bedroom at night with a gun, toying with the idea. He grew up to be six feet nine inches tall and weighed twenty stone (280 pounds). He also had sex fantasies about corpses. In spite of his powerful sexual interest in women from an early age, he was pathologically shy; when his sister once joked with him about wanting to kiss his teacher he replied, 'If I kissed her I'd have to kill her first.' Which is precisely what he did to his victims in manhood. Like the English sex murderer Christie, he killed women because he would have been impotent with a living woman.

At thirteen Ed ran away to his father, who promptly

returned him to his mother. He was then sent to live with his father's parents on a ranch in California. His mother rang her ex-husband to warn him that he was taking a risk in sending Ed to live with them; she said, 'You might wake up one day and find they've been killed.' Which is exactly what happened.

When he lost his temper with his domineering grandmother one day in August 1963, he pointed a rifle at the back of her head, and killed her. He then stabbed her repeatedly. When his grandfather came home, he shot him before he could enter the house. Then he telephoned his mother, and waited for the police to arrive. Donald Lunde, a psychiatrist who examined him later, remarked: 'In his way, he had avenged the rejection of both his mother and father.'

After five years in mental hospitals, he was sent back to his mother. She moved to Santa Cruz, where she became administrative assistant in a college of the University of California. She and Ed had violent, screaming quarrels, usually about trivial subjects. Kemper had evidently come to loathe her. He bought a motorcycle and wrecked it, suing the motorist involved. Then did the same thing with a second motorcycle. Using the insurance money he bought himself a car, and began driving around, picking up hitch-hikers, preferably female.

And on 7 May 1972, he committed his first sex murders, picking up Anita Luchese and Mary Anne Pesce, both students of Fresno State College, in Berkeley. He produced his gun, drove to a quiet spot, and made Anita climb into the boot while he handcuffed Mary Ann and put a plastic bag over her head. She seemed unafraid of him, and tried to talk to him reasonably. He stabbed her several times in the back, then in the abdomen; finally he cut her throat. After this he went to the boot and stabbed the other girl repeatedly. He then drove home – his mother was out – carried the bodies up to his apartment, and decapitated and dissected them. Later, he buried the pieces in the mountains.

On 14 September 1972 he picked up fifteen-year-old Aiko

Koo, a Eurasian girl hitch-hiking to a dance class in San Francisco. He produced his gun, drove her to the mountains, and then taped her mouth. When he tried to suffocate her by placing his fingers up her nostrils she fought fiercely. When she was dead, he laid her on the ground, and raped her, achieving orgasm within seconds. He took her back to his apartment, cut off the head and hands, and dissected the body, becoming sexually excited as he cut off the head. He took the remains out to the mountains above Boulder Creek and buried them.

On 8 January 1973 he picked up Cynthia Schall who usually hitched a lift to Cabrillo College. He produced the gun, drove her to the little town of Freedom, and stopped on a quiet road. For a while he played a cat-and-mouse game with her, telling her he had no intention of harming her, enjoying the sensation of power. Then he shot her, dumped the body in the boot, and drove home. She was a heavy girl, and he staggered with her into his bedroom, placing her in his closet. His mother came home, and Kemper talked to her and behaved normally. As soon as she was gone the next morning, he took out the body and engaged in various sex acts. Then he dissected it with an axe in the shower, and drove out to Carmel, with the body in plastic sacks, and threw them off cliffs. This time, parts of the body were discovered only a day later and positively identified.

After yet another a violent quarrel with his mother on 5 February, he drove to the local campus, and picked up Rosalind Thorpe, who was just coming out of a lecture. Shortly afterwards, he picked up 21-year-old Allison Lui. As they drove along in the dark, he shot Rosalind in the head. As Allison Lui covered her face with her hands, he shot her several times in the face.

He put both bodies in the boot, and drove home. His mother was at home, so he could not carry them in. Unable to wait, he took his big hunting knife (which he called 'the General') and hacked off both their heads in the boot. The next morning, when his mother had gone to work, he carried Allison Lui into the bathroom, cleaned off the blood, and had sexual intercourse with the headless corpse. He also cleaned up Rosalind Thorpe, although it is not clear whether he again performed necrophilia. He placed both bodies back in the boot, cut off Alice Lui's hands, then drove to the coast highway south of Pacifia and disposed of the heads; the bodies were dumped in Eden Canyon, Alameda. They were found nine days later.

Shortly after this, a policeman checking through gun licences realised that Ed Kemper had a criminal record, and had not declared this. He drove to Kemper's house, and found him in his car with a young blonde girl. Kemper handed over the gun, and the policeman drove off. His call probably saved the life of the blonde hitch-hiker.

This minor brush with the police evidently shook Kemper. He felt that he was going to 'blow up' soon: that is, commit a crime so obvious that he would be caught. So he decided to kill his mother while he still had the chance.

On the morning of Easter Sunday, 1973, Kemper walked into his mother's bedroom and hit her on the head with a hammer. Then he cut off her head with the General and dumped the body in a closet. He felt sick, and went out for a drive. Then he saw an acquaintance who owed him $10 and they went for a drive in his friend's car; without prompting, the man offered him the $10. Kemper, showing the odd moral landscape typical of serial killers, later said that this return of the money 'saved his [the acquaintance's] life'.

But Ed still needed to kill somebody. So he rang a friend of his mother's, Sara Hallett, and invited her for dinner with himself and his mother. When she arrived, she was breathless, and said, 'Let's sit down. I'm dead tired.' Kemper took this as a cue, and hit her, then strangled her. Later, in removing her head, he discovered he had broken her neck.

That night he slept in his mother's bed. The next day he drove west in Mrs Hallett's car. Then, using money he had taken from the dead woman, he rented a Hertz car. At one

146

point he was stopped by a policeman for speeding, and fined $25 on the spot. The policeman did not notice the gun on the back seat.

Kemper was expecting a manhunt, but when, after three days, there was still no news on the radio of the finding of the bodies, he stopped in Pueblo, Colorado, and telephoned the Santa Cruz police to confess to being 'the co-ed killer'. They asked him to call back later. He did, several times, before he finally convinced them that he was serious. So they sent a local policeman to arrest him.

In custody in Pueblo, Ed showed himself eager to talk loquaciously about the killings, describing them all in detail – even how he had buried the head of one victim in the garden, facing towards the house, so he could imagine her looking at him, and how he had cut out his mother's larynx and dropped it in the ash can 'because it seemed appropriate after she had bitched me so much.' He explained that he had driven to Pueblo before turning himself in because he was afraid that if he went straight to the local police they might shoot first and ask questions later, and he was 'terrified of violence'.

Kemper was adjudged legally sane, and sentenced to life imprisonment for his eight murders.

The BTK Strangler

Wichita, the largest city in Kansas, is a mid-sized and prosperous community with half a million inhabitants and a low crime rate; the last place in the world you would associate with sadistic murder.

That changed suddenly after 15 January 1972, the date of one of the most horrific crimes in the history of the Midwest. On that day, 15-year-old Charles Otero returned from school to find that his mother, father and two siblings had been killed. His mother and father, their wrists and ankles bound, lay dead in their bedroom. His nine-year-old brother Joe, wearing a hood, was dead in his bedroom. His 11-year-old sister Josephine had been hanged from a pipe in the basement, wearing only a shirt and socks. Two more children – Danny, 15, and Carmen, 13 – had also been at school during the killing spree.

Although there were semen traces all over the house, there had been no rape. Since all four had been strangled with cords, it looked as if the killer was a sadist who gained pleasure from the act of strangulation, and the sense of power it gave him to watch people suffer. This had been a well-known sexual perversion since the case of the strangler Vincent Verzeni was described in *Psychopathia Sexualis* by Richard von Krafft-Ebing in 1886. The killer had probably used a gun to gain control, then taken his time – about an hour and a half – in terrorising and killing them. It seemed likely he had gained entrance when the father – 38-year-old Puerto Rican, Joseph

149

Otero – was taking Charlie and two more children to school. He had then tied up the mother, Julie, 34, and her two children and waited for Joseph to return. It had obviously been carefully planned.

The police had no leads, but nine months later, a tip to look in a certain library book revealed a letter from the killer, promising more murders. He declared, 'I find it hard to control myself,' and admitted that he felt he was possessed by a monster. Naturally the press pounced on such a lurid story and soon the murderer had a media nickname: 'the B.T.K. Strangler' (short for 'Bind Torture Kill') often shortened to just 'BTK.'

Three months after the Otera murders, 20-year-old Kathryn Bright and her 19-year-old brother Kevin came home soon after midday to find an intruder with a gun, who told them he needed money to escape from the police. He tied Kathryn, then took Kevin into the bedroom and tried to strangle him. When Kevin resisted he was shot in the head. Then he heard sounds of distress from his sister, and dragged himself into the next room, only to be shot again; in spite of this he succeeded in escaping and getting help. But it was too late: Kathryn had been stabbed three times in the stomach and later died in hospital. The killer had also tried to strangle her.

The murders then ceased for three years. The next victim was 26-year-old mother of three, Shirley Vian, found strangled on 17 March 1977, on her bed; her three children, locked in the bathroom, had escaped through a tiny window; the killer later admitted he had intended to kill them too.

Nine months later, on 8 December 1977, it was the murderer himself who rang the police and told them that a girl named Nancy Fox had been killed. The call was quickly traced, but police found only a dangling public phone. 25-year-old secretary Nancy Fox had been strangled in the night, and semen indicated that the killer had masturbated over her.

Then came an eight-year gap, and the next victim, 53-year-old widow Marine Hedge, was strangled in her home on 27

April 1985. The killer took her body in the boot of her car to a nearby Lutheran church where he took photographs of the body in various types of bondage, before driving the body to a ditch, where he covered it over. Her disappearance was not attributed to BTK.

The strangler would later reveal that women like Marine Hedge were his 'projects', observed and stalked for days or weeks before he struck.

This was also true of his next victim, a 28 -year-old married woman named Vicki Wegerle, to whose house he gained entry on 16 September 1986, by claiming to be a telephone repairman; he strangled her after holding her at gunpoint, then took photos of her. Although he thought she was dead when he left her, she actually lived for a short time. Her husband found her dying on his return from work.

The killer gained entry to the house of the eleventh and final victim, Delores Davis, 62, on 19 January 1991 by hurling a concrete block through her plate-glass window, then telling her he was on the run and needed food and money. He handcuffed her, pretended he was leaving, then went back and strangled her. Then he took her body in the boot of her own car and dumped it under a bridge.

For thirteen years nothing further was heard from BTK. But on 19 March 2004, the newsrooom of the Wichita Eagle received a letter from him acknowledging responsibility for the death of Vicki Wegerle – whose husband had been chief suspect since 1986 – and enclosing a photograph of her driver's license and photographs of her body.

Immediately, the fear was back again. But it proved unnecessary. BTK was about to make the mistake he had been so careful to avoid for thirty years, and it came about because of his craving to play games with the police.

There were no less than eleven communications between March 2004 and February 2005, including a letter describing the Otero murders, cards with images of bondage of children on them, and even a misleading 'autobiography', giving false details of his life, which led to a public appeal to anyone who might recognise the writer. There was also a cereal box containing a bound doll with a plastic bag over its head, and another containing a bound doll symbolising Josephine Otero.

Then BTK made his mistake; he asked the police if he could send a message on a floppy disk, and on being assured (via a newspaper advertisement) that it would be acceptable, he sent one to a television station. But electronic traces on the disk indicated it had been formerly used by the Christ Lutheran Church in Wichita by someone called 'Dennis.'

A man named Dennis Rader, aged 60, president of the church council, was kept under observation, and his daughter was approached by the police for a blood sample. The DNA proved to be the same as in the semen left at crime scenes and, on 25 February 2005, Rader was arrested and charged. He seemed almost relieved, and quickly confessed.

The trial, from 27 June 2005 to 19 August, ended with the expected guilty verdict, and Rader received ten life sentences which would last 175 years. He is presently serving them at the El Dorado Correctional Facilty, Kansas.

Herb Mullin

Herbert Mullin was born on 18 April 1947 in Salinas, California. His mother was a devout Catholic and Mullin's upbringing was, according to his later confession, oppressively religious. But he seems to have been a completely normal boy, and was even voted by his class 'most likely to succeed'. By the age of seventeen he had a girlfriend, to whom he was engaged, and a close male friend named Dean; both were members of a group of school athletes who called themselves the Zeros. But Dean's death in a motor accident in July 1965 seems to have marked the beginning of the schizophrenia that led Mullin to commit thirteen murders.

Mullin arranged his bedroom as a kind of shrine round his friend's picture, and told his girlfriend that he was afraid he was homosexual. When he became eligible for call-up in the army, he decided to become a conscientious objector; his girlfriend, whose father was a military man, broke off their engagement.

In February 1969, when he was twenty-one, Herb announced that he was going to India to study religion, and his family noted that he seemed to be becoming 'more and more unrealistic'. A month later, at a family dinner, he began obsessively repeating everything his brother-in-law said and did. His family then persuaded him to commit himself to a mental hospital. He remained there for six weeks, but was unco-operative, and continued to talk about yoga and his (for middle-class Americans in the late 1960s) odd religious ideas.

By October 1969 Mullin was suffering from full-blown paranoid schizophrenia, hearing voices that told him to shave his head and burn his penis with a lighted cigarette. He had been smoking pot and taking LSD for a number of years, and this undoubtedly contributed to his mental derangement. Back in a mental home, he wrote dozens of letters to people he had never met, signing himself 'a human sacrifice, Herb Mullin'. He was given anti-psychotic drugs and, after a month, was discharged.

In June 1970 he went to Hawaii, against his parents' advice, and was soon in a mental hospital. His parents had to provide money for his return and he was escorted onto the plane by a policeman. Back in Santa Cruz he behaved strangely and got in trouble with the police. In June 1971 he moved to San Francisco and lived in cheap hotels; when evicted from his hotel in September 1972, he returned home – still highly disturbed. He had began receiving what he believed were telepathic messages, ordering him to kill.

On 13 October 1972 he was driving along a deserted stretch of highway in the Santa Cruz mountains when he saw an old man walking along. He stopped the car and asked the man to take a look at the engine; as the tramp bent obligingly over the car, Mullin hit him with a baseball bat, killing him. He left the body – later identified as Lawrence White – by the roadside and drove off.

On 24 October Herb picked up a Cabrillo College student, Mary Guilfoyle. As they drove towards downtown Santa Cruz, he stabbed her in the heart with a hunting knife, killing her instantly. Then he took her to a deserted road, and began cutting open the body with the knife, pulling out the internal organs. He left her there to the vultures, and drove off – her skeleton was found four months later. A week later, on 2 November, he entered the confessional of St Mary's Church, Los Gatos, and stabbed to death Father Henri Tomei. Herb had originally entered the church in the hope that religion would somehow prevent him from killing again, but he didn't even get to the point of confessing before he killed the priest.

Now the voices in Mullin's head seemed to be from potential victims, begging him to kill them. In December 1972 he bought a gun. On 25 January 1973 he drove out to Branciforte Drive, looking for Jim Gianera, the man who, years before, had introduced him to pot; he now believed Gianera had deliberately set out to destroy his mind. The door of the primitive cabin in which Gianera had lived was opened by 29-year-old Kathy Francis, who told him that Gianera no longer lived there. She gave him Gianera's address in Santa Cruz. Mullin drove there, and shot down Gianera; then, as the dying man's wife bent over him, he stabbed her in the back, then shot her. Then he went back to the cabin, and killed Kathy Francis and her two small sons, sleeping in the same bed. Kathy Francis's husband had been out of town at the time.

On 30 January, Mullin went to discuss his problems with a Lutheran minister in Santa Cruz, explaining mysteriously that 'Satan gets into people and makes them do things they don't want to.' He did not elaborate.

On 6 February Mullin was hiking aimlessly in the state park in Santa Cruz when he saw a makeshift tent. He told the four teenage boys inside that they were camping illegally and that he would have to report them. The boys, all in their teens, tried to talk him out of it. Suddenly, Mullin pulled out his revolver and shot them in rapid succession. They brought the number of his victims up to twelve.

A few days later, Mullin was preparing to deliver firewood to his parents' house when the mental voices told him he had to kill someone. It was 13 February. He stopped his station-wagon, went up to an old man, Fred Perez, who was working in the garden, and shot him. A neighbour looking out of her window saw the station-wagon driving away, and Fred Perez lying face down. She called the police, and within minutes Mullin was under arrest.

At his trial Mullin explained his reasons for killing. He was convinced that he was averting natural disasters – like another San Francisco earthquake – and had saved thousands of lives. Murder, he said, decreases natural disasters. He was found sane by legal standards, and guilty of ten murders – he was not charged with all thirteen. He will become eligible for parole in the year 2020.

In his book on the killings, *The Die Song*, psychiatrist Donald T. Lunde argues that Governor Reagan's economic measures, which forced the closure of many mental hospitals in California and thus indirectly deprived Mullin of treatment, was a false economy that ultimately cost both money and lives.

Peter Sutcliffe, the 'Yorkshire Ripper'

During the second half of the 1970s, the killer who became known as the Yorkshire Ripper caused the same kind of fear among prostitutes in the north of England as his namesake in the Whitechapel of 1888.

His reign of terror began in Leeds on a freezing October morning in 1975, when a milkman discovered the corpse of a woman on a recreation ground; her trousers had been pulled down below her knees, and her bra was around her throat. The whole of the front of the body was covered with blood; pathologists later established that she had been stabbed fourteen times. Before that, she had been knocked unconscious by a tremendous blow that had shattered the back of her skull. She was identified as a twenty-eight-year-old prostitute, Wilma McCann, who had left her four children alone to go on a pub crawl. Her killer seemed to have stabbed and slashed her in a frenzy.

Three months later, on 20 January 1976, a man on his way to work noticed a prostrate figure lying in a narrow alleyway in Leeds, covered with a coat. Like Wilma McCann, Emily Jackson had been half-stripped, and stabbed repeatedly in the stomach and breasts. She had also been knocked unconscious by a tremendous blow from behind. When the police established that the forty-two-year-old woman was the wife of a roofing contractor, and that she lived in the respectable suburb of Churwell, they assumed that the killer had selected her at random and crept up behind her with some blunt instrument. Further investigation revealed the surprising fact that this apparently normal housewife supplemented her income with prostitution, and that she had had sexual intercourse shortly before death – not necessarily with her killer. The pattern that was emerging was like that of the Jack the Ripper case: a sadistic maniac who preyed on prostitutes. Just as in Whitechapel in 1888, there was panic among the prostitutes of Leeds, particularly in Chapeltown, the red-light area where Emily Jackson had been picked up. But as no further 'Ripper' murders occurred in 1976, the panic subsided.

It began all over again more than a year later, on 5 February 1977, when a twenty-eight-year-old woman named Irene Richardson left her room in Chapeltown looking for customers, and encountered a man who carried a concealed hammer and a knife. Irene Richardson had been struck down from behind within half an hour of leaving her room; then her attacker had pulled off her skirt and tights, and stabbed her repeatedly. The wounds indicated that, like Jack the Ripper, he seemed to be gripped by some awful compulsion to expose the victim's intestines. Now the murders followed with a grim repetitiveness that indicated that the serial killer was totally in the grip of his obsession.

During the next three and a half years, the man whom the press christened the Yorkshire Ripper murdered ten more women, bringing his total to thirteen, and severely injured three more. Most of the victims were prostitutes, but two were young girls walking home late at night, and one of them a civil servant. With one exception, the method was always the same: several violent blows to the skull, which often had the effect of shattering it into many pieces, then stab wounds in the breast and stomach. In many cases the victim's intestines spilled out. The exception was a civil servant named Marguerite Walls, who was strangled with a piece of rope on 20 August 1979, after being knocked unconscious from behind. One victim who recovered – forty-two-year-old Maureen Long – was able to describe her attacker.

On 27 July 1977 she had been walking home through central Bradford after an evening of heavy drinking when a man in a white car offered her a lift. As she stepped out of the car near her front door, the man struck her a savage blow on the head, then stabbed her several times. But before he could be certain she was dead, a light went on in a nearby gypsy caravan and he drove away. She recovered after a brain operation, and described her attacker as a young man with long blond hair – a detail that later proved to be inaccurate. Her mistake may have saved the Ripper from arrest three months later.

A prostitute named Jean Jordan was killed near some allotments in Manchester on 1 October 1977. When the body was found nine days later – with twenty-four stab wounds – the police discovered a new £5 note in her handbag. Since it had been issued on the other side of the Pennines, in Yorkshire, it was obviously a vital clue. The police checked with the banks, and located twenty-three firms in the Leeds area who had paid their workers with £5 notes in the same sequence. Among the workers who were interviewed was a thirty-one-year-old lorry driver named Peter Sutcliffe, who worked at T. and W. H. Clark (Holdings) Ltd, and lived in a small detached house at 6 Garden Lane in Bradford. But Sutcliffe had dark curly hair and a beard, and his wife Sonia was able to provide him with an alibi. The police apologized and left, and the Yorkshire Ripper was able to go on murdering for three more years.

As the murders continued – four in 1977, three in 1978, three in 1979 – the police launched the largest operation that had ever been mounted in the north of England, and thousands of people were interviewed. Police received three letters signed 'Jack the Ripper', threatening more murders, and a cassette on which a man with a 'Geordie' accent taunted George Oldfield, the officer in charge of the case; these later proved to be false leads. The cassette caused the police to direct enormous efforts to the

159

Wearside area, and increased the murderer's sense of invulnerability. The final murder took place more than a year later. Twenty-year-old Jacqueline Hill, a Leeds University student, had attended a meeting of voluntary probation officers on 17 November 1980, and caught a bus back to her lodgings soon after 9 p.m. An hour later, her handbag was found near some waste ground by an Iraqi student, and he called the police. It was a windy and rainy night, and they found nothing. Jacqueline Hill's body was found the next morning on the waste ground. She had been battered unconscious with a hammer, then undressed and stabbed repeatedly. One wound was in the eye – Sutcliffe later said she seemed to be looking at him reproachfully, so he drove the blade into her eye.

This was the Ripper's last attack. On 2 January 1981 a black prostitute named Olive Reivers had just finished with a client in the centre of Sheffield when a Rover car drove up, and a bearded man asked her how much she charged; she said it would be £10 for sex in the car, and climbed in the front. He seemed tense and asked if she would object if he talked for a while about his family problems. When he asked her to get in the back of the car, she said she would prefer to have sex in the front; this may have saved her life – Sutcliffe had stunned at least one of his victims as she climbed into the back of the car. He moved on top of her, but was unable to maintain an erection. He moved off her again, and at this point a police car pulled up in front. Sutcliffe hastily told the woman to say she was his girlfriend. The police asked his name, and he told them it was Peter Williams. Sergeant Robert Ring and PC Robert Hydes were on patrol duty, and they were carrying out a standard check. Ring noted the number plate then went off to check it with the computer; while he radioed, he told PC Hydes to get into the back of the Rover. Sutcliffe asked if he could get out to urinate and Hydes gave permission: Sutcliffe stood by an oil storage tank a few feet away, then got back into the car. Meanwhile, the sergeant had discovered that the number plates did not belong to the Rover, and told Sutcliffe he would have to return to the police station.

In the station, Sutcliffe again asked to go to the lavatory and was given permission. It was when the police made him empty his pockets and found a length of clothes-line that they began to suspect that they might have trapped Britain's most wanted man. To begin with, Sutcliffe lied fluently about why he was carrying the rope and why he was in the car with a prostitute.

It was the following day that Sergeant Ring learned about Sutcliffe's brief absence from the car to relieve himself, and went to look near the oil storage tank. In the leaves, he found a ball-headed hammer and a knife. Then he recalled Sutcliffe's trip to the lavatory at the police station. In the cistern he found a second knife. When Sutcliffe was told that he was in serious trouble, he suddenly admitted that he was the Ripper, and confessed to eleven murders. (It seems odd that he got the number wrong – he was later charged with thirteen – but it is possible that he genuinely lost count. He was originally suspected of fourteen murders, but the police later decided that the killing of another prostitute, Jean Harrison – whose body was found in Preston, Lancashire – was not one of the series. She had been raped and the semen was not of Sutcliffe's blood group.)

A card written by Sutcliffe and displayed in his lorry read: 'In this truck is a man whose latent genius, if unleashed, would rock the nation, whose dynamic energy would overpower those around him. Better let him sleep?' The story that began to emerge was of a lonely and shy individual, brooding and introverted, who was morbidly fascinated by prostitutes and red-light areas.

He was born on 2 June 1946, the eldest of five children and his mother's favourite. His school career was undistinguished and he left at fifteen. He drifted aimlessly from job to job, including one as a gravedigger in the Bingley cemetery, from which he was dismissed for bad timekeeping. (His later

161

attempt at a defence of insanity rested on a claim that a voice had spoken to him from a cross in the cemetery telling him he had a God-given mission to kill prostitutes.)

In 1967, when he was twenty-one, he met a sixteen-year-old Czech girl, Sonia Szurma, in a pub, and they began going out together. It would be another seven years before they married. The relationship seems to have been stormy; at one point, she was going out with an ice-cream salesman, and Sutcliffe picked up a prostitute 'to get even'. He was unable to have intercourse, and the woman went off with a £10 note and failed to return with his £5 change. When he saw her in a pub two weeks later and asked for the money, she jeered at him and left him with a sense of helpless fury and humiliation. This, he claimed, was the source of his hatred of prostitutes.

In 1969 he made his first attack on a prostitute, hitting her on the head with a sock full of gravel. In October of that year, he was caught carrying a hammer and charged with being equipped for theft; he was fined £25. In 1971 he went for a drive with a friend, Trevor Birdsall, and left the car in the red-light area of Bradford. When he returned ten minutes later he said, 'Drive off quickly,' and admitted that he had hit a woman with a brick in a sock. Sutcliffe was again driving with Birdsall in 1975 on the evening that Olive Smelt was struck down with a hammer. In 1972 Sonia Szurma went to London for a teacher's training course and had a nervous breakdown; she was diagnosed as schizophrenic.

Two years later, she and Sutcliffe married, but the marriage was punctuated by violent rows – Sutcliffe said he became embarrassed in case the neighbours heard the shouts, implying that it was she who was shouting rather than he. He also told the prostitute Olive Reivers that he had been arguing with his wife 'about not being able to go with her', which Olive Reivers took to mean that they were having sexual problems. Certainly, this combination of two introverted people can hardly have improved Sutcliffe's mental condition.

Sutcliffe's first murder – of Wilma McCann – took place in

the year after he married Sonia. He admitted: 'I developed and played up a hatred for prostitutes.' Unlike the Düsseldorf sadist of the 1920s, Peter Kürten, Sutcliffe never admitted to having orgasms as he stabbed his victims; but anyone acquainted with the psychology of sexual criminals would take it for granted that this occurred, and that in most of the cases where the victim was not stabbed, or was left alive, he achieved orgasm at an earlier stage than usual. The parallels are remarkable. Kürten, like Sutcliffe, used a variety of weapons, including a hammer. On one occasion when a corpse remained undiscovered, Kürten also returned to inflict fresh indignities on it. Sutcliffe had returned to the body of Jean Jordan and attempted to cut off the head with a hacksaw. It was when he pulled up Wilma McCann's clothes and stabbed her in the breast and abdomen that Sutcliffe realized that he had discovered a new sexual thrill. With the second victim, Emily Jackson, he pulled off her bra and briefs, then stabbed her repeatedly – he was, in effect, committing rape with a knife. Sutcliffe was caught in the basic trap of the sex criminal: the realization that he had found a way of inducing a far more powerful sexual satisfaction than he was able to obtain in normal intercourse, and that he was pushing himself into the position of a social outcast. He admitted sobbing in his car after one of the murders, and being upset to discover that Jayne MacDonald had not been a prostitute (and later, that her father had died of a broken heart). But the compulsion to kill was becoming a fever, so that he no longer cared that the later victims were not prostitutes. He said, probably with sincerity, 'The devil drove me.' Sutcliffe's trial began on 5 May 1981. He had pleaded not guilty to murder on grounds of diminished responsibility, and told the story of his 'mission' from God. But a warder had overheard him tell his wife that if he could convince the jury that he was mad, he would only spend ten years in a 'loony bin'. The Attorney-General, Sir Michael Havers, also pointed out that Sutcliffe had at first behaved perfectly normally, laughing at the idea that he might be mentally abnormal, and had introduced the talk of 'voices' fairly late in his admissions to the police. On 22 May Sutcliffe was found guilty of murder, and jailed for life, with a recommendation that he should serve at least thirty years.

Dennis Nilsen

On the evening of 8 February 1983, a drains maintenance engineer named Michael Cattran was asked to call at 23 Cranley Gardens, in Muswell Hill, north London, to find out why tenants had been unable to flush their toilets since the previous Saturday. Although Muswell Hill is known as a highly respectable area of London – it was once too expensive for anyone but the upper middle classes – No. 23 proved to be a rather shabby house, divided into flats. A tenant showed Cattran the manhole cover that led to the drainage system. When he removed it, he staggered back and came close to vomiting; the smell was unmistakably decaying flesh. And when he had climbed down the rungs into the cistern, Cattran discovered what was blocking the drain: masses of rotting meat, much of it white, like chicken flesh. Convinced this was human flesh, Cattran rang his supervisor, who decided to come and inspect it in the morning.

When they arrived the following day, the drain had been cleared. And a female tenant told them she had heard footsteps going up and down the stairs for much of the night. The footsteps seemed to go up to the top flat, which was rented by a thirty-seven-year-old civil servant named Dennis Nilsen. Closer search revealed that the drain was still not quite clear; there was a piece of flesh, six inches square, and some bones that resembled fingers. Detective Chief Inspector Peter Jay, of Hornsey CID, was waiting in the hallway of the house that evening when Dennis Nilsen walked in from his day at the office – a Jobcentre in Kentish Town. He told Nilsen he wanted to talk to him about the drains. Nilsen invited the policeman into his flat, and Jay's face wrinkled as he smelled the odour of decaying flesh. He told Nilsen that they had found human remains in the drain, and asked what had happened to the rest of the body. 'It's in there, in two plastic bags,' said Nilsen, pointing to a wardrobe.

In the police car, the Chief Inspector asked Nilsen whether the remains came from one body or two. Calmly, without emotion, Nilsen said: 'There have been fifteen or sixteen altogether.' At the police station Nilsen, a tall man with metal-rimmed glasses, seemed eager to talk. (In fact, he proved to be something of a compulsive talker, and his talk overflowed into a series of school exercise books in which he later wrote his story for the use of Brian Masters, a young writer who contacted him in prison.) He told police that he had murdered three men in the Cranley Gardens house – into which he moved in the autumn of 1981 – and twelve or thirteen at his previous address, 195 Melrose Avenue, Cricklewood.

The plastic bags from the Muswell Hill flat contained two severed heads, and a skull from which the flesh had been stripped – forensic examination revealed that it had been boiled. The bathroom contained the whole lower half of a torso, from the waist down, intact. The rest was in bags in the wardrobe and in the tea chest. At Melrose Avenue, thirteen days and nights of digging revealed many human bones, as well as a chequebook and pieces of clothing. The self-confessed mass murderer – he seemed to take a certain pride in being 'Britain's biggest mass murderer' – was a Scot, born at Fraserburgh on 23 November 1945. His mother, born Betty Whyte, married a Norwegian soldier named Olav Nilsen in 1942. It was not a happy marriage; Olav was seldom at home, and was drunk a great deal; they were divorced seven years after their marriage.

In 1954, Mrs Nilsen married again and became Betty Scott.

Dennis grew up in the house of his grandmother and grandfather, and was immensely attached to his grandfather, Andrew Whyte, who became a father substitute. When Nilsen was seven, his grandfather died and his mother took Dennis in to see the corpse. This seems to have been a traumatic experience; in his prison notes he declares, 'My troubles started there.' The death of his grandfather was such a blow that it caused his own emotional death, according to Nilsen.

Not long after this, someone killed the two pigeons he kept in an air raid shelter, another severe shock. His mother's remarriage when he was nine had the effect of making him even more of a loner. In 1961, Nilsen enlisted in the army, and became a cook. It was during this period that he began to get drunk regularly, although he remained a loner, avoiding close relationships. In 1972 he changed the life of a soldier for that of a London policeman, but disliked the relative lack of freedom – compared to the army – and resigned after only eleven months. He became a security guard for a brief period, then a job interviewer for the Manpower Services Commission. In November 1975, Nilsen began to share a north London flat – in Melrose Avenue – with a young man named David Gallichan, ten years his junior. Gallichan was later to insist that there was no homosexual relationship, and this is believable. Many heterosexual young men would later accept Nilsen's offer of a bed for the night, and he would make no advances, or accept a simple 'No' without resentment.

But in May 1977, Gallichan decided he could bear London no longer, and accepted a job in the country. Nilsen was furious; he felt rejected and deserted. The break-up of the relationship with Gallichan – whom he had always dominated – seems to have triggered the homicidal violence that would claim fifteen lives. The killings began more than a year later, in December 1978.

Around Christmas, Nilsen picked up a young Irish labourer in the Cricklewood Arms, and they went back to his flat to continue drinking. Nilsen wanted him to stay over the New Year but the Irishman had other plans. In a note he later wrote for his biographer Brian Masters, Nilsen gives as his motive for this first killing that he was lonely and wanted to spare himself the pain of separation. In another confession he also implies that he has no memory of the actual killing. Nilsen strangled the unnamed Irishman in his sleep with a tie. Then he undressed the body and carefully washed it, a ritual he observed in all his killings. After that he placed the body under the floorboards where – as incredible as it seems – he kept it until the following August. He eventually burned it on a bonfire at the bottom of the garden, burning some rubber at the same time to mask the smell.

In November 1979, Nilsen attempted to strangle a young Chinese man who had accepted his offer to return to the flat; the Chinese man escaped and reported the attack to the police. But the police believed Nilsen's explanation that the Chinese man was trying to 'rip him off' and decided not to pursue the matter.

The next murder victim was a twenty-three-year-old Canadian called Kenneth James Ockendon, who had completed a technical training course and was taking a holiday before starting his career. He had been staying with an uncle and aunt in Carshalton after touring the Lake District. He was not a homosexual, and it was pure bad luck that he got into conversation with Nilsen in the Princess Louise in High Holborn around 3 December 1979. They went back to Nilsen's flat, ate ham, eggs and chips, and bought £20 worth of alcohol. Ockendon watched television, then listened to rock music on Nilsen's hi-fi system. Then he sat listening to music wearing earphones, watching television at the same time. This may have been what cost him his life; Nilsen liked to talk, and probably felt 'rejected'. 'I thought bloody good guest this . . .' And some time after midnight, while Ockendon was still wearing the headphones, he strangled him with a flex. Ockendon was so drunk that he put up no struggle. And Nilsen was also so drunk that after the murder, he sat down, put on the headphones, and went on playing music for hours.

When he tried to put the body under the floorboards the next day, rigor mortis had set in and it was impossible. He had to wait until the rigor had passed. Later, he dissected the body. Ockendon had large quantities of Canadian money in his moneybelt, but Nilsen tore this up. The rigorous Scottish upbringing would not have allowed him to steal. Nilsen's accounts of the murders are repetitive, and make them sound mechanical and almost identical.

The third victim in May 1980, was a sixteen-year-old butcher named Martyn Duffey, who was also strangled and placed under the floorboards. Number four was a twenty-six-year-old Scot named Billy Sutherland – again strangled in his sleep with a tie and placed under the floorboards.

Number five was an unnamed Mexican or Filipino, killed a few months later. Number six was an Irish building worker. Number seven was an undernourished down-and-out picked up in a doorway. (He was burned on the bonfire all in one piece.)

The next five victims, all unnamed, were killed equally casually between late 1980 and late 1981. Nilsen later insisted that all the murders had been without sexual motivation – a plea that led Brian Masters to entitle his book on the case *Killing for Company*. There are moments in Nilsen's confessions when it sounds as if, like so many serial killers, he felt as if he was being taken over by a Mr Hyde personality or possessed by some demonic force.

In October 1981, Nilsen moved into an upstairs flat in Cranley Gardens, Muswell Hill. On 25 November, he took a homosexual student named Paul Nobbs back with him, and they got drunk. The next day, Nobbs went into University College Hospital for a check-up, and was told that bruises on his throat indicated that someone had tried to strangle him. Nilsen apparently changed his mind at the last moment.

The next victim, John Howlett, was less lucky. He woke up

as Nilsen tried to strangle him and fought back hard; Nilsen had to bang his head against the headrest of the bed to subdue him. When he realized Howlett was still breathing, Nilsen drowned him in the bath. He hacked up the body in the bath, then boiled chunks in a large pot to make them easier to dispose of. (He also left parts of the body out in plastic bags for the dustbin men to take away.)

In May 1982, another intended victim escaped – a drag artiste called Carl Stottor. After trying to strangle him, Nilsen placed him in a bath of water, but changed his mind and allowed him to live. When he left the flat, Stottor even agreed to meet Nilsen again – but decided not to keep the appointment. He decided not to go to the police.

The last two victims were both unnamed, one a drunk and one a drug addict. In both cases, Nilsen claims to be unable to remember the actual killing. Both were dissected, boiled and flushed down the toilet. It was after this second murder – the fifteenth in all – that the tenants complained about blocked drains, and Nilsen was arrested. The trial began on 24 October 1983, in the same court where Peter Sutcliffe had been tried two years earlier. Nilsen was charged with six murders and two attempted murders, although he had confessed to fifteen murders and seven attempted murders. He gave the impression that he was enjoying his moment of glory. The defence pleaded diminished responsibility, and argued that the charge should be reduced to manslaughter. The jury declined to accept this, and on 4 November 1983, Nilsen was found guilty by a vote of 10 to 2, and sentenced to life imprisonment.

Ted Bundy

During the 1970s, it became increasingly clear that America's law enforcement agencies were facing a new problem: the killer who murdered repeatedly and compulsively – not just half a dozen times, like Jack the Ripper, or even a dozen, like the Boston Strangler, but twenty, thirty, forty, even a hundred times.

In Houston, Texas, a homosexual with a taste for boys, Dean Corll, murdered about thirty teenagers – the precise number has never been established – and buried most of the bodies in a hired boatshed; Corll was shot to death by his lover and accomplice, Wayne Henley, in August 1973.

In 1979 Chicago builder John Gacy lured thirty-three boys to his home and buried most of the bodies in a crawl space under his house.

In 1983 a drifter named Henry Lee Lucas experienced some kind of religious conversion, and confessed to 360 murders, mostly of women, killed and raped as he wandered around the country with his homosexual companion Ottis Toole.

In 1986, in Ecuador, another drifter named Pedro Lopez confessed to killing and raping 360 young girls. Lopez has so far claimed the highest number of victims – Lucas is believed to have exaggerated, although his victims undoubtedly run to more than a hundred.

During the seventies, the killer who was most responsible for making Americans aware of this new type of criminal was a personable young law student named Theodore Robert Bundy. On 31 January 1974, a student at the University of Washington, in Seattle, Lynda Ann Healy, vanished from her room; the bedsheets were bloodstained, suggesting that she had been struck violently on the head. During the following March, April and May, three more girl students vanished; in June, two more.

In July, two girls vanished on the same day. It happened at a popular picnic spot, Lake Sammanish; a number of people saw a good-looking young man, with his arm in a sling, accost a girl named Janice Ott and ask her to help him lift a boat onto the roof of his car; she walked away with him and did not return. Later, a girl named Denise Naslund was accosted by the same young man; she also vanished. He had been heard to introduce himself as 'Ted'.

In October 1974 the killings shifted to Salt Lake City; three girls disappeared in one month. In November the police had their first break in the case: a girl named Carol DaRonch was accosted in a shopping centre by a young man who identified himself as a detective, and told her that there had been an attempt to break into her car; she agreed to accompany him to headquarters to view a suspect. In the car he snapped a handcuff on her wrist and pointed a gun at her head; she fought and screamed, and managed to jump from the car. That evening, a girl student vanished on her way to meet her brother. A handcuff key was found near the place from which she had been taken.

Meanwhile, the Seattle police had fixed on a young man named Ted Bundy as a main suspect. For the past six years he had been involved in a close relationship with a divorcée named Meg Anders, but she had called off the marriage when she realized he was a habitual thief. After the Lake Sammanish disappearances, she had seen a photofit drawing of the wanted 'Ted' in the *Seattle Times* and thought it looked like Bundy; moreover, 'Ted' drove a Volkswagen like Bundy's. She had seen crutches and plaster of Paris in

172

Bundy's room, and the coincidence seemed too great; with immense misgivings, she telephoned the police.

They told her that they had already checked on Bundy; but at the suggestion of the Seattle police, Carol DaRonch was shown Bundy's photograph. She tentatively identified it as resembling the man who had tried to abduct her, but was obviously far from sure. (Bundy had been wearing a beard at the time.) In January, March, April, July and August 1975, more girls vanished in Colorado. (Their bodies – or skeletons – were found later in remote spots.)

On 16 August 1975, Bundy was arrested for the first time. As a police car was driving along a dark street in Salt Lake City, a parked Volkswagen launched into motion; the policeman followed and it accelerated. He caught up with the car at a service station, and found in the car a pantyhose mask, a crowbar, an ice pick and various other tools; there was also a pair of handcuffs. Bundy, twenty-nine years old, seemed an unlikely burglar. He was a graduate of the University of Washington and was in Utah to study law; he had worked as a political campaigner, and for the Crime Commission in Seattle. In his room there was nothing suspicious – except maps and brochures of Colorado, from which five girls had vanished that year. But strands of hair were found in the car, and they proved to be identical with those of Melissa Smith, daughter of the Midvale police chief, who had vanished in the previous October.

Carol DaRonch had meanwhile identified Bundy in a police line-up as the fake policeman, and bloodspots on her clothes – where she had scratched her assailant – were of Bundy's group. Credit card receipts showed that Bundy had been close to various places from which girls had vanished in Colorado. In theory, this should have been the end of the case – and if it had been, it would have been regarded as a typical triumph of scientific detection, beginning with the photofit drawing and concluding with the hair and blood evidence. The evidence was, admittedly, circumstantial, but taken all together, it formed a powerful case. The central objection to it became apparent as soon as Bundy walked into court. He looked so obviously decent and clean-cut that most people felt there must be some mistake.

He was polite, well-spoken, articulate, charming, the kind of man who could have found himself a girlfriend for each night of the week. Why *should* such a man be a sex killer? In spite of which, the impression he made was of brilliance and plausibility rather than innocence. For example, he insisted that he had driven away from the police car because he was smoking marijuana, and that he had thrown the joint out of the window. The case seemed to be balanced on a knife-edge – until the judge pronounced a sentence of guilty of kidnapping. Bundy sobbed and pleaded not to be sent to prison; but the judge sentenced him to a period between one and fifteen years.

The Colorado authorities now charged him with the murder of a girl called Caryn Campbell, who had been abducted from a ski resort where Bundy had been seen by a witness. After a morning courtroom session in Aspen, Bundy succeeded in wandering into the library during the lunch recess and jumping out of the window. He was recaptured eight days later, tired and hungry, and driving a stolen car. Legal arguments dragged on for another six months – what evidence was admissible and what was not. And on 30 December 1977, Bundy escaped again, using a hacksaw blade to cut through an imperfectly welded steel plate above the light fixture in his cell.

He made his way to Chicago, then south to Florida; there, near the Florida State University in Tallahassee, he took a room. A few days later, a man broke into a nearby sorority house and attacked four girls with a club, knocking them unconscious; one was strangled with her pantyhose and raped; another died on her way to hospital. One of the strangled girl's nipples had been almost bitten off, and she had a bite mark on her left buttock. An hour and a half later, a student woke up when she heard bangs next door, and a girl whimpering. She dialled the number of the room, and as the telephone rang, someone could be heard running out.

Cheryl Thomas was found lying in bed, her skull fractured but still alive. Three weeks later, on 6 February 1978, Bundy – who was calling himself Chris Hagen – stole a white Dodge van and left Tallahassee; he stayed in the Holiday Inn, using a stolen credit card. The following day a twelve-year-old girl named Kimberly Leach walked out of her classroom in Lake City, Florida, and vanished. Bundy returned to Tallahassee to take a girl out for an expensive meal – paid for with a stolen credit card – then absconded via the fire escape, owing large arrears of rent.

At 4 a.m. on 15 February, a police patrolman noticed an orange Volkswagen driving suspiciously slowly, and radioed for a check on its number; it proved to be stolen from Tallahassee. After a struggle and a chase, during which he tried to kill the policeman, Bundy was captured yet again. When the police learned his real name, and that he had just left a town in which five girls had been attacked, they suddenly understood the importance of their capture. Bundy seemed glad to be in custody, and began to unburden himself. He explained that 'his problem' had begun when he had seen a girl on a bicycle in Seattle, and 'had to have her'. He had followed her, but she escaped. 'Sometimes,' he admitted, 'I feel like a vampire.'

On 7 April, a party of searchers along the Suwannee River found the body of Kimberly Leach in an abandoned hut; she had been strangled and sexually violated. Three weeks later, surrounded by hefty guards, Bundy allowed impressions of his teeth to be taken, for comparison with the marks on the buttocks of the dead student, Lisa Levy. Bundy's lawyers persuaded him to enter into 'plea bargaining': in exchange for a guarantee of life imprisonment – rather than a death sentence – he would confess to the murders of Lisa Levy, Margaret Bowman and Kimberly Leach. But Bundy changed his mind at the last moment and decided to sack his lawyers. Bundy's trial began on 25 June 1979, and the evidence against him was damning; a witness who had seen him leaving the student house after the attacks; a pantyhose mask found in the room of Cheryl Thomas, which resembled the one found in Bundy's car; but above all, the fact that Bundy's teeth matched the marks on Lisa Levy's buttocks.

The highly compromising taped interview with the Pensacola police was judged inadmissible in court because his lawyer had not been present. Bundy again dismissed his defence and took it over himself; the general impression was that he was trying to be too clever. The jury took only six hours to find him guilty on all counts. Judge Ed Cowart pronounced sentence of death by electrocution, but evidently felt some sympathy for the good-looking young defendant. 'It's a tragedy for this court to see such a total waste of humanity. You're a bright young man. You'd have made a good lawyer . . . But you went the wrong way, partner. Take care of yourself . . .'

Bundy was taken to Raiford prison, Florida, where he was a placed on death row. On 2 July 1986, when he was due to die a few hours before Gerald Stano, both were granted a stay of execution. The Bundy case illustrates the immense problems faced by investigators of serial murders. When Meg Anders – Bundy's mistress – telephoned the police after the double murder near Lake Sammanish, Bundy's name had already been suggested by three people. But he was only one of 3,500 suspects. Later Bundy was added to the list of one hundred 'best suspects' which investigators constructed on grounds of age, occupation and past record. Two hundred thousand items were fed into computers, including the names of 41,000 Volkswagen owners, 5,000 men with a record of mental illness, every student who had taken classes with the dead girls, and all transfers from other colleges they had attended. All this was programmed into thirty-seven categories, each using a different criterion to isolate the

176

suspect. Asked to name anyone who came up on any three of these programs, the computer produced 16,000 names. When the number was raised to four, it was reduced to 600. Only when it was raised to twenty-five was it reduced to ten suspects, with Bundy seventh on the list.

The police were still investigating number six when Bundy was detained in Salt Lake City with burgling tools in his car. Only after that did Bundy become suspect number one. And by that time he had already committed a minimum of seventeen murders. (There seems to be some doubt about the total, estimates varying between twenty and forty; Bundy himself told the Pensacola investigators that it ran into double figures.)

Detective Robert Keppel, who worked on the case, is certain that Bundy would have been revealed as suspect number one even if he had not been arrested. But in 1982, Keppel and his team were presented with another mass killer in the Seattle area, the so-called Green River Killer, whose victims were mostly prostitutes picked up on the 'strip' in Seattle. Seven years later, in 1989, he had killed at least forty-nine women, and the computer had still failed to identify an obvious suspect number one.

The Bundy case is doubly baffling because he seems to contradict the basic assertions of every major criminologist from Lombroso to Yochelson. Bundy is not an obvious born criminal, with degenerate physical characteristics; there is (as far as is known) no history of insanity in his family; he was not a social derelict or a failure. In her book *The Stranger Beside Me*, his friend Ann Rule describes him as 'a man of unusual accomplishment'. How could the most subtle 'psychological profiling' target such a man as a serial killer? The answer to the riddle emerged fairly late in the day, four years after Bundy had been sentenced to death. Before his conviction, Bundy had indicated his willingness to co-operate on a book about himself, and two journalists, Stephen G. Michaud and Hugh Aynesworth, went to interview him in

177

prison. They discovered that Bundy had no wish to discuss guilt, except to deny it, and he actively discouraged them from investigating the case against him. He wanted them to produce a gossipy book focusing squarely on himself, like best-selling biographies of celebrities such as Frank Sinatra. Michaud and Aynesworth would have been happy to write a book demonstrating his innocence, but as they looked into the case, they found it impossible to accept this; instead, they concluded that he had killed at least twenty-one girls. When they began to probe, Bundy revealed the characteristics that Yochelson and Samenow had found to be so typical of criminals: hedging, lying, pleas of faulty memory, and self-justification: 'Intellectually, Ted seemed profoundly dissociative, a compartmentalizer, and thus a superb rationalizer.' Emotionally, he struck them as a severe case of arrested development: 'he might as well have been a twelve-year-old, and a precocious and bratty one at that. So extreme was his childishness that his pleas of innocence were of a character very similar to that of the little boy who'll deny wrongdoing in the face of overwhelming evidence to the contrary.' So Michaud had the ingenious idea of suggesting that Bundy should 'speculate on the nature of a person capable of doing what Ted had been accused (and convicted) of doing'. Bundy embraced this idea with enthusiasm, and talked for hours into a tape recorder. Soon Michaud became aware that there were, in effect, two 'Teds' – the analytical human being, and an entity inside him that Michaud came to call the 'hunchback'. (We have encountered this 'other person' – Mr Hyde – syndrome in many killers, including Peter Sutcliffe.)

After generalizing for some time about violence in modern society, the disintegration of the home, and so on, Bundy got down to specifics, and began to discuss his own development. He had been an illegitimate child, born to a respectable young girl in Philadelphia. She moved to Seattle to escape the stigma, and married a cook in the Veterans' Hospital. Ted was an oversensitive and self-conscious child who had all the

178

usual daydreams of fame and wealth. And at an early stage he became a thief and something of a habitual liar – as many imaginative children do. But he seems to have been deeply upset by the discovery of his illegitimacy.

Bundy was not, in fact, a brilliant student. Although he struck his fellow students as witty and cultivated, his grades were usually Bs.

In his late teens he became heavily infatuated with a fellow student, Stephanie Brooks, who was beautiful, sophisticated, and came of a wealthy family. Oddly enough, she responded and they became 'engaged'. To impress her he went to Stanford University to study Chinese; but he felt lonely away from home and his grades were poor. 'I found myself thinking about standards of success that I just didn't seem to be living up to.' Stephanie wearied of his immaturity, and threw him over – the severest blow so far. He became intensely moody. 'Dogged by feelings of worthlessness and failure', he took a job as a busboy in a hotel dining room. And at this point, he began the drift that eventually turned him into a serial killer.

He became friendly with a drug addict. One night, they entered a cliffside house that had been partly destroyed by a landslide, and stole whatever they could find. 'It was really thrilling.' He began shoplifting and stealing 'for thrills', once walking openly into someone's greenhouse, taking an eight-foot tree in a pot, and putting it in his car with the top sticking out of the sunroof. He also became a full-time volunteer worker for Art Fletcher, the black Republican candidate for Lieutenant-Governor. He enjoyed the sense of being a 'somebody' and mixing with interesting people. But Fletcher lost, and Bundy became a salesman in a department store. He met Meg Anders in a college beer joint, and they became lovers – she had a gentle, easy-going nature, which brought out Bundy's protective side. But she was shocked by his kleptomania. In fact, the criminal side – the 'hunchback' – was now developing fast. He acquired a taste for violent pornography – easy to buy openly in American shops.

Once walking round the university district he saw a girl undressing in a lighted room. This was the turning point in his life. He began to devote hours to walking around hoping to see more girls undressing. He was back at university, studying psychology, but his night prowling prevented him from making full use of his undoubted intellectual capacities. He obtained his degree in due course – this may tell us more about American university standards than about Bundy's abilities – and tried to find a law school that would take him. He failed all the aptitude tests and was repeatedly turned down.

A year later, he was finally accepted – he worked for the Crime Commission for a month, as an assistant, and for the Office of Justice Planning. His self-confidence increased by leaps and bounds. When he flew to San Francisco to see Stephanie Brooks, the girl who had jilted him, she was deeply impressed and willing to renew their affair. He was still having an affair with Meg Anders, and entered on this new career as a Don Juan with his usual enthusiasm. He and Stephanie spent Christmas together and became 'engaged'. Then he dumped her as she had dumped him. By this time, he had committed his first murder. For years, he had been a pornography addict and a peeping Tom. ('He approached it almost like a project, throwing himself into it, literally, for years.')

Then the 'hunchback' had started to demand 'more active kinds of gratification'. He tried disabling women's cars, but the girls always had help on hand. He felt the need to indulge in this kind of behaviour after drinking had reduced his inhibitions. One evening, he stalked a girl from a bar, found a piece of heavy wood, and managed to get ahead of her and lie in wait. Before she reached the place where he was hiding, she stopped at her front door and went in. But the experience was like 'making a hole in a dam'. A few evenings later, as a woman was fumbling for her keys at her front door, he struck her on the head with a piece of wood. She collapsed, screaming, and he ran away. He was filled with remorse and swore he would never do such a thing again.

But six months later he followed a woman home and peeped in as she undressed. He began to do this again and again. One day, when he knew the door was unlocked, he sneaked in, entered her bedroom, and jumped on her. She screamed and he ran away. Once again, there was a period of self-disgust and revulsion. This was in the autumn of 1973.

On 4 January 1974, he found a door that admitted him to the basement room of eighteen-year-old Sharon Clarke. Now, for the first time, he employed the technique he later used repeatedly, attacking her with a crowbar until she was unconscious. Then he thrust a speculum, or vaginal probe, inside her, causing internal injuries. But he left her alive.

On the morning of 1 February 1974, he found an unlocked front door in a students' rooming house and went in. He entered a bedroom at random; twenty-one-year-old Lynda Healy was asleep in bed. He battered her unconscious, then carried the body out to his car. He drove to Taylor Mountain, twenty miles east of Seattle, made her remove her pyjamas, and raped her. When Bundy was later 'speculating' about this crime for Stephen Michaud's benefit, the interviewer asked: 'Was there any conversation?' Bundy replied: 'There'd be some.' Since this girl in front of him represented not a person, but again the image of something desirable, the last thing expected of him would be to personalize this person.' So Lynda Healy was bludgeoned to death; Bundy always insisted that he took no pleasure in violence, but that his chief desire was 'possession' of another person. Now the 'hunchback' was in full control, and there were five more victims over the next five months. Three of the girls were taken to the same spot on Taylor Mountain and there raped and murdered – Bundy acknowledged that his sexual gratification would sometimes take hours.

The four bodies were found together in the following year. On the day he abducted the two girls from Lake Sammanish,

Bundy 'speculated' that he had taken the first, Janice Ott, to a nearby house and raped her, then returned to abduct the second girl, Denise Naslund, who was taken back to the same house and raped in view of the other girl; both were then killed, and taken to a remote spot four miles north-east of the park, where the bodies were dumped. By the time he had reached this point in his 'confession', Bundy had no further secrets to reveal; everything was obvious. Rape had become a compulsion that dominated his life. When he moved to Salt Lake City and entered the law school there – he was a failure from the beginning as a law student – he must have known that if he began to rape and kill young girls there, he would be establishing himself as suspect number one. This made no difference; he had to continue. Even the unsuccessful kidnapping of Carol DaRonch, and the knowledge that someone could now identify him, made no difference. He merely switched his activities to Colorado.

Following his arrest, conviction and escape, he moved to Florida, and the compulsive attacks continued, although by now he must have known that another series of murders in a town to which he had recently moved must reduce his habitual plea of 'coincidence' to an absurdity. It seems obvious that by this time he had lost the power of choice. In his last weeks of freedom, Bundy showed all the signs of weariness and self-disgust that had driven Carl Panzram to contrive his own execution. Time finally ran out for Bundy on 24 January 1989. Long before this, he had recognized that his fatal mistake was to decline to enter into plea bargaining at his trial; the result was a death sentence instead of life imprisonment. In January 1989, his final appeal was turned down and the date of execution fixed. Bundy then made a last-minute attempt to save his life by offering to bargain murder confessions for a reprieve – against the advice of his attorney James Coleman, who warned him that this attempt to 'trade over victims' bodies' would only create hostility that would militate against further stays of execution.

In fact, Bundy went on to confess to eight Washington murders, and then to a dozen others. Detective Bob Keppel, who had led the investigation in Seattle, commented: 'The game-playing stuff cost him his life.' Instead of making a full confession, Bundy doled out information bit by bit. 'The whole thing was orchestrated,' said Keppel. 'We were held hostage for three days.' And finally, when it was clear that there was no chance of further delay, Bundy confessed to the Chi Omega Sorority killings, admitting that he had been peeping through the window at girls undressing until he was carried away by desire and entered the building. He also mentioned pornography as being one of the factors that led him to murder. Newspaper columnists showed an inclination to doubt this, but Bundy's earlier confessions to Michaud leave no doubt that he was telling the truth.

At 7 a.m., Bundy was led into the execution chamber at Starke State prison, Florida; behind plexiglass, an invited audience of forty-eight people sat waiting. As two warders attached his hands to the arms of the electric chair, Bundy recognized his attorney among the crowd; he smiled and nodded. Then straps were placed around his chest and over his mouth; the metal cap with electrodes was fastened onto his head with screws and his face was covered with a black hood. At 7.07 a.m. the executioner threw the switch; Bundy's body went stiff and rose fractionally from the chair. One minute later, as the power was switched off, the body slammed back into the chair. A doctor felt his pulse and pronounced him dead. Outside the prison, a mob carrying 'Fry Bundy!' banners cheered as the execution was announced.

Richard Ramirez the 'Night Stalker'

Throughout 1985 handgun sales in Los Angeles soared. Many suburbanites slept with a loaded pistol by their beds. A series of violent attacks upon citizens in their own homes had shattered the comfortable normality of middle-class life. Formerly safe neighbourhoods seemed to be the killer's favourite targets. The whole city was terrified.

The attacks were unprecedented in many ways. Neither murder nor robbery seemed to be the obvious motive, although both frequently took place. The killer would break into a house, creep into the main bedroom and shoot the male partner through the head with a .22. He would then rape and beat the wife or girlfriend, suppressing resistance with threats of violence to her or her children. Male children were sometimes sodomized, the rape victims sometimes shot. On occasion he would ransack the house looking for valuables while at other times he would leave empty-handed without searching.

During the attacks he would force victims to declare their love for Satan. Survivors described a tall, slim Hispanic male with black, greasy hair and severely decayed teeth. The pattern of crimes seemed to be based less upon a need to murder or rape but a desire to terrify and render helpless. More than most serial killers the motive seemed to be exercising power. The killer also had unusual methods of victim selection. He seemed to be murdering outside his own

185

racial group, preferring Caucasians and specifically Asians. He also seemed to prefer to break into yellow houses. In the spring and summer of 1985 there were more than twenty attacks, most of which involved both rape and murder. By the end of March the press had picked up the pattern and splashed stories connecting the series of crimes. After several abortive nicknames, such as the 'Walk-In Killer' or the 'Valley Invader', the *Herald Examiner* came up with the 'Night Stalker', a name sensational enough to stick. Thus all through the hot summer of 1985 Californians slept with their windows closed. One policeman commented to a reporter: 'People are armed and staying up late. Burglars want this guy caught like everyone else. He's making it bad for their business.'

The police themselves circulated sketches and stopped anyone who looked remotely like the Night Stalker. One innocent man was stopped five times. Despite these efforts and thorough forensic analysis of crime scenes there was little progress in the search for the killer's identity. Things were obviously getting difficult for the Night Stalker as well. The next murder that fitted the pattern occurred in San Francisco, showing perhaps that public awareness in Los Angeles had made it too taxing a location. This shift also gave police a chance to search San Francisco hotels for records of a man of the Night Stalker's description.

Sure enough, while checking the downmarket Tenderloin district police learned that a thin Hispanic with bad teeth had been staying at a cheap hotel there periodically over the past year. On the last occasion he had checked out the night of the San Francisco attack. The manager commented that his room 'smelled like a skunk' each time he vacated it and it took three days for the smell to clear. Though this evidence merely confirmed the police's earlier description, the Night Stalker's next shift of location was to prove more revealing. A young couple in Mission Viejo were attacked in their home. The Night Stalker shot the man through the head while he slept, then raped his partner on the bed next to the body. He then tied

186

her up while he ransacked the house for money and jewellery. Before leaving he raped her a second time and forced her to fellate him with a gun pressed against her head. Unfortunately for the killer, however, his victim caught a glimpse of him escaping in a battered orange Toyota and memorized the licence plate. She immediately alerted the police. LAPD files showed that the car had been stolen in Los Angeles's Chinatown district while the owner was eating in a restaurant. An all-points bulletin was put out for the vehicle, and officers were instructed not to try to arrest the driver, merely to observe him. However, the car was not found.

In fact, the Night Stalker had dumped the car soon after the attack, and it was located two days later in a car park in Los Angeles's Rampart district. After plain-clothes officers had kept the car under surveillance for twenty-four hours, the police moved in and took the car away for forensic testing. A set of fingerprints was successfully lifted. Searching police fingerprint files for a match manually can take many days and even then it is possible to miss correlations. However, the Los Angeles police had recently installed a fingerprint database computer system, designed by the FBI, and it was through this that they checked the set of fingerprints from the orange Toyota. The system works by storing information about the relative distance between different features of a print, and comparing them with a digitized image of the suspect's fingerprint. The search provided a positive match and a photograph.

The Night Stalker was a petty thief and burglar. His name was Ricardo Leyva Ramirez. The positive identification was described by the forensic division as 'a near miracle'. The computer system had only just been installed, this was one of its first trials. Furthermore, the system only contained the fingerprints of criminals born after 1 January 1960. Richard Ramirez was born in February 1960.

The police circulated the photograph to newspapers, and it was shown on the late evening news. At the time, Ramirez was in Phoenix, buying cocaine with the money he had stolen in Mission Viejo. On the morning that the papers splashed his name and photograph all over their front pages, he was on a bus on the way back to Los Angeles, unaware that he had been identified. He arrived safely and went into the bus station toilet to finish off the cocaine he had bought. No one seemed to be overly interested in him as he left the station and walked through Los Angeles. Ramirez was a Satanist, and had developed a belief that Satan himself watched over him, preventing his capture.

At 8.15 a.m. Ramirez entered Tito's Liquor Store at 819 Towne Avenue. He selected some Pepsi and a pack of sugared doughnuts; he had a sweet tooth that, coupled with a lack of personal hygiene, had left his mouth with only a few blackened teeth. At the counter other customers looked at him strangely as he produced three dollar bills and awaited his change. Suddenly he noticed the papers' front pages, and his faith in Satan's power must have been shaken.

He dodged out of the shop and ran, accompanied by shouts of, 'It is him! Call the cops!' He pounded off down the street at a surprising speed for one so ostensibly unhealthy. Within twelve minutes he had covered two miles. He had headed east. He was in the Hispanic district of Los Angeles. Ever since the police had confirmed that the Night Stalker was Hispanic there had been a great deal of anger among the Hispanic community of Los Angeles. They felt that racial stereotypes were already against them enough without their being associated with psychopaths. Thus more than most groups, Hispanics wanted the Night Stalker out of action. Ramirez, by now, was desperate to get a vehicle. He attempted to pull a woman from her car in a supermarket lot until he was chased away by some customers of the barber's shop opposite. He carried on running, though exhausted, into the more residential areas of east Los Angeles.

There, he tried to steal a 1966 red Mustang having failed to notice that the owner, Faustino Pinon, was lying underneath repairing it. As Ramirez attempted to start the car Pinon grabbed him by the collar and tried to pull him from the driver's seat. Ramirez shouted that he had a gun, but Pinon carried on pulling at him even after the car had started, causing it to career into the gatepost. Ramirez slammed it into reverse and accelerated into the side of Pinon's garage, and the vehicle stalled. Pinon succeeded in wrenching Ramirez out of his car, but in the following struggle Ramirez escaped, leaping the fence and running off across the road.

There he tried to wrestle Angelina De La Torres from her Ford Granada. 'Te voy a matar! (I'm going to kill you!),' screamed Ramirez. 'Give me the keys!' but again he was thwarted and he ran away, now pursued by a growing crowd of neighbours. Manuel De La Torres, Angelina's husband, succeeded in smashing Ramirez on the head with a gate bar and he fell, but he managed to struggle up and set off running again before he could be restrained. Incredibly, when Ramirez had developed a lead, he stopped, turned round and stuck his tongue out at his pursuers, then sped off once more. His stamina could not hold indefinitely, however, and it was De La Torres who again tackled him and held him down.

It is possible that Ramirez would have been lynched there and then had not a patrolman called to the scene arrived. Coincidentally the patrolman was the same age as the killer, and he too was called Ramirez. He reached the scene just as the Night Stalker disappeared under the mob. He drove his patrol car to within a few feet of where Ramirez was restrained, got out and prepared to handcuff the captive. 'Save me. Please. Thank God you're here. It's me, I'm the one you want. Save me before they kill me,' babbled Ramirez. The patrolman handcuffed him and pushed him into the back of the car. The crowd was becoming restless, and the car was kicked as it pulled away. Sixteen-year-old Felipe Castaneda, part of the mob that captured Ramirez, remarked, 'He should never, *never* have come to East LA. He might have been a

189

tough guy, but he came to a tough neighbourhood. He was Hispanic. He should have known better.'

The Night Stalker was in custody, at first in a police holding cell and then in Los Angeles county jail. While in police care he repeatedly admitted to being the 'Night Stalker' and begged to be killed. The case against Ramirez was strong. The murder weapon, a .22 semi-automatic pistol, was found in the possession of a woman in Tijuana, who had been given it by a friend of Ramirez. Police also tried to track down some of the jewellery that Ramirez had stolen and fenced, by sending investigators to his birthplace El Paso, a sprawling town on the Texas–Mexico border. Questioning his family and neighbours revealed that Ramirez's early life had been spent in petty theft and smoking a lot of marijuana. He had never joined any of the rival teenage gangs that fight over territory throughout El Paso, preferring drugs and listening to heavy metal.

It had been common knowledge that Ramirez was a Satanist; a boyhood friend, Tom Ramos, said he believed that it was Bible study classes that had turned the killer that way. The investigators also found a great deal of jewellery stashed at the house of Ramirez's sister Rosa Flores. The police were also hoping to find a pair of eyes that Ramirez had gouged from one of his victims that had not been found in any previous searches. Unfortunately they were not recovered.

The evidence against Ramirez now seemed unequivocal. In a controversial move, the mayor of Los Angeles said that whatever went on in court, he was convinced of Ramirez's guilt. This was later to prove a mainstay in a defence argument that Ramirez could not receive a fair trial in Los Angeles. The appointed chief prosecutor in the case was deputy District Attorney P. Philip Halpin, who had prosecuted the 'Onion Field' cop-killing case twenty years earlier. Halpin hoped to end the trial and have Ramirez in the gas chamber in a relatively short period of time. The prosecutor drew up a set of initial charges and submitted them as quickly as possible. A public defender was appointed to represent Ramirez. However, Ramirez's family had engaged an El Paso lawyer, Manuel Barraza, and Ramirez eventually rejected his appointed public defender in favour of the El Paso attorney. Barraza did not even have a licence to practise law in California. Ramirez accepted, then rejected, three more lawyers, finally settling upon two defenders, Dan and Arturo Hernandez. The two were not related, although they often worked together. The judge advised Ramirez that his lawyers did not even meet the minimum requirements for trying a death-penalty case in California, but Ramirez insisted, and more than seven weeks after the initial charges were filed, pleas of not guilty were entered on all counts. The Hernandezes and Ramirez seemed to be trying to force Halpin into making a mistake out of sheer frustration, and thus to create a mistrial. After each hearing the Hernandezes made pleas for, and obtained, more time to prepare their case. Meanwhile one prosecution witness had died of natural causes, and Ramirez's appearance was gradually changing. He had had his hair permed, and his rotten teeth replaced. This naturally introduced more uncertainty into the minds of prosecution witnesses as to Ramirez's identity. The racial make-up of the jury was contested by the defence, which caused delays. The defence also argued, with some justification, that Ramirez could not receive a fair trial in Los Angeles, and moved for a change of location. Although the motion was refused it caused yet more delays.

In the end it took three and a half years for Ramirez's trial to finally get under way. Halpin's case was, in practical terms, unbeatable. The defence's only real possibility of success was in infinite delay. For the first three weeks of the trial events progressed relatively smoothly. Then Daniel Hernandez announced that the trial would have to be postponed as he was suffering from nervous exhaustion. He had a doctor's report that advised six weeks rest with psychological counselling. It seemed likely that a mistrial would be declared. Halpin tried

191

to argue that Arturo Hernandez could maintain the defence, even though he had failed to turn up at the hearings and trial for the first seven months. However, this proved unnecessary as the judge made a surprise decision and denied Daniel Hernandez his time off, arguing that he had failed to prove a genuine need. Halpin by this stage was actually providing the Hernandezes with all the information that they required to mount an adequate defence, in order to move things along and prevent mistrial. For the same reasons the judge eventually appointed a defence co-counsel, Ray Clark. Clark immediately put the defence on a new track: Ramirez was the victim of a mistaken identity. He even developed an acronym for this defence – SODDI or Some Other Dude Did It. When the defence case opened Clark produced testimony from Ramirez's father that he had been in El Paso at the time of one of the murders of which he was accused. He also criticized the prosecution for managing to prove that footprints at one of the crime scenes were made by a size eleven-and-a-half Avia trainer without ever proving that Ramirez actually owned such a shoe.

When the jury finally left to deliberate, however, it seemed clear that they would find Ramirez guilty. Things were not quite that easy, however. After thirteen days of deliberation juror Robert Lee was dismissed for inattention and replaced by an alternative who had also witnessed the case. Two days later, juror Phyllis Singletary was murdered in a domestic dispute. Her live-in lover had beaten her then shot her several times. She was also replaced. At last on 20 September 1989 after twenty-two days of deliberation the jury returned a verdict of guilty on all thirteen counts of murder, twelve of those in the first degree.

The jury also found Ramirez guilty of thirty other felonies, including burglary, rape, sodomy and attempted murder. Asked by reporters how he felt after the verdict, Ramirez replied, 'Evil.' There remained only the selection of sentence. At the hearing Clark argued that Ramirez might actually have been possessed by the devil, or that alternatively he had been driven to murder by overactive hormones. He begged the jury to imprison Ramirez for life rather than put him on Death Row. If the jury agreed, Clark pointed out, 'he will never see Disneyland again', surely punishment enough. After five further days of deliberation, the jury voted for the death penalty. Again, reporters asked Ramirez how he felt about the outcome as he was being taken away. 'Big deal. Death always went with the territory. I'll see you in Disneyland.'

Any attempt to trace the source of Ramirez's violent behaviour runs up against an insurmountable problem. No external traumas or difficulties seem to have brutalized him. He had a poor upbringing, he was part of a racial minority, but these things alone cannot explain such an incredibly socio-pathic personality. Ramirez seems to have created himself. He was an intelligent and deeply religious child and early teenager. Having decided at some stage that counter-culture and drug taking provided a more appealing lifestyle, he developed pride in his separateness. In the El Paso of his early manhood, people would lock their doors if they saw him coming down the street. He was known as 'Ricky Rabon', Ricky the thief, a nickname he enjoyed as he felt it made him 'someone'. By the time he moved to Los Angeles, he was injecting cocaine and probably committing burglaries to support himself. He let his teeth rot away, eating only childish sugary foods. He refused to wash. He listened to loud heavy metal music. It has been argued that it was his taste in music that drove him to murder and Satanism, but this would seem to be more part of the mood of censorship sweeping America than a genuine explanation. Anyone who takes the trouble to listen to the music in question, particularly the AC/DC album cited by American newspapers at the time of the murders, will find that there is little in it to incite violence.

Ramirez's obvious attempts to repel others in his personal behaviour, and his heavy drug use seem more likely sources of violence than early poverty or music. His assumed 'otherness' seems in retrospect sadly underdeveloped, having never progressed beyond a teenager's need to appal staid grown-up society. This is not to say that Ramirez was unintelligent. His delaying of his trial and his choice of the Hernandezes to continue the delays shows that he had worked out the most effective method of staying alive for the longest period either before or soon after he was captured. His remarks in court upon being sentenced were not particularly original, yet they are articulate: 'It's nothing you'd understand but I do have something to say. I don't believe in the hypocritical, moralistic dogma of this so-called civilized society. I need not look beyond this room to see all the liars, haters, the killers, the crooks, the paranoid cowards – truly *trematodes* of the Earth, each one in his own legal profession. You maggots make me sick – hypocrites one and all . . . I am beyond your experience. I am beyond good and evil, legions of the night, night breed, repeat not the errors of the Night Prowler [a name from an AC/DC song] and show no mercy. I will be avenged. Lucifer dwells within us all. That's it.' Ramirez remains on Death Row. Since his conviction he has received fan mail from dozens of women, many enclosing sexual photographs of themselves. Most of these 'followers' are probably just looking for a cheap thrill, like children who lean over the edge of a bear pit at a zoo – he's caged, so they can play at titillating him. None, however, should have any illusions about what he would have done to them if it had been *their* house he broke into during his 1985 rampage.

Yet Ramirez gained at least one devoted and genuine friend – his wife. In October 1996 he married Doreen Lioy – a forty-one-year-old freelance magazine editor with a reported IQ of 152 – in a non-religious ceremony in the San Quentin prison. Afterwards Doreen said: 'The facts of his case ultimately will confirm that Richard is a wrongly convicted man, and I believe fervently that his innocence will be proven to the world.'

Jeffrey Dahmer

By the early 1990s, police experts thought they had a fairly good idea of the typical serial killer 'type': a male loner, yet sometimes capable of great charm, who harboured a compulsive need to kill. They tended to have low-paid, low-skilled jobs – so the fictional psychiatrist and serial killer Hannibal Lector was a pure fantasy. Serial killers usually murdered strangers and usually, after the act, hid the body and got away from the crime scene. And they tended to hunt everyday people, avoiding higher risk targets like politicians and celebrities. Yet the cases that came to light through the 1990s often flew in the face of these assumptions.

Jeffrey Dahmer didn't try to get rid of the bodies of his victims – he treasured them, what he didn't eat that is, in his small flat. Fred West wasn't a loner who killed strangers – with his wife Rose he also murdered their lovers and one of their own children. Dr Harold Shipman was a well-respected general practitioner and family man – and may have murdered over 250 of his patients. Andrew Cunanan hunted and killed one of the world's most famous fashion designers, and the Florida Highway Killer turned out to be a woman.

By the beginning of the 1990s it began to seem that the American public had become shock-proof where serial killers were concerned. Killer 'duos' like the Hillside Stranglers, or Lucas and Toole, killed to satisfy their sexual appetites. 'Sunset Slayer' Douglas Clark and his mistress Carol Bundy confessed to a taste for playing with the severed heads of their female victims. In 1985, the suicide of a man named Leonard Lake, and the flight of his companion Charles Ng, led the police to a house in Calaveras County, California, and to a cache of videos showing the sexual abuse and torture of female victims – the number seems to have exceeded thirty. Ex-convict Gerald Gallego and his mistress Charlene Williams made a habit of abducting and murdering teenage girls, who were first subjected to an orgy of rape and lesbian advances, all in the search for the 'perfect sex slave'. In Chicago, a group of four young men, led by twenty-seven-year-old Robin Gecht, abducted at least fifteen women, and subjected them to an orgy of rape and torture – which included amputation and ritual eating of the breasts – in the course of 'Satanic' ceremonies. There was also evidence to link the New York Killer 'Son of Sam' – David Berkowitz, who casually shot strangers in cars – with a Satanic cult. It was hard to imagine how human depravity could go any further. In spite of which, the revelations that burst onto television screens in late July 1991 caused nationwide shock.

Just before midnight on 22 July, a young black man came running out of an apartment building in Milwaukee, Wisconsin, with a handcuff dangling from his wrist, and told two police patrolmen that a madman had tried to kill him, and threatened to cut out his heart and eat it. He led the police to the apartment of thirty-one-year-old Jeffrey Dahmer, where they demanded entrance. Dahmer at first behaved reasonably, claiming to be under stress after losing his job and drinking too much, but when the police asked for the handcuff key, he became hysterical and abusive, and had to be taken into custody. The police soon realized that Dahmer's two-room apartment was a mixture of slaughter house and torture chamber. A freezer proved to contain severed heads, another some severed hands and a male genital organ, while five skulls – some painted grey – were found in various boxes.

Back at the police station, Dahmer confessed to killing

196

seventeen youths, mostly blacks. He also confessed that the plastic bags of human 'meat' in the freezer were intended to be eaten, and described how he had fried the biceps of one victim in vegetable oil. The threat to eat the heart of Tracy Edwards – the latest intended victim – had been no idle bluff.

The first problem was to find out the identities of the men to whom these skulls, bones and genitals belonged. Back at police headquarters, Dahmer was obviously relieved to be co-operating; he seemed glad that his career of murder was over. It had all started, he admitted, when he was only eighteen years old, in 1978. That first victim had been a hitchhiker. It was almost ten years before he committed his next murder. But recently the rate of killing had accelerated – as it often does with serial killers – and there had been no less than three murders in the last two weeks. He had attempted to kill Tracy Edwards only three days after his last murder.

Dahmer was also able to help the police towards establishing the identities of the victims – which included twelve blacks, one Laotian, one Hispanic and three whites. Some of their names he remembered; the police had to work out the identities of others from identity cards found in Dahmer's apartment, and from photographs shown to parents of missing youths. All Dahmer's confessions were sensational; but the story of one teenage victim was so appalling that it created outrage around the world.

Fourteen-year-old Laotian Konerak Sinthasomphone had met Dahmer in front of the same shopping mall where the killer was later to pick up Tracy Edwards; the boy agreed to return to Dahmer's apartment to allow him to take a couple of photographs. Unknown to Konerak, Dahmer was the man who had enticed and sexually assaulted his elder brother three years earlier. Dahmer had asked the thirteen-year-old boy back to his apartment in September 1988, and had slipped a powerful sleeping draught into his drink, then fondled him sexually. Somehow, the boy succeeded in staggering out into the street and back home. The police were notified, and

Dahmer was charged with second-degree sexual assault and sentenced to a year in a correction programme, which allowed him to continue to work in a chocolate factory.

Now the younger brother Konerak found himself in the same apartment. He was also given drugged coffee, and then, when he was unconscious, stripped and raped. After that, Dahmer went out to buy some beer – he had been a heavy drinker since schooldays. On his way back to the apartment Dahmer saw, to his horror, that his naked victim was talking to two black teenage girls, obviously begging for help.

Dahmer hurried up and tried to grab the boy; the girls clung on to him. One of them succeeded in ringing the police, and two squad cars arrived within minutes. Three irritable officers wanted to know what the trouble was about. When Dahmer told them that the young man was his lover, that they lived together in the nearby apartments, and that they had merely had a quarrel, the policemen were inclined to believe him – he looked sober and Konerak looked drunk. 'They decided to move away from the gathering crowd, and adjourned to Dahmer's apartment. There Dahmer showed them Polaroid pictures of the boy in his underwear, to convince him that they were really lovers (the police had no way of knowing that the photographs had been taken that evening), and told them that Konerak was nineteen.

Meanwhile, Konerak sat on the settee, dazed but probably relieved that his ordeal was over. His passivity was his undoing – his failure to deny what Dahmer was saying convinced the police that Dahmer must be telling the truth. They believed Dahmer and went off, leaving Konerak in his apartment. The moment the police had left, Dahmer strangled Konerak, violated the corpse, then took photographs as he dismembered it.

After stripping the skull of flesh, he painted it grey – probably to make it look like a plastic replica. Back at District Three station house, the three policemen made their second mistake of the evening – they joked about the homosexual quarrel they had just broken up. But a tape recorder happened to be switched on, and when Dahmer was arrested two months later and admitted to killing the Laotian boy, the tape was located and played on radio and television. The story caused universal uproar. On 26 July, four days after Dahmer's arrest, the three policemen – John Balcerzak, Joseph Gabrish and Richard Portubcan – were suspended from duty with pay. (Later, administrative charges were filed against them, but finally dismissed.)

Public anger was now transferred from Jeffrey Dahmer to the police department. Police Chief Philip Arreola found himself assailed on all sides, subjected to harsh criticism from his own force for not supporting his own men (in the following month, the Milwaukee Police Association passed a vote of no- confidence in him), and from Milwaukee's blacks and Asians for racism. Dahmer's first murder had taken place in 1968, when he was eighteen. According to Dahmer's confession, he had found himself alone in the family house at 4480 West Bath Road; his father had already left, and his mother and younger brother David were away visiting relatives. He had been left with no money, and very little food in the broken refrigerator. That evening, he explained, he decided to go out and look for some company. It was not hard to find.

A nineteen-year-old white youth, who had spent the day at a rock concert, was hitch-hiking home to attend his father's birthday party. When an ancient Oldsmobile driven by someone who looked about his own age pulled up, the boy climbed in. They went back to Dahmer's house and drank some beer, and talked about their lives. Dahmer found he liked his new friend immensely. But when the boy looked at the clock and said he had to go, Dahmer begged him to stay. The boy refused. So Dahmer picked up a dumbbell, struck him on the head, then strangled him. He then dragged the body to the crawl space under the house, and dismembered it with a carving knife. It sounds an impossible task for an eighteen-year-old, but Dahmer was not without experience – he had always had a morbid interest in dismembering animals. He had wrapped up the body parts in plastic bags.

But after a few days, the smell began to escape. Dahmer's mother was due back soon, and was sure to notice the stench. He took the plastic bags out to the wood under cover of darkness and managed to dig a shallow grave – the soil was rock-hard. But even with the bags now underground, he still worried – children might notice the grave. So he dug them up again, stripped the flesh from the bones, and smashed up the bones with a sledgehammer. He scattered them around the garden, and the property next door. When his mother returned a few days later, there was nothing to reveal that her son was now a killer.

Unfortunately, Dahmer was unable to recall the name of his victim. The Milwaukee police telephoned the police of Bath Township and asked them if they had a missing person case that dated from mid-1978. They had. On 18 June, a youth named Stephen Mark Hicks had left his home in Coventry Township to go to a rock concert. Friends had driven him there, and they agreed to rendezvous with him that evening to take him home. Hicks failed to turn up at the meeting place, and no trace of him was ever found.

For nine years after killing Stephen Hicks, Dahmer kept his homicidal impulses under control. A period of three years in the army had ended with a discharge for drunkenness. After a short stay in Florida, he had moved in with his grandmother Catherine, in West Allis, south of Milwaukee. But he was still drinking heavily, and was in trouble with the police for causing a disturbance in a bar. His family was relieved when he at last found himself a job – in the Ambrosia Chocolate Company in Milwaukee.

Dahmer soon discovered Milwaukee's gay bars, where he became known as a monosyllabic loner. But it was soon observed that he had a more sinister habit. He would sometimes engage a fellow customer in conversation, and offer him a drink. These drinking companions often ended up in a drugged coma. Yet Dahmer's intention was clearly not to commit rape. He seemed to want to try out his drugs as a kind of experiment, to see how much he had to administer, and how fast they worked. But other patrons noticed, and when one of Dahmer's drinking companions ended up unconscious in hospital, the owner of Club Bath Milwaukee told him that he was barred.

On 8 September 1986, two twelve-year-old boys reported to the police that Dahmer had exposed himself to them and masturbated. Dahmer alleged that he had merely been urinating. He was sentenced to a year on probation, and told his probation officers, with apparent sincerity: 'I'll never do it again.' (Judges and probation officers were later to note that Dahmer had a highly convincing manner of donning the sackcloth and ashes.)

This period ended on 9 September 1987. A year of good behaviour had done nothing to alleviate Dahmer's psychological problems; on the contrary, they had built up resentment and frustration. Six days after his probation ended, the frustration again exploded into murder. On 15 September, Dahmer was drinking at a gay hang-out called Club 219, and met a twenty-four-year-old man called Stephen Tuomi. They decided to go to bed, and adjourned to the Ambassador Hotel, where they took a room that cost $43.88 for the night. Dahmer claims that he cannot recall much of that night, admitting that they drank themselves into a stupor. When Dahmer woke up, he says Tuomi was dead, with blood coming from his mouth, and strangulation marks on his throat. It was a terrifying situation – alone in a hotel room with a corpse, and the desk clerk likely to investigate whether the room had been vacated at any moment. Dahmer solved it by going out and buying a large suitcase, into which he stuffed the body. Then he got a taxi to take him back to his grandmother's house in West Allis, where he had his own basement flat – the driver helped him to drag the heavy case indoors. There, says Dahmer, he dismembered the body, and stuffed the parts into plastic bags which were put out for the garbage collector. He performed his task of disposal so efficiently that the police were unable to find the slightest sign of it, and decided not to charge Dahmer with the murder.

Clearly, this second murder was a watershed in Dahmer's life. The earlier murder of Stephen Hicks might have been put behind him as a youthful aberration, committed in a mood of psychological stress. But the killing of Stephen Tuomi was a deliberate act – whether Dahmer was fully sober or not. Since Tuomi had gone to the room specifically to have sex, there could be no reason whatever to kill him – unless Dahmer's needs involved more than an act of mutual intercourse: that is, unless they actually involved killing and dissecting his sexual partner, as he had killed and dissected animals as a teenager. As a result of the murder of Stephen Tuomi, Dahmer seems to have acknowledged that murder was, in fact, what he needed to satisfy his deviant sexual impulse. The fifteen murders that followed leave no possible doubt about it. Precisely four months later, on 16 January 1988, Dahmer picked up a white young male prostitute named James Doxtator at a bus stop outside Club 219, and asked him if he would like to earn money by posing for a video. They went back to West Allis on the bus, and had sex in the basement. Then Dahmer gave the boy a drink heavily laced with sleeping potion, and, when he was unconscious, strangled him. With his grandmother's garage at his disposal, getting rid of the body was easy.

He told the police that he cleaned the flesh from the bones with acid, then smashed the bones with a sledgehammer, and scattered them around like those of his first victim. What he does not seem to have admitted is that the murder and dismemberment of James Doxtator was his primary purpose when he invited the boy back home. The police interrogator looked up from his notebook to ask if there was anything distinctive about Doxtator by which he might be identified; Dahmer recalled that he had two scars near his nipples that looked like cigarette burns. Doxtator's mother later confirmed that her son had such scars.

Two months elapsed before Dahmer killed again. On 24 March 1988, in a bar called the Phoenix not far from Club 219, he met a twenty-three-year-old homosexual named Richard Guerrero, who was virtually broke. Attracted by the graceful, slightly built Hispanic youth, Dahmer made the same proposals that he had made to the previous victim and, like the previous victim, Guerrero accompanied him back to his grandmother's house. There they had oral sex, and Guerrero was given a drugged drink. When he was unconscious, Dahmer strangled him, then dismembered the body in the garage.

Guerrero's frantic family hired a private detective and circulated flyers with their son's description. They also hired a psychic. But they were still searching three years later, when Dahmer confessed to the murder. Dahmer's grandmother was becoming concerned about the awful smells that came from the garage. Dahmer said it was garbage, but it seemed to persist even when the sacks had been collected. Dahmer's father Lionel came to investigate, and found a black, sticky residue in the garage. Dahmer, confronted with this evidence, said he had been using acid to strip dead animals of their flesh and fur, as he had done in childhood.

In September 1988, Catherine Dahmer finally decided she could no longer put up with the smells and her grandson's drunkenness. On 25 September, Dahmer moved into an apartment at 808 N. 24th Street. There can be no doubt that Dahmer intended to use his new-found freedom to give full rein to his morbid sexual urges. But an unforeseen hitch occurred. Within twenty-four hours, the four-time murderer was in trouble with the police: 26 September 1988 was the day he met a thirteen-year-old Laotian boy named Sinthasomphone, lured him back to his apartment and drugged him. But the elder brother of later victim Konerak somehow managed to escape, and Dahmer was charged with sexual assault and enticing a child for immoral purposes. He spent a week in prison, then was released on bail. On 30 January 1990 he was found guilty; the sentence would be handed out four months later. But even the possibility of a long prison sentence could not cure Dahmer of his obsessive need to kill and dismember.

When he appeared in court to be sentenced on 23 May 1989, he had already claimed his fifth victim. Anthony Sears was a good-looking twenty-three-year-old who dreamed of becoming a male model; he had a girlfriend and had just been appointed manager of a restaurant. On 25 March, he went drinking in a gay bar called LaCage with a friend called Jeffrey Connor, and Dahmer engaged them in conversation. By the time the bar closed, Sears had agreed to accompany Dahmer back to his grandmother's home. (Dahmer seems to have been worried that the police were watching his own apartment.)

Once there, they had sex, then Dahmer offered Sears a drink. The grim routine was repeated almost without variation: strangulation, dismemberment and disposal of the body parts in the garbage. Dahmer seems to have decided to preserve the skull as a memento; he painted it, and later took it with him when he moved into the Oxford Apartments. The Assistant DA, Gale Shelton, had recognized instinctively that a man who would drug a teenage boy for sex was highly dangerous, and needed to be kept out of society for a long time. Arguing for a prison sentence of five years, she described Dahmer as evasive, manipulative, uncooperative and unwilling to change. Dahmer's lawyer Gerald Boyle argued that the assault on the Laotian boy was a one-off offence, and would never happen again. Dahmer himself revealed considerable skill as an actor in representing himself as contrite and self-condemned. 'I am an alcoholic and a homosexual with sexual problems.' He described his appearance in court as a 'nightmare come true', declared that he was now a changed man, and ended by begging the judge: 'Please don't destroy my life.'

Judge William Gardner was touched by the appeal. This clean-cut boy obviously needed help, and there was no psychiatric help in prison. So he sentenced Dahmer to five years on probation, and a year in a house of correction, where he could continue to work at the chocolate factory during the day. From the Community Correctional Center in Milwaukee, Dahmer addressed a letter to Judge Gardner, stating, 'I have always believed a man should be willing to assume responsibility for the mistakes he makes in life. The world has enough misery in it without my adding to it. Sir, I assure you that it will never happen again. That is why, Judge Gardner, I am requesting a sentence modification.'

Dahmer was released from the Correctional Center two months early – on 2 March 1990. Eleven days later, he moved into the Oxford Apartments. Two more victims followed in quick succession. Thirty-three-year-old Eddie Smith, an ex-jailbird, was picked up in the gay Club 219, drugged with one of Dahmer's Mickey Finns, then strangled and dismembered. A few weeks later, on 14 June, twenty-eight-year-old Eddie Smith was killed in the same way and his body disposed of in garbage bags. So far, Dahmer's murders seem to have been due to a compulsive drive to kill and dismember. Now a new development occurred: psychological sadism.

In April 1991, Eddie Smith's sister Carolyn received a telephone call from a soft-spoken man who told her that Eddie was dead; when she asked how he knew he replied: 'I killed him', and hung up. Dahmer's career of slaughter almost came to an abrupt end on 8 July 1990; it was on that day that he made the mistake of varying his method.

He approached a fifteen-year-old Hispanic boy outside a gay bar, and offered him $200 to pose for nude photographs. The boy returned to room 213 and removed his clothes. But instead of offering him the usual drugged drink, Dahmer picked up a rubber mallet and hit him on the head. It failed to knock him unconscious, and the boy fought back as Dahmer tried to strangle him. Somehow, the boy succeeded in calming

205

his attacker. And, incredibly, Dahmer allowed him to go, even calling a taxi. The boy had promised not to notify the police. But when he was taken to hospital for treatment, he broke his promise. For a few moments, Dahmer's future hung in the balance. But when the boy begged them not to allow his foster-parents to find out that he was homosexual, the police decided to do nothing about it. When he saw his probation officer, Donna Chester, the next day, Dahmer looked depressed and unshaven. He said he had money problems and was thinking of suicide. She wanted to know how he could have money problems when he was earning $1,500 a month, and his apartment cost less than $300 a month. He muttered something about hospital bills. And during the whole of the next month, Dahmer continued to complain of depression and stomach pains, and to talk about jumping off a high building. Donna Chester suggested that he ought to find himself another apartment in a less run-down area. She was unaware that Dahmer was an addict who now urgently needed a fix of his favourite drug: murder.

It happened a few weeks later, on 3 September 1990. In front of a bookstore on 27th, Dahmer picked up a young black dancer named Ernest Miller, who was home from Chicago, where he intended to start training at a dance school in the autumn. They had sex in apartment 213, then Dahmer gave him a drugged drink, and watched him sink into oblivion. Perhaps because he had not killed for three months, Dahmer's craving for violence and its nauseating aftermath was stronger than usual. Instead of strangling his victim, Dahmer cut his throat. He decided that he wanted to keep the skeleton, so after cutting the flesh from the bones, and dissolving most of it in acid, he bleached the skeleton with acid. He also kept the biceps, which he put in the freezer.

Soon after Ernest Miller's disappearance, his grandmother began receiving telephone calls; the voice at the other end of the line made choking and groaning noises, and sometimes cried: 'Help me, help me.' Neighbours were beginning to notice the smell of decaying flesh; some of them knocked on Dahmer's door to ask about it. Dahmer would explain politely that his fridge was broken and that he was waiting to get it fixed.

The last victim of 1990 died almost by accident. Twenty-three-year-old David Thomas had a girlfriend and a three-year-old daughter; nevertheless he accepted Dahmer's offer to return to his apartment in exchange for money. Dahmer gave him a drugged drink, but then decided that Thomas was not his type after all, and that he had no desire for sex. But since Thomas was now drugged, and might be angry when he woke up, he killed him anyway. But he filmed the dismemberment process, and took photographs of his severed head; Thomas's sister later identified him by the photographs. He had committed nine murders; there were eight still to go.

The first murder of the new year was a nineteen-year-old black homosexual named Curtis Straughter, whose ambition was to become a male model; Dahmer picked him up in freezing, rainy weather on 18 February 1991. While they were engaging in oral sex in the evil-smelling apartment, Straughter began to flag as the sleeping potion took effect. Dahmer took a leather strap and strangled him, then dismembered the body and recorded the process on camera. Once again, he kept the skull.

On 25 March there occurred an event that psychiatrists believe may be responsible for the final spate of multiple murder. It was on that day that Dahmer's mother Joyce contacted him for the first time in five years. Joyce Dahmer – now Flint – was working as an AIDS counsellor in Fresco, California, and it may have been her contact with homosexuals that led her to telephone her son. She spoke openly about his homosexuality – for the first time – and told him she loved him. The call was a good idea – or would have been if she had made it a few years earlier. Now it was too late; Dahmer had gone too far in self-damnation.

The murder of nineteen-year-old Errol Lindsey on 7 April has a quality of *déjà-vu*. The police report states bleakly that Dahmer met Lindsey on a street corner and offered him money to pose for photographs. Lindsey was drugged and strangled; then Dahmer had oral sex with the body. Errol Lindsey was dismembered, but Dahmer kept his skull. Thirty-one-year-old Tony Hughes was a deaf mute who loved to dance. When Dahmer accosted him outside Club 219 on 24 May, he had to make his proposition in writing – $50 for some photographs. Hughes was given the sleeping potion, then strangled and dismembered. Dahmer had become so casual that he simply left the body lying in the bedroom for a day or so before beginning the dismemberment process – it was, after all, no more dangerous than having an apartment full of skulls and body parts.

With victim number thirteen, Dahmer again varied his method and came close to being caught. This was the fourteen-year-old Laotian boy – already mentioned – Konerak Sinthasomphone. Instead of strangling him after drugging him and committing rape, Dahmer went out to buy a pack of beer. Konerak woke up and almost escaped. But the Milwaukee police returned him, and his skull ended as yet another keepsake.

Sunday 30 June was the day of Chicago's Gay Pride Parade, and Dahmer decided to attend, taking a Greyhound bus for the ninety-mile trip. After watching the parade, Dahmer went to the police station to report that a pickpocket had taken his wallet. But he seems to have had enough money left to approach a young black he met at the Greyhound bus station, another aspiring model named Matt Turner. They travelled back to Milwaukee on the bus, then to Dahmer's apartment by cab. (Dahmer often earned more than $300 a week at the chocolate factory, which explains his frequent extravagance with cabs.) In his later confession, Dahmer said nothing about sex; but he admitted to drugging Turner, strangling him with a strap, then dismembering him and cutting off his head, keeping the skull.

Five days later, Dahmer was back in Chicago, looking for another victim. In a gay club on Wells Street he met twenty-three-year-old Jeremiah Weinberger, and invited him back to Milwaukee. Weinberger consulted a former room mate, Ted Jones, about whether he should accept. 'Sure, he looks OK,' said Jones. He was later to comment ruefully: 'Who knows what a serial killer looks like?'

Dahmer and Weinberger spent Saturday in room 213 having sex; Dahmer appeared to like his new acquaintance. But when, the following day, Weinberger looked at the clock and said it was time to go, Dahmer offered him a drink. Weinberger's head joined Matt Turner's in a plastic bag in the freezer. But Dahmer was nearing the end of his tether, and even drink could not anaesthetize him for long. Neighbours kept complaining about the smell, and he solved this by buying a fifty-seven-gallon drum of concentrated hydro-chloric acid, and disposing of some of the body parts that were causing the trouble. All this meant he was frequently late for work, or even absent. On 15 July 1991 the Ambrosia Chocolate Company finally grew tired of his erratic behaviour and fired him. His reaction was typical. The same day he picked up a twenty-four-year-old black named Oliver Lacy, took him back to his apartment, and gave him a drugged drink. After strangling him, he sodomized the body. But the murder spree was almost over.

Four days later, the head of the final victim joined the others in the freezer. He was twenty-five-year-old Joseph Bradeholt, an out-of-work black who was hoping to move from Minnesota to Milwaukee with his wife and two children. But he accepted Dahmer's offer of money for photographs, and willingly joined in oral sex in room 213. After that, he was drugged, strangled and dismembered. His body was placed in the barrel of acid, which was swiftly turning into a black, sticky mess. That Dahmer's luck finally ran out may have been due to the carelessness that leads to the downfall of so many multiple murderers.

The last intended victim, Tracy Edwards, was a slightly built man, and should have succumbed to the drug like all the others. For some reason, he failed to do so; it seems most likely that Dahmer failed to administer a large enough dose. Equally puzzling is the fact that, having seen that the drug had failed to work, he allowed Edwards to live, and spent two hours watching a video with him. Was the homicidal impulse finally burning itself out? Dahmer knew that if he failed to kill Tracy Edwards, he would be caught; yet, with a large knife in his hand, he allowed him to escape from the apartment. It sounds as if he recognized that the time had come to try to throw off the burden of guilt and rejoin the human race.

On 27 January Wisconsin's worst mass murderer came to trial in Milwaukee before Judge Lawrence Gram, entering a plea of guilty but insane. On 15 February the jury rejected Dahmer's plea and found him guilty of the fifteen murders with which he had been charged. (In two cases, the prosecution had decided the evidence was insufficient.) He was sentenced to fifteen terms of life imprisonment (Wisconsin has no death penalty).

Dahmer proved a model prisoner (as most captured serial killers tend to be) and was soon allowed to mix with the general prison population, eating his meals in the cafeteria and given light janitorial work to do. His two appointed partners on the clean-up detail were Jesse Anderson, a white man who had murdered his wife and tried to pin the blame on a black man, and Christopher Scarver, a black delusional schizophrenic, convicted for murder, and convinced he was the son of God. On the morning of 28 November 1994, Scarver beat both Anderson and Jeffrey Dahmer to death with a broom handle.

Andrei Chikatilo

On 14 April 1992, just two months after Jeffrey Dahmer was sentenced, another trial – this time in Russia – drew the attention the world's press. The accused was a forty-eight-year-old grandfather named Andrei Chikatilo, and he was charged with the murder of fifty-three women and children. The story that unfolded was one of the most savage and dramatic cases of serial crime ever to be uncovered. On 24 December 1978 the mutilated body of nine-year-old Lena Zakotnova was found in the Grushevka River where it flows through the Soviet mining city of Shakhti. It had been tied in a sack and dumped in the water some forty-eight hours before its discovery. She had been sexually assaulted and partially throttled, and her lower torso had been ripped open by multiple knife wounds. Lena was last seen after leaving school on the afternoon of her death. A woman named Burenkova reported seeing a girl of Lena's description talking to a middle-aged man at a nearby tram stop, and they walked away together. The Shakhti police soon arrested a suspect. Aleksandr Kravchenko had been in prison for a similar murder in the Crimea.

At the time he had been too young to be executed, so served six years of a ten-year sentence. He was the prime suspect from the beginning of the investigation and when he was caught attempting a burglary the police decided to charge him with the murder. Unconcerned at the fact that Kravchenko was only twenty-five, not 'middle-aged', the Shakhti police soon extracted a confession. In the dock Kravchenko insisted that it had been beaten out of him, but this carried little weight with the judge (Soviet trials had no juries; a judge both decided guilt and passed sentence). Kravchenko was found guilty and sentenced to fifteen years in a labour camp.

There was a public outcry at the leniency of the sentence, and the prosecution, as allowed in Soviet law, appealed to increase it to death. A new judge agreed and Kravchenko was executed by a single shot in the back of the head in 1984. By that time the real killer of Lena Zakotnova had murdered at least sixteen other women and children.

Born in the Ukrainian farm village of Yablochnoye on 6 October 1936, Andrei Romanovich Chikatilo was soon well acquainted with death. Stalin, in his drive to communize the peasantry, had reduced the Ukraine to a chaos of starvation and fear. In his first ten years, Chikatilo witnessed as much state-condoned brutality and killing as any front-line soldier. When he was five years old, Chikatilo's mother told him about the disappearance of one of his cousins, seven years previously, and that she believed he had been kidnapped and eaten. The gruesome story made a deep impression on Chikatilo. For years afterwards, he later admitted, he would brood on the story and re-create his cousin's sufferings in his imagination. There can be little doubt that this strongly influenced his sexual development. Even as a boy, Chikatilo was an ardent Soviet. He was fascinated by a novel called *Molodaya Gvardiya*, or *The Young Guard*, which concerned the heroic exploits of a group of young Russian partisans fighting the Germans in the vast Soviet forests, eventually dying to a man, proclaiming unshaken loyalty to Stalin. A predictably bloody tale, it also contained several scenes in which prisoners were tortured for information.

This positive, even heroic depiction of torture in isolated woodland made a deep impression on the child. At school Chikatilo had few friends and was painfully shy. He was nicknamed Baba – meaning woman – because he had chubby breasts and lived in terror that his chronic bed-wetting and

212

short-sightedness would be discovered by his classmates. His weak sight was something of an obsession with him and it was not until he was thirty that he eventually obtained a pair of glasses, so keen was he to conceal the defect. As he grew into his teens, however, his chubbiness turned to size and strength – his new nickname was 'Andrei Sila' meaning 'Andrew the Strong'.

Mentally, however, Chikatilo remained a loner. By his late teens he had shyly attempted several relationships with girls, but all had quickly failed. His major problem was a conviction that he was impotent. Like a lot of teenage boys, he was so scared during his first attempts at sex that he failed to achieve an erection. As the years went on he became convinced that he was incapable of a normal sex life. It was during his national service that he first experienced orgasm with a girl, and that was because she suddenly decided that things were going too far and tried to break his hold on her. She had no chance against his abnormal strength and he was surprised at the sexual passion her struggles aroused in him. He held her for only a few moments before releasing her unharmed, but had already ejaculated into his trousers.

Thinking about it afterwards, he realized that it was her fear and his power over her that had excited him so much. He had started to find sex and violence a stimulating concoction. In the years following his national service he moved out of the Ukraine, east to Russia, where job prospects and the standard of living were better. He found work as a telephone engineer and a room in Rodionovo-Nesvetayevsky, a small town just north of the large industrial city of Rostov.

A short while afterwards his mother, father and sister came to live with him in this comparative luxury. His younger sister, Tatyana, was worried that he was not married at twenty-seven and, after several failed matchmaking attempts, introduced him to a twenty-four-year-old girl called Fayina. Chikatilo was as shy as usual, but Fayina found this attractive. Things went well with the courtship and they were married in 1963. He still thought of himself as impotent and made embarrassed excuses

213

on their wedding night. A week later Fayina persuaded him to try again and, with some coaxing, the marriage was consummated. Even so, Chikatilo showed no enthusiasm for sex. His dammed sexual drives were by then pushing him in other, more unwholesome directions.

In 1971 he passed a correspondence degree course in Russian philology and literature from the Rostov University. With the new qualification, the thirty-five-year-old Chikatilo embarked upon a fresh career as a teacher. He found that he lacked all aptitude for the work. His shyness encouraged the pupils either to ignore his presence or openly to mock him. Other members of staff disliked his odd manner and his tendency to self-pity, so he was virtually shunned by all. Yet he soon found himself enjoying the work as his sexual fantasies began to centre around children. Over the next seven years Chikatilo committed numerous indecent assaults on his pupils. Apart from voyeurism, these included surreptitious groping, excessive beatings and, on one occasion, mouthing the genitals of a sleeping boy in a school dormitory. His sexual drive to dominate and control had centred on children as the easiest targets and, as time went on, he developed a taste for fantasizing about sadism. The oddest part of the situation was the inaction of the authorities. Chikatilo was forced to resign from several teaching jobs for his behaviour, but his record remained spotless each time. In the Soviet teaching system the failure of one teacher reflected on his colleagues and superiors as well, so they simply passed him on and pretended that nothing had happened.

In 1978, the Chikatilos and their two children moved to the town of Shakhti. Fayina had heard the rumours of his sexual misdemeanours, but had chosen to ignore them. He behaved quite normally towards their own son and daughter, aged nine and eleven, and she was unable to believe that a man who could barely produce one erection a month could marshal the sexual energy to be a pervert.

Chikatilo now bought an old shack in the slum end of town and began to invite down-and-out young women back with offers of food and vodka. There he would request them to perform sexual acts – notably fellatio – that he would never have requested from his strait-laced wife. He would often be unable to achieve erection, but this seemed to matter less with the kind of derelicts who accepted his invitation. Yet his real interest remained pre-pubescent children, and on 22 December 1978 he persuaded one to follow him to his shack. Lena Zakotnova had caught his eye as soon as he saw her waiting at the tram stop. He had sidled up to her and started chatting. She soon revealed to the grandfatherly stranger that she desperately needed to go to the toilet and he persuaded her to follow him to his shack.

Once through the door he dropped his kindly façade and started to tear at her clothes. Muffling her screams by choking her with his forearm, he blindfolded her with her scarf and tried to rape her. Once again he failed to achieve an erection, but ejaculated anyway. Ecstatically he pushed his semen into her with his fingers and ruptured her hymen. The sight of the blood caused him to orgasm again and filled him with sexual excitement. Pulling out a pocket knife he stabbed at her repeatedly, ripping open her whole lower torso.

When he returned to his senses he felt terrified – he knew he would face the death sentence if caught. Wrapping the corpse in a few sacks, he crept outside, crossed the street and a stretch of wasteland and dropped Lena in the fast-flowing Grushevka River. The autopsy later showed that she was still alive when she hit the water.

After watching the bundle float away, Chikatilo went home. But in his agitation he forgot to turn off the light in the shack. His neighbours on the slum street had not seen the pair arrive or heard Lena's muffled screams. However, one of them did note that Chikatilo's light had been left on all night and mentioned it to a policeman asking questions from door to door. Chikatilo was called in for questioning.The police soon guessed that the sullen teacher was using the shack for assignations, but this was not incriminating in itself. What interested them was the fact that some very young girls had been seen entering and leaving with Chikatilo, and a few enquiries at his old schools had revealed his taste for paedophilia.

He was called in for questioning nine times in all. Then the police transferred their attention to Kravchenko. They did not even examine the shack for traces of blood. Chikatilo continued teaching until 1981, when staff cuts made him redundant. On 3 September 1981, six months after losing his job, he killed again.

He was now working as a supply clerk for a local industrial conglomerate. This involved travelling around, often to the other side of the country, to obtain the necessary parts and supplies to run the Shakhti factory.

It would undoubtedly have been better if Chikatilo had remained a schoolteacher. In a restricted environment his opportunities would have been confined. The new job allowed him to travel, and spend as much time as he liked doing it. Now he was free to hunt at will.

He met Larisa Tkachenko at a bus stop outside the Rostov public library. She was a seventeen-year-old absentee from boarding school who was used to exchanging the odd fling for a nice meal and a drink or two. Her usual dates were young soldiers, but when the middle-aged man asked if she wanted to go to a local recreation area she agreed without much hesitation.

After a short walk they found themselves on a gravel path leading through a deserted stretch of woodland. Away from possible onlookers Chikatilo could not keep his hands off her any longer. He threw her down and started to tear at her trousers. Although she almost certainly expected to have sex with him, this was too frightening for her and she started to fight back. His already overstretched self-control snapped and he bludgeoned her with his heavy fists in an ecstasy of sadosexual release. To stifle her cries he rammed earth into her mouth then choked her to death. He bit off one of her nipples as he ejaculated over the corpse.

216

This time he did not come back to earth with a jolt as he had after killing Lena Zakotnova. He ran around the corpse waving her clothes and howling with joy. He later said, 'I felt like a partisan' – a reference to his childhood favourite novel *The Young Guard*. After half an hour he calmed down, covered Larisa's corpse with some branches and hid her clothes. She was found the next day, but no clues to the identity of the killer were discovered.

The murder of Lena Zakotnova had made Chikatilo aware of the basic nature of his desires; the murder of Larisa Tkachenko made him aware that he wanted to go on killing. All serial killers seem to cross this mental Rubicon. The initial horror and guilt gives way to an addiction to hunting that transcends all social and moral boundaries. And they never seem to break the habit; once hooked, they usually continue until they are caught or die. There are instances of serial killers 'going into remission' for years at a time but, like recovering alcoholics, the urge to re-indulge is always with them.

Strangely, however, being caught does stop the homicidal behaviour. Serial killers, like Jeffrey Dahmer, are more often the victims of violence in jail than they are a danger to others. Under the eye of authority, the urge to kill seems to be suppressed . . . until they are released, that is. Any degree of freedom can reignite the urge to kill in a 'reformed' serial killer.

Ten months after his second murder, on 12 June 1982, Chikatilo killed again. Thirteen-year-old Lyuba Biryuk left her home in the little settlement of Zaplavskaya to get some shopping from the nearby village of Donskoi Posyulok. She was last seen alive waiting at a local bus stop, but apparently decided to walk home in the warm sunshine. Chikatilo fell in step with her and started a conversation. Children always found his manner reassuring, but as soon as they came to a secluded stretch of path he attacked and tried to rape her. Failing, as usual, he pulled a knife from his pocket and stabbed wildly at her until her struggles and screams ceased. He covered her body, hid her clothes and shopping in the undergrowth and escaped unobserved. She was found two weeks later. In the heat of the southern Russian summer she had decayed to no more than a skeleton.

Chikatilo killed six more times that year: once in July, twice in August, twice in September and once in December. Four of these were girls ranging in age from ten to nineteen but the other two were boys, aged fifteen and nine. This bisexual choice of victims would confuse the police investigation later on. Indeed, in the early stages of linking the murders some of the boys were officially reclassified as girls (despite their male names) because officers could not believe the killer could be attracted to both sexes.

In fact, as any competent criminal psychologist could have told them, the sex of the victims was almost immaterial. Chikatilo wanted to be in total control of his victims. As such, boys served his purpose just as well as girls. Most of these victims were killed in the Rostov region, but two he killed on his business trips to other Soviet republics. Even when the majority of his victims had been linked into one investigation, these, and others killed outside the Rostov district, were not connected until Chikatilo himself confessed to them. A police force with more experience of serial crime would have quickly noted a linking pattern in the murders. All the victims were children or teenagers who had somehow been lured to secluded, usually wooded areas. They had been savagely attacked, sexually assaulted and usually butchered with a long-bladed knife. Most strikingly, in almost every case, wounds were found around the eyes of the victim. After killing a ten-year-old girl called Olya Stalmachenok on 11 December 1982, Chikatilo lay low once again. His next murder did not take place until mid-June 1983: a fifteen-year-old-Armenian girl called Laura Sarkisyan. Her body was never found and the murder only came to light when Chikatilo confessed to it.

The next month he met a thirteen-year-old girl in the Rostov train station. He recognized her as Ira Dunenkova, the little sister of one of his casual girlfriends from teaching days. It was obviously a risk to approach somebody who could – even tenuously – be linked to himself, but from her ragged clothes he quickly realized that she had become one of the innumerable vagrants than haunted every Soviet city, despite their official non-existence.

He persuaded her to go for a walk with him in the nearby stretch of heath called Aviators' Park. Reaching a quiet spot, he tried to have sex with her and, failing to get an erection, he used a more reliable instrument: a kitchen knife. Chikatilo killed three more times that summer. On uncertain dates he killed Lyuda Kutsyuba, aged twenty-four and a woman aged between eighteen and twenty-five whose identity has not been discovered. On 8 August he persuaded seven-year-old Igor Gudkov to follow him to Aviators' Park and then butchered him.

This brought his number of victims to fourteen, of which about half had been discovered by the police. Even for an area with a high – if unofficial – crime rate like Rostov, over half a dozen murdered children was enough to catch the attention of the central authorities in Moscow. A team of investigators was sent to assess the situation in September 1983. Their report was highly critical of the inept handling of the murders by the local police and concluded that six victims were definitely the work of one sexual deviant. The report was accepted and its suggestions quickly implemented, but, as was typical of the Soviet system, the public were not warned of the danger. Shielded by public ignorance, Chikatilo killed three more people before the turn of the year: a twenty-two-year-old woman called Valya Chuchulina and Vera Shevkun, a prostitute aged nineteen; and finally, on 27 December, a fourteen-year-old boy called Sergei Markov, his seventeenth victim that year. The following year, 1984, was to prove the most terrible in Chikatilo's murderous career. Between January and September he murdered fifteen women and children.

Chikatilo's method of hunting victims was time-consuming and, fortunately, rarely successful. He would hang around train stations, bus stops, airports and other public places, and would approach potential victims and strike up an innocuous conversation. If they warmed to him he would offer them the bait. To children he would propose going to his home to watch videos – then a rare luxury in Rostov. He might also make the same suggestion to young adults, or he might offer to take them, via 'a little-known short cut', to some place they wanted to go. To vagrants or prostitutes he would simply offer vodka, food or money for sex in the woods.

On 9 January, he killed seventeen-year-old Natalya Shalapinina in Aviators' Park. Then on 21 February he killed a forty-four-year-old tramp called Marta Ryabyenko in almost exactly the same spot. On 24 March Chikatilo killed a ten-year-old girl, Dima Ptashnikov, just outside the town of Novoshakhtinsk. Nearby, police found a footprint in a patch of mud which they were convinced belonged to the murderer. It was little enough, but it was their first solid piece of forensic evidence, and it improved the flagging morale of the investigators.

In May 1984, Chikatilo took his greatest risk ever. Haunting the Rostov train station, he bumped into an ex-girlfriend, Tanya Petrosyan, a thirty-two-year-old divorcée whom he had not seen for six years. He invited her for a picnic, but she replied that she had no time then. Common sense dictated that he should have left it at that. If he made a date for a later time she might tell other people about it. Even so, he took her address. A few days later he arrived at Tanya's house carrying a new doll for her eleven-year-old daughter. He was also carrying a knife and a hammer. He later insisted that he had only wanted sex from Tanya, but he now carried his killing tools as a matter of habit. He found himself being introduced to Tanya's elderly mother, and was told that Sveta, the daughter, would have to go with them on the picnic.

They took a train to a nearby stretch of woodland. As Sveta played with her doll a little way off, Chikatilo and Tanya undressed and started to have oral sex. After a while Chikatilo tried to enter Tanya, but failed. It was then that she made the greatest mistake of her life; she jeered at his inability. Seeing red, he grabbed the knife from his pocket and drove it into the side of her head. Then he beat her to a pulp with the hammer. Hearing her mother's dying screams, Sveta tried to run away, but Chikatilo soon caught her. He knocked her down and then killed her with dozens of blows from the knife and hammer. The attack was so furious that he completely beheaded the little girl. Afterwards he dressed himself and caught the train home.

Tanya's mother was old and mentally subnormal. She waited for three days before contacting the police, and even then could not remember what the stranger had looked like. Once again, Chikatilo's luck had held.

He had now killed twenty-two victims, and over the next four months this rose to thirty-two. Most were in the Rostov area, but three he killed on business trips: two in Tashkent and one in Moscow. As usual his targets were of both sexes, aged between eleven and twenty-four. He would have doubtless killed more that year, but at last his luck seemed to run out. He was arrested on suspicion of being the Rostov serial killer on 14 September 1984.

Inspector Aleksandr Zanasovski had questioned Chikatilo for acting suspiciously at the Rostov train station two weeks previously. On the evening of 13 September he spotted him again, this time across the square at the Rostov bus station. Again he noted that Chikatilo was trying to strike up conversations with young people with almost manic persistence. Zanasovski followed Chikatilo until four the next morning. In that time they travelled backwards and forwards on various forms of public transport with no destination ever becoming apparent. Eventually, when Chikatilo appeared to receive oral sex from a young lady on a public bench, the inspector arrested him. In the briefcase that the suspect had carried all night the police found a jar of Vaseline, a length of rope and a kitchen knife with an eight-inch blade.

Yet still Chikatilo's incredible luck held. When the forensic department tested his blood, the case fell apart. The semen

221

found on and around the victims proved to belong to a 'secreter'; that is, a man who secretes minute amounts of blood into his spittle and semen. The tests had shown the killer to have 'AB' blood – Chikatilo was type 'A'. Despite this major setback, the investigators found it hard to believe that he was innocent. Under Soviet law they could only hold a suspect for a maximum of ten days without preferring charges but they needed more time to build a case against him. They checked his previous record, learned about a reported theft of the two rolls of linoleum, so booked him on that. On 12 December 1984 Chikatilo was found guilty by the people's court of the crime of theft of state property, and sentenced to a year of correctional labour. However, since he had already spent three months in jail, the judge waived the sentence.

On 1 August 1985 Chikatilo went back to killing. The victim was eighteen-year-old Natalya Pokhlistova, a mentally subnormal transient he met during a business trip to Moscow.

They went off to a deserted spot and tried to have sex. When he failed he mutilated her with a knife then strangled her. Chikatilo killed again that month. On 27 August 1986 he murdered Irina Gulyayeva. Like his last victim, she was an eighteen-year-old, mentally subnormal vagrant. He met her in Shakhti – the place where he killed for the very first time – and butchered her in the nearby woods. She was his thirty-fourth victim, and the last for a year and nine months. On 16 May 1987 Chikatilo killed a thirteen-year-old boy called Oleg Makarenkov in Siberia.

He killed twice more in 1987, both in areas far from Rostov. The thirty-sixth victim was a twelve-year-old boy called Ivan Bilovetski, killed in Chikatilo's native Ukraine on 29 July. The thirty-seventh was Yura Tereshonok, aged sixteen, outside Leningrad on 15 September.

Once again, he ceased killing for the winter months, perhaps because it was harder to get people to accompany him into snowbound woods. Some time in April 1988, he killed an unidentified woman in the Krasny region. Then, on 14 May, he butchered nine-year-old Lyosha Voronko near the Ilovaisk train station in the Ukraine. His last victim that year, bringing the sum total to forty, was fifteen-year-old Zhenya Muratov, on 14 July. The following year, on 1 March 1989, he killed indoors for the first time since his first victim, Lena Zakotnova. Tatyana Ryzhova, a fifteen-year-old runaway, was induced to follow Chikatilo to an apartment that belonged to his daughter, Ludmila. The place had been empty since Ludmila had divorced her husband and moved in with her parents. Chikatilo had the job of swapping it for two smaller apartments ('swapping' was the typical method of property dealing in the Soviet Union). It was a task he was in no hurry to complete since it provided the perfect place to bring prostitutes. He gave Tatyana food and vodka, and tried to have sex with her. Soon she became restless and started to shout. Chikatilo tried to quiet her, but when she started to scream, he silenced her by stabbing her in the mouth. Some of the neighbours heard Tatyana's screams, but did nothing; wife beating was a common occurrence in the Soviet Union.

When Chikatilo had ceased to mutilate Tatyana he realized his danger. Somehow he had to get her body out of the apartment without being seen. He was in a populated area and for all he knew the police might already be on their way. He solved the problem by cutting off her head and legs and wrapping them in her clothes. Then he mopped the bloody floor and went out to steal a sled to remove the body. Finding one nearby, he set off into the night with Tatyana's remains firmly tied down.

All seemed to be going well until he tried to pull the sled over a rail crossing and it stuck due to the thin snow cover. To his horror he saw a stranger walking towards him and wondered if he should either run or try to kill the witness. The man pulled level with him and, without a word, helped Chikatilo lift the burdened sled across the tracks, then went on his way. Tatyana's mutilated body was found stuffed into some nearby pipes on 9 March 1989.

Chikatilo killed four more times that year. On 11 May he

murdered eight-year-old Sasha Dyakonov in Rostov. Travelling to the Vladimir region to the north-east, he killed ten-year-old Lyosha Moiseyev on 11 May. In mid-August he killed Yelena Varga, aged nineteen, on another business trip, this time to the Rodionovo-Nesvetayevski region. Finally, he murdered Alyosha Khobotov on 28 August. He met ten-year-old Khobotov outside a video salon (a Soviet equivalent of a movie house) in the town of Shakhti. The boy happily told him that he preferred horror movies above all others. Chikatilo replied that he owned a video machine and a large collection of horror videos. Alyosha jumped at his offer to view them.

Chikatilo led his victim through the local graveyard to a quiet spot where a shovel stood by an open grave. He had dug the trench himself some time earlier in a fit of suicidal depression. Now, in a different mood, he bit out Alyosha's tongue, cut off his genitals and threw him, still alive, into the pit. Then he filled in the grave.

On 14 January 1990, he murdered eleven-year-old Andrei Kravchenko. As with the last victim, he picked up Andrei outside the Shakhti video salon by offering to show him horror movies. The following 7 March, he persuaded a ten-year-old boy called Yaroslav Makarovto to follow him to a party. He led him into the Rostov Botanical Gardens, then molested and butchered him. His next victim was Lyubov Zuyeva, a thirty-one-year-old mentally handicapped woman whom he met on a train to Shakhti some time in April. He persuaded her to have sex with him in the woods, then stabbed her to death.

On 28 July he persuaded thirteen-year-old Vitya Petrov, waiting for a late train with his family at Rostov station, to follow him to the Botanical Gardens. Once out of the sight of others, he killed him. Strangely enough, Chikatilo had tried to pick up Vitya's younger brother, Sasha, only a few hours earlier, but had been scolded away by the boys' mother. Chikatilo's fiftieth victim was eleven-year-old Ivan Fomin, killed on a river beach in Novcherkassk on 14 August. The corpse was found three days later. Chikatilo now decided to make a journey to

Moscow. For some months he had been involved in a petty dispute with some Assyrian builders over garages that had been built next to his son's house, blocking the light. Since his son was away doing his national service, Chikatilo had made strenuous complaints via official channels, but nothing had happened. Growing increasingly paranoid, Chikatilo decided that some sort of illegal conspiracy was being directed against him, and in Moscow demanded audiences with both President Gorbachev and parliamentary head Anatoly Lukyanov. Needless to say he was granted neither, but stayed on for a few days in the 'tent city' of protesters that had steadily grown outside the Kremlin since the introduction of glasnost. After that he had to return to work, so he packed up his tent and protest sign and went back to Rostov.

On 17 October 1990 he met a mentally handicapped sixteen-year-old called Vadim Gromov on the Novocherkassk train. He persuaded the young man to get off the train with him at the wooded station of Donleskhoz by offering to take him to a party. Gromov's body was found just over two weeks later, by which time Chikatilo had murdered again. This time the victim was sixteen-year-old Vitya Tishchenko, who disappeared after buying train tickets from the Shakhti station on the last day of October. He was found, mutilated, three days later. Oddly enough, the investigators were now beginning to feel more optimistic. For most of the inquiry, morale had been abysmal. The police had always been undermanned and badly organized, and it had been easy for Chikatilo to play games with them. He would kill in Rostov, and when the police concentrated their manpower in that area, he would kill in Shakhti or Novocherkassk, throwing them into confusion.

Now, the killer was becoming careless. The woman in the Shakhti ticket office reported seeing a tall middle-aged man in dark glasses hanging around when Tishchenko bought the tickets. Her teenage daughter added that she had seen the same man trying to pick up a boy several days before. With this rough description and increased manpower, the investigation at last seemed to have a chance. If only the killer would return to one of his known murder locations they might get him before he murdered again.

This was exactly what Chikatilo did, but, once again, the police missed him. His fifty-third victim was a twenty-two-year-old girl called Sveta Korostik, whom he killed in the woods outside Donleskhoz train station. Only one policeman had been posted there to check the identities of any suspicious persons alighting on the platform.

Sveta's body was found a week later. But when Sergeant Igor Rybakov, the officer on duty at the station on the day of Sveta's murder, was questioned, an amazing fact emerged. He had interviewed a suspicious-looking man that day and had sent a report in but, for some reason, it had not been processed.

Rybakov said that at 4 p.m. on 6 October, he had observed a large, mud-spattered, middle-aged man emerge from the forest and wash his hands in the dribble of water flowing from the platform fire hydrant. The sergeant would probably have ignored him, taking him for one of the many mushroom pickers that frequented the station, but noticed that he was wearing a grey suit, odd attire for rain-soaked woods. He asked for identification, and was handed a passport that bore the name Andrei Romanovich Chikatilo. The man explained that he had been visiting a friend. The officer studied Chikatilo and noticed that his hand was bandaged and there was a streak of red liquid on his cheek. Nevertheless, he allowed him to board a train and leave.

Chikatilo's name was checked and the investigators learned of the Lena Zakotnova questioning, the paedophilia and the 1984 arrest. But for the fact that his blood group was wrong he would have been a prime suspect. It was at this point that somebody remembered a circular that had been sent around to all Soviet police departments. Japanese scientists had discovered that in one case in a million, the blood type secreted into the semen and the actual blood type can be different. It was just possible that Chikatilo might be such a person. Chikatilo was initially placed under twenty-four-hour surveillance, but the fear that he might commit another murder or commit suicide led the investigators to arrest him on 20 November 1990. He offered no resistance and came quietly. His semen type was tested and proved to be 'AB'; the same as that found on the bodies of the victims. Now certain they had the right man, the police wanted a confession. After days of relentless questioning, Chikatilo slowly began to admit the truth. He started by confessing to molesting children while he had been a schoolteacher, but eventually described fifty-five sex murders, including that of Lena Zakotnova. The stunned police – who had only linked thirty-six victims to the Rostov murderer – had now to admit that they had executed an innocent man for Lena's killing. Chikatilo was finally charged with the brutal murder of fifty-three women and children. Over the next year and a half, he was studied by doctors and criminologists. During that time he led officers to undiscovered bodies and, with a shop dummy and a stage knife, acted out how he had killed each victim. His habits had become fixed over the years. For example, he would usually bite off the victim's tongue and nipples. Wounds on or around the eyes were almost invariable. He would cut or bite off the boys' penises and scrotums and throw them away like so much rubbish. With the girls and women he would cut out the uterus and chew it manically as he stabbed at them. The psychiatrists ruled that this was not technically cannibalism, since he did not swallow the flesh, but was in fact motivated by the same impulse that makes people give love bites in the height of sexual passion. Chikatilo simply commented, 'I did not want to bite them so much as chew them. They were so beautiful and elastic.'

Chikatilo's wife was stunned when she was told of the reason for his arrest. She had thought he was being persecuted for protesting about the Assyrian garages and, at first, refused to believe that the man she had been married to for twenty-five years was a monster. He had always been a loving, if weak-willed father to their children and doted on their grandchildren.

How could he have concealed over a decade of slaughter from her? Yet, when Chikatilo himself admitted the crimes to her face she was forced to accept the terrible truth. She cursed him and left, never to speak to him again. For their part, the police believed that she had known nothing of her husband's activities and provided her with a change of identity and a home in another part of the country.

The trial opened on 14 April 1992. The shaven-headed Chikatilo raved and shouted from the cage that held and protected him from the angry public. At one point he even stripped off his clothes and waved his penis at the court shouting, 'Look at this useless thing! What do you think I could do with that?' His extreme behaviour might well have been motivated by the fact that his only hope of escaping execution was a successful insanity plea. The defence tried to prove that Chikatilo was driven by an insane and undeniable need to kill and was not in control of his actions during the murders. They had little chance of convincing the judge, since Chikatilo clearly planned many of the killings, and had long dormant periods when he did not kill.

On 14 October 1992, as Chikatilo received individual sentences for fifty-two murders, the court was filled with shrieks that often drowned the judge's voice. But at one point, Judge Akubzhanov showed unexpected agreement with one of Chikatilo's arguments, when he accepted that it was the refusal of the Soviet Union to acknowledge the high national level of crime that had contributed to Chikatilo's long immunity. Sixteen months later, on 14 February 1994, Andrei Chikatilo was executed by a single shot in the back of the neck, fired from a small calibre Makarov pistol.

Aileen Wuornos

In Chikatilo, nicknamed in the Western newspapers 'The Red Ripper', the Soviet Union suffered one of the most savage serial killers on record. But, even before his execution, the American media was claiming another 'first' in serial murder: the first female serial killer. This, of course, has to be immediately qualified by admitting that murderesses like Anna Zwanziger and Gesina Gottfried were serial poisoners. But these women had specific motives for getting rid of individual victims: usually profit, sometimes revenge, occasionally a mere passing grudge. If by serial killer we mean someone who experiences a psychopathic need to kill, devoid of apparent motive, then Aileen Wuornos probably qualifies as America's first genuine female serial killer.

Twelve days before Christmas 1989, two friends, scrap-metal hunting in the woods outside Ormond Beach, Florida, found a male corpse wrapped in an old carpet. The body had been there for about two weeks and was badly decomposed due to Florida's almost perpetually hot weather. However, the forensics lab managed to identify the victim as Richard Mallory, a fifty-one-year-old electrician from the town of Clearwater. The autopsy showed that he had been shot three times in the chest and once in the neck with a .22 calibre handgun. Because of the proximity of Daytona Beach – a notorious crime black spot – and the overall lack of evidence, the investigating officers made only routine efforts to find the

229

perpetrator. In all likelihood Mallory had been shot in a fight or a mugging, then hidden in the woods to avoid detection. Such crimes took place with depressing regularity around Daytona, and the chances of catching the killer were minimal.The police were forced to reappraise the situation, however.

Over the next twelve months, five more victims were discovered in almost identical circumstances. A forty-three-year-old construction worker, David Spears, was found on 1 June 1990, shot six times with a .22 handgun. Five days later the corpse of rodeo worker Charles Carskaddon, aged forty, was found covered with an electric blanket with nine bullet holes in him. A fifty-year-old truck driver called Troy Burress was found on 4 August, killed by two .22 calibre bullets. On 12 September, a fifty-six-year-old child abuse investigator, Charles Humphreys, was found shot six times in the torso and once in the head. Finally, on 19 November, the body of Walter Gino Antonio was found, shot dead by four .22 calibre bullets. In each case the victim was a middle-aged, apparently hetero-sexual male. They all appeared to have been killed in or near their cars, just off one of the state highways, and hidden in nearby scrub or woodland. Some were partially stripped, but no evidence of sexual or physical abuse could be found. Used prophylactics found near some of the bodies suggested that they had been involved in a sexual encounter before they were murdered. In every case, money, valuables and the victim's vehicle had been stolen. The cars were generally found dumped shortly after the murder with the driver's seat pulled well forward, as if to allow a comparatively short person to reach the drive pedals.

When it was found that the same handgun was being used in each of the killings the police were forced to accept that they might have a serial killer on their hands; yet, disturbingly, the murders did not fit any known pattern. As we have seen again and again in the preceding chapters, serial crime always has a sexual element to it. Why would a heterosexual serial murderer strip and kill middle-aged men? On the other hand, if the killer was homosexual, why was there no evidence of direct sexual abuse?

It was the FBI's psychological profiling unit that provided the startling answer: the killer was probably a woman. Predictably, media attention, which had been minimal up to then, grew exponentially when this was revealed. Confusing as the case was, at least the Florida police had a solid lead. Many serial killers steal from their victims, but usually valueless things like underclothes or removed body parts, and do so entirely for souvenir purposes. The Florida Highway Killer, whatever her other motives, was taking cash and valuables from the victims. These might be traced if and when she used or sold them.

As it turned out, the killer made an even more serious blunder. On 4 July 1990 she and her girlfriend skidded off the road in a car she had stolen from Peter Seims, a sixty-five-year-old part-time missionary she had killed in early June somewhere in southern Georgia. Witnesses told the police that they had seen the two women – one tall and blonde, the other a short, heavy-set brunette – abandon the damaged Pontiac Sunbird after removing the licence plates.

Police took detailed descriptions of the pair, but did not initially connect them with the highway killings. When it became clear that they were looking for a female killer they rereviewed the Seims case and, since he was still missing, added him to the list. They also issued artist's impressions of the two women with the request for further information. It seemed the case was taking a new turn; they might have a pair of female serial killers on their hands.

By December 1990, the police had two names to attach to the artist's sketches, thanks to tips from members of the public.The brunette was possibly one Tyria J. Moore, a twenty-eight-year-old occasional hotel maid; and the blonde could be her live-in lover, a thirty-four-year-old prostitute who went under several names, one of them being Lee

Wuornos. Shortly afterwards, a routine check on a Daytona pawn shop revealed several items that had belonged to Richard Mallory. The pawn ticket that went with the belongings was made out to a Cammie Green, but the statutory thumbprint – that all Florida pawn tickets must carry – proved to be that of Wuornos.

The police arrested her outside the Last Resort bikers' bar on 9 January 1991. Shortly afterwards, Tyria Moore was located at her sister's home in Pennsylvania. Strangely enough, the officers who went to pick her up did not arrest her. Instead they took Moore to a nearby motel. What took place there has never been made clear, but it has been alleged that a deal was struck and, possibly, a contract signed. To understand these claims fully it is necessary to look at the influence of the media on the investigation, and vice versa. Movies like *The Silence of the Lambs*, *Thelma and Louise* and *Basic Instinct* had recently made serial killers and women outlaws two of the major money-spinners in the US entertainment industry. Even before Wuornos's arrest, up to fifteen movie companies were rumoured to be offering film contracts for the Highway Killer's story. An obvious target for such money would be the investigating officers.

By the time of her apprehension the police had ascertained that Tyria Moore could not have been directly involved in at least some of the murders. There were various witnesses who could swear that she was working as a motel maid at the time of these killings. If she was not charged with any criminal offence, the movie contract lawyers could bid for her story without infringing the 'Son of Sam' law. This ruling made it illegal for convicted felons to profit directly from their crimes. Any money from movies, books, press interviews and so forth went to the victims, or their families if the victim were dead.

It has been alleged that in return for immunity from prosecution – and a cut of the profits – Moore signed a contract with officers Binegar, Henry and Munster to sell her story, in conjunction with theirs, to a movie company.

232

Tyria Moore – who admitted that 'Lee' Wuornos had told her about at least one of the murders – agreed to help the prosecution in return for immunity from the charge of 'accessory after the fact'. She led officers to the creek where Wuornos had thrown the .22 revolver used in the murders and, under police supervision, made eleven bugged phone calls to Lee in prison. In them she claimed that she was still undiscovered by the police and urged Lee to confess. Wuornos, who was plainly still in love with Moore, tried to soothe her and agreed to make a statement. On 16 January 1991 Wuornos gave a three-hour videotaped confession in Volusia County Jail. In it she admitted to killing Mallory, Spears, Carskaddon, Seims, Burress, Humphreys and Antonio. She also gave details that only a witness to the murders could have known, apparently confirming her testimony. Defending her actions, she insisted that she had only gone to the woods with them to trade sex for money. Each of the seven men had tried to attack or rape her, she said, forcing her to kill them in self-defence. When asked why she was confessing, she replied that she wanted to clear Tyria Moore's name.

It was decided that Wuornos was to be tried for each murder separately. Her defence counsels contended that it would be prejudicial to the trial if the jury heard evidence connected with the other murders, but at the first trial, for the killing of Richard Mallory, Judge Uriel Blount Jr ruled otherwise. Florida's Williams Rule allowed evidence of similar offences to be revealed to a jury when the judge considered it important to the case. Of course, this seriously undermined Wuornos's claim that she had fired in self-defence. To believe that even a hard-working street prostitute had to kill seven men in the space of a single year stretched the jury's credulity to breaking point.

For some reason the defence lawyers declined to call character witnesses for the defendant and, incredibly, did not inform the court that Richard Mallory had previously served a prison sentence for rape. It is possible that this was done deliberately to increase the chances for a claim of mistrial at any ensuing appeal, but it left Lee Wuornos with hardly a leg to stand on in court. The jury found her guilty and Judge Blount sentenced her to the electric chair.

At a subsequent arraignment for three of the other murders, Wuornos pleaded unconditionally guilty and requested the death sentence without trial on the grounds that she wanted to 'be with Jesus' as soon as possible. It seems likely that this was an all-or-nothing gamble to win the judge's sympathy and receive life imprisonment instead of further death sentences. Wuornos became outraged when the judge complied with her request, shouting that she was being executed for being a rape victim. As she left the courtroom she loudly wished similar experiences on the judge's wife and children. Was Aileen Wuornos really a serial killer? If we discount her own defence, that she was a victim of circumstance, we are left with a tantalizing lack of motive for the murders. Some have argued that she killed simply for financial profit: robbing a client, then shooting him to silence the only witness. To support this view it has been pointed out that she was clearly desperate not to lose her lover, Tyria Moore. Moore appears to have been unwilling to work during the period of their relationship but, nevertheless, insisted on living in expensive motels. It seems clear that she knew Wuornos was prostituting herself to get money, but never objected to her lover's self-abasement – even after Lee had told her about the murder of Richard Mallory.

There may indeed be some truth in this theory, but it does not seem enough to explain the murder of seven men, none of whom would have appeared particularly well-off. A more likely theory is that Wuornos killed to revenge herself on men. She was brought up by her grandparents when her real parents abandoned her as a baby. She has claimed that she was regularly beaten and occasionally sexually abused by her grandfather throughout her childhood. When she was thirteen, she was driven into the woods and raped by a middle-aged friend of her grandparents. From her early teens on it appears that she made money through prostitution and claims to have been beaten up and raped by clients quite often. She had several affairs and was married to a man fifty years her senior, but they all ended acrimoniously. It was only with Tyria Moore that she seemed to be reasonably happy.

On the available evidence, it seems likely that the first victim, Richard Mallory, may well have raped Wuornos. Did this push her into serial crime? Over 1990 she admits to having had hundreds of clients, all but seven of whom she apparently had no trouble with. On the other hand, the similarities between the murder victims and the circumstances of the rape when she was thirteen are unmistakable. Perhaps her trigger was resistance or threat. She may indeed be telling the truth when she insisted that the men she killed threatened her and refused to pay after sex. This may have thrown her into a rage in which she – justifiably, in her view – shot them dead. Certainly most people who came in contact with her, sooner or later noted her savage temper and habit of specious self-justification.

For whatever the reason Wuornos killed, she caused a major stir in law enforcement circles. The possibility that she may be the start of a new trend in serial murder has disturbing ramifications. As Robert Ressler – former FBI agent and originator of the term 'serial killer' – said of the case: 'If Wuornos is said to be a serial killer we have to rewrite the rules.' Fortunately, to date, female serial crime remains all but unknown.

The drama of Lee Wuornos's story spawned two movies, an opera and several books before she was executed by lethal injection on 9 October 2002. As she was led out of the court, following her first conviction and death sentence in 1991, Wuornos had shouted: 'I'm going to Heaven now. You're all going to Hell!' Shortly after her death, an anonymous joker posted a message on a website that was hosting an online discussion about her execution. Signed Satan, it simply read: 'Umm . . . Could you guys take her back?'

Fred and Rose West

In the summer of 1993, Frederick and Rosemary West – a builder and his wife living at 25 Cromwell Street in Gloucester – were accused of sexually assaulting a young woman. The charges were eventually dropped after the accuser refused to give evidence, but in the meantime the Wests' children had been taken into care. It was there that foster-carers overheard the children talking about their older sister, Heather, being 'under the patio'. Questioned about this ominous phrase, the kids said that they had been told that Heather had been working in the Midlands for the past five years, but that their parents would still occasionally threaten them with being 'put under the patio with Heather'.

When the police checked the records against Heather West's National Insurance number, they found that she had never claimed any state benefits or National Health care, despite supposedly leaving home at the tender age of sixteen. The police applied for a warrant and entered 25 Cromwell Street to dig up the patio. When they found the dismembered skeleton of a young girl, Fred West was arrested. He admitted to killing sixteen-year-old Heather in 1987, but insisted his wife Rose knew nothing about it. As West refused to admit to anything else, the investigation might have rested there, but then the police had unearthed a third femur: evidently there was more than one body under the West patio.

Confronted with this fresh evidence, Fred West admitted to

two more killings, Shirley Robinson and Alison Chambers, whom he had sexually assaulted and killed in the late 1970s. However, he failed to mention the further six bodies – buried beneath his cellar and bathroom – partially, it seems, because he didn't want his beloved home damaged by more police digging. Later, however, under the pressure of intense questioning, he admitted these killings, plus a further three victims he had buried out in the Gloucestershire countryside.

Fred West was born in 1941, the son of a Gloucestershire cow-herder. The eldest of seven children, Fred was his mother's pet and, although living in poverty, seems to have had a fairly happy childhood. Happy, of course, does not necessarily mean normal. Fred later claimed that his father regularly committed incest with his daughters, using the logic: 'I made you, so I can do anything I like with you.' Fred also claimed to have had sex with his sisters, and to have even got one pregnant. That said, of course, Fred West was a habitual liar and was obsessed by his sexual fantasies, so there may have been no incest in the West family at all. Fred's obsession with sex seems to have dated from two accidents in his teens. The first came when he fell off his motorcycle and landed on his head. He was in a coma for a week, but recovered. The second came a few months after his convalescence. He put his hand up a girl's skirt at a local dance, and she reacted by pushing him off the fire escape they were standing on. He again landed on his head.

After his second recovery, Fred's previously good-natured demeanour was often shattered by fits of violent fury, and his attitude to sex became manic. It seems likely that Fred West suffered scarring to the pre-frontal lobes of the brain in one or both his accidents. Although such damage can often go otherwise unnoticed – with no effect on brain or body functions – in some individuals it can lead to violent behaviour and sexual hyperactivity. Indeed, scarring to the pre-frontal lobes of the brain is yet another common factor among certain serial killers. In custody, Fred told the police that he did not know

238

the identities of all his victims. The first three had been his girlfriend, then his first wife and, later, his first wife's daughter by another man – then, of course, there was Heather West.

Several other victims had been lodgers at 25 Cromwell Street, but the others he had picked up hitch-hiking or had simply abducted. Painstaking police investigation filled in the gaps in Fred's confession, but it is by no means certain that he told the whole truth as to the number of women and girls he had killed over the years.

Fred's first known victim was Anna McFall in 1967 – he seems to have killed her because she was pregnant with his baby and was pressuring him to marry her. After killing her he carefully dismembered her body and buried it and the foetus near the caravan they had been living in. He did not bury her fingers or toes, however, apparently retaining them as a keepsake.

Next, although it has never been proven, Fred West is likely to have been responsible for the kidnapping and disappearance of fifteen-year-old Mary Bastholm, from a Gloucester bus stop in 1968. Although she was not mentioned in Fred's lengthy confession, he had known her, often frequenting the café in which she worked as a waitress. Certainly abducting girls on the street, either by force or by simply offering them a lift, was Fred's favourite modus operandi. In the summer of 1971, Fred apparently killed eight-year-old Charmaine, his estranged wife Rena's daughter from a previous relationship. Fred had custody of both Charmaine and Anne-Marie, his daughter with Rena, and it took a few months for his wife to ask where her child was. When it became obvious she might go to the authorities, Fred got Rena drunk, strangled her, dismembered her and buried her under his then home in Midland Road, Gloucester.

By this time Fred had a new live-in-mistress: eighteen-year-old Rosemary Letts, soon to be Rose West. Rose had been born the daughter of a sadistic and disciplinarian father and a manic depressive mother. Indeed, Daisy, her mum, was given electro-shock therapy while pregnant with Rose; nobody is certain what effect a series of massive electric jolts to a mother's brain might have on her developing foetus, but it is hardly likely to have been beneficial.

After this difficult start, Rose's life did not get much better. Her father, a low-paid manual labourer, used any excuse to beat and maltreat his five children. His method of punishing them for going to bed too late, for example, was to drench them and their bedding with buckets of cold water. Little wonder, then, that at fifteen, Rose ran off with one of the few men to have shown her any kindness; unfortunately, that man was Fred West.

By the time Rose moved in with him, Fred almost certainly had developed the habit of raping, torturing and killing strangers; but he never harmed her. Monster as he was, he genuinely loved his wife.

In 1972 he killed Linda Gough, aged twenty-one, and Lucy Partington, also aged twenty-one and buried them beneath his new home at 25 Cromwell Street. The following year he killed schoolgirl Carol Cooper, fifteen. In 1975 he killed Juanita Mott, nineteen, and Shirley Hubbard, fifteen. West killed no one (that we know of) in 1976, but in 1977 he murdered Therese Siegenthaler, twenty-one – a Swiss hitch-hiker he referred to as 'Tulip' because he thought she was Dutch – and Alison Chambers, aged seventeen. In 1978 he killed Shirley Robinson, eighteen, a lodger and lover heavily pregnant with Fred's baby. He then claims to have given up murder until May 1987, when he killed his eldest daughter Heather during a row. However, many believe that Fred West killed other victims and buried them in as yet undiscovered graves in the local countryside. Fred West hanged himself in his cell on New Year's Day 1995, before he could be tried; but the horror was not yet over. As the police investigation continued, it had become increasingly clear that Fred's insistence that his second wife, Rosemary, knew nothing about the murders was a lie. Evidence given by the six surviving West children, and by friends and acquaintances, clearly indicated that Rose was fully involved in Fred's sexual predations. Further evidence came from a former beauty queen, Caroline Raine, who reported being abducted and sexually assaulted by *both* Fred and Rose West.

Then there was the circumstantial yet damning fact that eight-year-old Charmaine – the daughter of Fred's first wife, Rena, by another man – had been killed while Fred was in prison for petty theft and failure to pay fines. The most likely candidate for that murder was the then seventeen-year-old lover Rose – resentful at being left in charge of another woman's child and often seen to mistreat Charmaine. Fred's involvement in that murder, whatever he later confessed, almost certainly stretched no further than burying the corpse under their kitchen floor when he eventually got out of jail. Yet Fred's dark gallantry in protecting Rose also had the side effect of tying her to him, murders and all: they both had monstrous secrets now. When Rose's father once tried to persuade her to leave Fred, he noticed that a seemingly innocuous phrase from Fred clearly upset Rose terribly. Fred had implored Rose to stay with the words: 'Come on, Rosie, you know what we've got between us.' At the trial, held in October 1995, the prosecution claimed that Rose had helped in all ten of the killings that had taken place since 1972. The jury agreed (although there remains some doubt as to whether Rose actually helped kill Heather West, her own daughter). She was sentenced to ten life terms in jail. Fred West's beloved home at 25 Cromwell Street, where he and Rose raped, tortured, murdered, dismembered and buried the bodies of their victims, was levelled by Gloucester Council in 1996.

Theodore Kaczynski, the 'Unabomber'

On 25 May 1978, a small parcel bomb mildly wounded a security guard at Illinois's Northwestern University. This was the first amateurish attack made by the serial killer who later became known as the 'Unabomber'. Over the next eighteen years, the Unabomber sent home-made, but increasingly sophisticated parcel bombs to educational establishments, technology companies and corporate businesses.

Police were doubly flummoxed by this method of attack: not only was the killer murdering strangers – the first and greatest problem in serial crime investigation – but he or she was also striking from a distance, using the unwitting US Postal Service as an accomplice. There were no personal links to lead to the killer from the victims and no possibility of chance eyewitnesses identifying the murderer.

Between May 1978 and December 1985, the Unabomber is known to have sent out nine, fortunately non-fatal, parcel bombs. Two were intercepted and defused, but the others injured eighteen people, some seriously. One of these bombs – that wounded United Airlines President Percy A. Wood – earned the bomb maker the media nickname the 'Un.A.bomber', later simplified to the 'Unabomber'. December 1985, in Sacramento California, saw the first fatal Unabomber attack. Hugh C. Scrutton tried to remove a package left lying in the car park behind his computer rental shop. It exploded, killing him. This bomb had not been delivered by the Postal Service, it had been simply left in the parking lot. It seemed likely, therefore, that the killer had put it there in order to watch, from a distance, the result of their handiwork. Unfortunately, nobody had seen the booby trap bomb being planted.

The next bombing followed the same pattern. On 20 February 1987 a bomb was left in the parking lot outside a computer firm in Salt Lake City. This time, however, a secretary in the firm spotted the bomber placing the booby trap. She thought it odd that the tall man in the hooded sweatshirt and aviator dark glasses should leave a lump of wood with nails sticking out of it right where it might damage somebody's tyres but, unfortunately, before she could alert anyone her boss, Gary Wright, drove into the lot, got out of his car and kicked the lump of wood out of the path of his tyres. The resulting explosion took off his leg, but did not kill him.

Police were delighted to have a description of the Unabomber – if a bit sketchy – and plastered the artist's reconstruction all over the national media. Any doubt that the Unabomber meant his bombs to kill had been removed by the last two attacks: both bombs had been packed with metal fragments, designed to shred their victims with flying shrapnel. But at least he seemed to have given up killing from a distance – the temptation to see the results of his murders obviously had been too great to ignore. Unfortunately the publication of the witness description removed this advantage. The Unabomber stopped sending bombs for six years – presumably frightened that the police might identify him – but when he struck again he did so via the US Mail. On 22 June 1993 a parcel bomb badly injured Dr Charles Epstein, a leading geneticist at the University of California, partly destroying his hand and sending shrapnel through his chest and across his face. Only swift medical aid saved his life.

The next day a similar parcel bomb badly hurt computer scientist Dr David Gelernter of Yale University. He lost most of his right hand, and the sight and hearing on his right side. He too survived, but only with extensive medical treatment.

On 10 December 1994 a parcel bomb killed New York advertising executive Thomas Mosser. Some doubted that this was a genuine Unabomber attack until it was pointed out that one of Mosser's corporate clients was the Exxon oil company – responsible, in many people's eyes, for recklessly polluting the environment. Less than five months later, on 24 April, timber industry lobbyist Gilbert B. Murray picked up a parcel, supposedly sent by a firm called 'Closet Dimensions'. As Murray picked up the package, one of his staff members joked: 'It's heavy. Must be a bomb.' The blast was particularly powerful, destroying Murray's head and upper body, but not killing anyone else. Fortunately, he was to be the Unabomber's last victim.

In 1995, in the wake of the Oklahoma bombing, the Unabomber sent a 'manifesto' to the *Washington Post* and the *New York Times* – threatening to blow up a passenger jet if it were not promptly published. It proved to be a rambling screed that attacked big business, environmentally damaging government policies, academic and scientific research . . . and progress in general. The opening paragraph read:

The Industrial Revolution and its consequences have been a disaster for the human race. They have greatly increased the life-expectancy of those of us who live in 'advanced' countries, but they have destabilized society, have made life unfulfilling, have subjected human beings to indignities, have led to widespread psychological suffering (in the Third World to physical suffering as well) and have inflicted severe damage on the natural world. The continued development of technology will worsen the situation. It will certainly subject human beings to greater indignities and inflict greater damage on the natural world, it will probably lead to greater social disruption and psychological suffering, and it may lead to increased physical suffering even in 'advanced' countries.

It was plain that the Unabomber believed that all development since the Industrial Revolution was dangerous and damnable. He was evidently a well-educated, well-read man, and many of the things he stated were simply extreme extensions of mainstream environmentalism. But he was also delusional and self-justifying, insisting that his bombing campaign had been the only way to make the media pay attention to his message. It may have been true that there were few avenues to attack modern technology through the conventional, pro-technology US media, but killing to get people's attention completely undermined the credibility of his manifesto.

And the fact that he had almost certainly watched the explosions that killed Hugh C. Scrutton and crippled Gary Wright placed the Unabomber firmly in the serial killer category. Whatever environmental and political self-justification he offered, he was not an eco-terrorist: he was a sadist.

Fortunately, the manifesto was the last terror package the Unabomber was ever to send. David Kaczynski, in Montana, read the Unabomber's manifesto and realized with horror that it sounded just like the rantings of his hermit-like older brother Theodore. Most telling was the reversal of the old homily: 'you can't have your cake and eat it'. The Unabomber, insisting that the positive uses of technology were not worth the negative side effects, wrote: 'you can't eat your cake and have it'. This was a family habit, picked up from the Kaczynski brothers' mother, and its inclusion convinced David that Theodore was the Unabomber.

With natural misgivings, David Kaczynski informed the FBI, who raided Theodore's isolated Montana cabin and found plenty of proof that he was the Unabomber. Theodore J. Kaczynski had been a brilliant academic – in 1967, at just twenty-five, he had been appointed Assistant Professor of Mathematics at Berkeley University, California – but, in 1969, Kaczynski suffered a total emotional breakdown and had subsequently become a recluse. Living in an isolated log cabin, Kaczynski believed he followed a life that was in tune with nature – making bombs with some parts carefully hand-carved from wood and roiling in hatred for the modern world.

In 1996 Ted Kaczynski was sentenced to four life sentences, with parole permanently denied.

The Monsters of the Andes

In April 1980 a Colombian man was arrested in Ambato, Ecuador, when he tried to abduct an eleven-year-old Indian girl from the market place. A few days earlier, the rain-swollen river had overflowed its banks and revealed the bodies of four missing girls; ever since then, police had been looking for a multiple sex killer. The prisoner, thirty-one-year-old Pedro Alonzo Lopez, denied that he had anything to do with the murders. A priest who posed as a fellow prisoner finally extracted a confession; soon, Lopez had told police that he had raped and killed about three-hundred-and-sixty girls, and would lead them to some of the burial sites.

Lopez later told the story of his life to American journalist Ron Laytner. The seventh son of a prostitute in Tolima, Colombia – with twelve brothers and sisters – he was thrown out of the house by his mother at the age of eight for sexually fondling one of his sisters. Kindly neighbours took him in, but the next day his mother took him to the edge of town and left him. He took a day to find his way home, laughing at his success. The next day his mother took him on a bus to another town and left him there. That night, a man found the crying child and promised to be a father to him; in fact he took him to an empty building and raped him.

In Bogota, where he was begging in the streets, a visiting

American family sent him to a school for orphans, but a woman schoolteacher tried to seduce him when he was twelve, and he ran away after stealing money.

At the age of eighteen, in prison for stealing a car, he was grabbed by four male prisoners and raped. He swore revenge. It took two weeks to manufacture a knife; then he lured the rapists, one by one, into a dark cell and killed three of them; the fourth stumbled on the bodies and fled, screaming, from the cell. Two years were added to his prison sentence – the murders were looked on as self-defence.

Once out of prison, he began abducting and raping young girls, preferably under the age of twelve. He would then kill them and bury the bodies. They were mostly Indians, and no one paid much attention to their disappearance.

Once the Ayacucho Indians caught him carrying off a nine-year-old girl and, after torturing him, prepared to bury him alive. An American missionary intervened and took the bound rapist in her jeep to the nearest Peruvian police outpost. The police were not interested, and sent him back across the border into Colombia, where he continued to murder girls – his total was by this time around a hundred.

Later he returned to Ecuador because, as he explained to Laytner, its girls are more gentle and trusting than those of Colombia.

His method was always the same – to walk around markets until he saw a girl with 'a certain look of innocence and beauty'. He would follow the girl, if necessary for days, until her mother left her alone. Then he would approach her and tell her that he had a present for her mother. He would lead her by the hand to the outskirts of the town. If night fell while he did this, he would forcibly keep the child with him, trying to sooth her with promises and gentle words. But as soon as the sun had risen he would rape and simultaneously strangle her. He would only kill the children in daylight, he later said, because he wanted to see the life drain from their eyes. He added that he had always hoped one day to rape and kill a white child –

he was attracted by fair hair – but tourists tended to keep too close an eye on their children.

In April 1980, the man who had become known as 'the Monster of the Andes' used his usual technique to lure away the eleven-year-old daughter of Carlina Ramon Poveda; but the frantic mother caught up with her daughter, walking hand in hand with her abductor. She denounced him shrilly, and when he called her a dirty Indian, summoned some Indian men to come and help her; they held Lopez down until the police arrived.

In hindsight, in the murders of the three men who raped Lopez in prison while he was still a teenager, we can see the typical response of a particular type of ruthless egotist to any humiliation; the sort of dangerous bully that the author A.E.Van Vogt called a 'Right Man', because such men cannot stand to be in the wrong or to be shamed. A Right Man will lie, self-delude and even, in extreme cases, kill to avoid admitting to even the tiniest fault.

While Lopez was making his endless list of self-excusing complaints to journalist Ron Laytner, he declared: 'I cannot see the sky. This is wrong, for I am the Man of the Century. I will be famous in history.' Asked to explain how he justified his murders, he told Laytner: 'The arrival of life is divine. It comes through the act of sex. And so if an innocent person dies in the act of sex, it is also divine. That person will find heaven without suffering in this world.'

This sounds curiously like the early twentieth-century US serial killer Carl Panzram's explanation that he was 'doing people good' by murdering them, since life was so vile that to kill someone was to do him a favour. A Right Man lives in a strange universe of fantasy and self-justification, and the 'anti-social type' serial killer 'punishes' society through murder; combined, such deep personality defects make a terrible mix.

Lopez later lowered his claimed number of murders to 140. It is not known if this modest self-reappraisal contributed to the prison authorities' decision to free him, on grounds of good behaviour, in early 1999. His model behaviour in prison did not, however, prevent the Ecuadorian government immediately deporting him to Colombia.

Political relations between Ecuador and Colombia have been very bad for a number of years. Unfortunately, instead of handing Lopez over to the Colombian authorities to stand trial for his crimes in that country, the Ecuadorians are said to have simply taken him over the Colombian border, at night, and released him: an act that might be seen as comparable to releasing a killer virus into the air of an enemy nation.

Lopez is on record as saying that, if freed, he would return to his 'mission' to rape and kill little girls. Even Victor Lascano, the governor of the Ambato Prison that held Lopez for twenty years, is quoted as saying of the release: 'God save the children. He is unreformed and totally remorseless. This whole nightmare may start again.'

Pedro Lopez's whereabouts are, at the time of writing, unknown.

By one of those grisly coincidences that are so frequent in the world of murder, a second 'Monster of the Andes' was operating in Ecuador within five years of the arrest of Lopez. He was Daniel Camargo Barbosa and, like Lopez, he came from Colombia. In 1985 he was serving a life sentence in Colombia for the rape and murder of a nine-year-old girl, but succeeded in escaping into Ecuador. During 1986, he raped and murdered seventy-one young girls. Most were lured to a quiet spot with a promise of sweets. Barbosa then raped them, then he bludgeoned or slashed them to death with astonishing ferocity. Most of his victims were lured from around the port area of the town of Guayaquil.

Barbosa was arrested in Quito when a policeman noticed bloodstains on his clothing. A slightly built man of fifty-seven, with a great deal of natural charm, Barbosa seemed an unlikely mass murderer. But, like so many serial killers, he was avid for 'recognition'; while under arrest he began to boast about his murders, then willingly led detectives to the sites of over fifty bodies. He even appeared on television, and when asked whether he had accomplices, replied proudly: 'No, I did it all myself.' Asked why he had committed his crimes, he explained: 'When one has been the victim of traumatic experiences in childhood, one grows up with the mental conditions for committing these acts' – a reply that indicates that, like so many serial killers, he possessed a relatively high I.Q.

Like Lopez, he was sentenced to just sixteen years in prison, the maximum possible sentence under Ecuadorian law at that time. However, unlike Lopez, Barbosa was not secretly released in his native Colombia after his sentence was over; he had been stabbed to death in prison on 13 November 1994. His killer was apparently the cousin of one of his many victims.

The Green River Killer

For over two decades the mystery of the Green River serial killer hung over the American Northwest. And not just police investigators were shamed by their lack of success in apprehending the killer, but so were local media organisations – one of whom publicly revealed the existence a police trap set for the murderer in the early days of the hunt. More than that, Washington State, seen by many as an idyllic, rural state, was revealed to have a darker underbelly: just like New York or Los Angeles, it was a place where many teenage girls ended up as prostitutes . . . and where the killer of such girls could escape justice for decades.

On 12 August 1982, a slaughterman discovered a bloated corpse floating in the slow-flowing Green River, near Seattle, in Washington State. The police pathologist succeeded in lifting an excellent set of prints from the swollen fingers, which enabled the criminal identification department to name the victim as 23-year-old Debra Lynn Bonner, known as 'Dub'; she was a stripper with a list of convictions as a prostitute. And she was, in fact, the second of literally dozens of women who would be found during the next three years.

The first victim had been found a month earlier, half a mile downstream, strangled with her own slacks, and had been identified as 16-year-old Wendy Coffield. In spite of her age, she had a record as a hardened professional prostitute – indeed, she was known to have worked as a 'trick roll':

someone who sets up her clients ('Johns') for robbery.

Within three days of the finding of Debra Bonner, Dave Reichert, the detective in charge of the case, heard that two more bodies had been found in the Green River. Both women were black, both were naked, and they had been weighted down to the river bottom with large rocks. They were only a few hundred yards upstream from the spot where Dub Bonner had been found and – much to police embarrassment – had almost certainly been there at the time her body was being hauled out of the water.

Keen not to repeat this mistake, Detective Reichert walked along the bank from the new crime scene, back towards the place where Dub Bonner had been found. This thoroughness paid off when he discovered another body. Like the other two, she was black, and was later identified as 16-year-old Opal Mills. The fact that rigor mortis had not yet disappeared meant that she had been left there in the past two days. This, in turn, meant that if the police had kept watch on the river after the first bodies were found, the killer would have almost certainly been caught.

In the light of such revelations, it is now hardly surprising that the local authorities' ineptitude would eventually make the Green River case doubly infamous.

The next – and perhaps worse – mistake occurred two days later, when a local TV station fatuously announced that the riverbank was now under round-the-clock surveillance. This destroyed any chance of catching the killer on a return visit.

The medical evidence on the other two women, Marcia Chapman and Cynthia Hinds, confirmed that the Green River Killer was a 'sick trick'; both women had pointed rocks jammed into their vaginas. Like the others, they were prostitutes working the Strip – the main road – leading to Seattle's Sea-Tac Airport.

On Saturday 28 August 1982, Kase Lee left her pimp's apartment to 'turn a trick', and vanished. The next day Terri Milligan took an hour off from soliciting to go for a meal;

apparently a car pulled up for her as she walked to the fast-food joint, and, unwilling to reject business, she climbed in. She was never seen alive again.

The following day, 15-year-old Debra Estes – known to the police as Betty Jones – was picked up by a blue-and-white pickup truck; the man drove her to remote woodland, made her undress at gun point, then ordered her to give him a blow job. After that he robbed her of $75 and left her with her hands tied. This man was pulled in by police who recognized the description of his pickup truck, and identified him as the attacker. But a lie-detector test established his innocence of the Green River murders. Confirming this, while he was still in custody, 18-year-old Mary Meehan, who was eight months pregnant, disappeared, and became victim number nine.

Within three weeks of her rape, Debra Estes was back working the street – an indication of the desperate necessity that drives many street prostitutes. She became the tenth victim of the Green River Killer. Six more victims in August, October, November and December would bring his total up to at least sixteen – the largest annual total for any US serial killer up to that time.

Yet it would be exceeded in the following year, 1983, when twenty-six women vanished, and the remains of eight of them were found near Sea-Tac Airport or close by. In March, special investigator Bob Keppel, known for his brilliant work on the Ted Bundy case, was asked to write a report on the investigation. It was devastating, with hundreds of examples of incompetence and failure to follow up on leads. For example, when the driving license of victim Marie Malvar was found at the airport, and the police were notified, they did not even bother to collect it – although it might well have contained the killer's fingerprints.

In 1984, four victims were found together on Auburn West Hill, six more in wooded areas along State Route 410, and two near Tigard, Oregon, the latter giving rise to the speculation that the killer had moved to live in a new location. In January a Green River Task Force of 36 investigators was formed, with a then staggering $2-million budget. By 1988 the cost of the investigation was to reach over $13 million.

Among the hundreds of suspects interviewed by the police was Gary Leon Ridgway, born in 1949, a mild-looking man with fishlike lips, who worked for the Kenworth Truck Plant and was known to pick up prostitutes – he even admitted being obsessed by them. He also confessed to choking a prostitute in 1982, but he claimed this was because she bit him and that he did her no permanent damage.

By 1986, with the investigation stalled, Ridgway's file was re-opened. His ex-wife was interviewed and mentioned his preference for sex in the open, often near the Green River. As a result, Ridgway was placed under surveillance. But still women disappeared – although no longer with quite the same frequency.

In December 1988, a television special on the case, 'Manhunt Live', led to 4,000 tips from the public, and to the arrest of 38-year-old William J. Stevens, who had a criminal record. But although both police and media believed the Green River Killer had been arrested, credit card receipts proved Stevens had been elsewhere at the time of some of the murders, and he was released.

And so throughout the 1990s, the case marked time. Reichert, the chief investigator, later admitted that his obsession with the killer had caused serious problems in his marriage.

Genetic fingerprinting had first been used in 1986, and had led to the solution of many murders. The main problem was likely to occur if there was not enough DNA material for testing, or if it was old. In 2001, a major breakthrough came when the Washington State crime lab acquired the equipment to extract usable DNA from old samples and multiply the quantity by the method known as STR, or short tandem repeats. (This is also known as the PCR, or polymerase chain reaction, which amplifies genetic samples by 'unzipping' the double-stranded DNA molecule, and making two exact copies.)

Now a major review of samples of semen evidence began. And by September 2001, it had paid off. Semen samples, taken from Opal Mills, Marcia Chapman and Carol Christensen, three of the earliest victims, proved to be from Gary Ridgway. Paint fragments and fibre evidence taken from the grave of Debra Estes in 1988 were also linked to Ridgway. So when Ridgway was finally arrested on November 30, 2001, he was charged with four counts of murder.

At first pleading innocent, he later agreed to change his plea to guilty to avoid the death penalty.

Ridgway's account of how he became a serial killer occupies the most fascinating chapter of Reichert's book: *Chasing the Devil*. As with many killers, the problems seem to have started with his upbringing. He was a chronic bed-wetter, and his mother would drag him out of bed and parade him in front of his brothers, then make him stand naked in a tub of cold water. His father seems to have been a timid nonentity. But as an employee of a mortuary he strongly influenced his son's fantasies by describing at length interrupting someone having sex with a corpse. Ridgway began to fantasise about this. When he saw his mother sunbathing he had sometimes imagined having sex with her, but now he dreamed of killing her and violating the body.

Like so many serial killers he was sadistic to animals, and once killed a cat by locking it in a refrigerator. He also claimed that, as a teenager, he once drowned a little boy by wrapping his legs around him and pulling him under the water. And later he would stab and injure another small boy, although he was never caught.

Joining the US Navy, Ridgeway was sent to the Philippines, and there began to use prostitutes regularly. They quickly became his lifelong obsession.

He had discovered he enjoyed choking people during a quarrel with his second wife, Marcia, when, on an angry impulse, he wrapped his arm round her neck from behind (a method also used by the Boston Strangler). He released her

259

before she was harmed, but Ridgeway had felt an addictive surge of sexual elation as he throttled her – thus dooming at least forty-eight young women to brutal deaths.

In 1975 Gary and Marcia had a son, Matthew, whom he adored. A resulting religious phase lasted until 1980, when the pair divorced. Yet – despite marriage, son and faith – Ridgeway constantly used prostitutes during this period. He was hooked, so to speak.

He embarked on killing after his divorce. Because he seemed a feeble-looking 'milquetoast', his victims felt no alarm about him, and allowed him to get behind them. He often took them back to his house, had sex, then killed them. Later, he found he preferred to kill them first and have sex with the bodies. He also confessed to revisiting the hidden bodies several times for more sex.

He even admitted to a fantasy – never carried out – of overpowering a prostitute then impaling her with an upright pole inserted into her vagina; a favourite practice of the historical Dracula, also known as Vlad the Impaler.

This apparently innocuous little man was able to carry on killing for many years – partly because he looked so harmless, partly through luck and largely through the general incompetence shown by investigators and the media at the start of the investigation. Detective Reichert emphasizes that Ridgway was full of self-pity, regarding himself as the main and helpless victim of his sinister urges.

On 5 November 5 2003, Ridgway pleaded guilty to 48 murders, and received 48 life sentences.

Leonard Lake and Charles Ng

One thing becomes very clear from the study of serial killers: that defiance and despair are part of the syndrome. The psychologist Joel Norris, the author of *Serial Killers: The Growing Menace*, writes of a killer who had 'reached the final stage of the serial murderer syndrome: he realised that he had come to a dead end with nothing but his own misery to show for it'.

Norris is writing about Leonard Lake, perhaps the most horrific serial killer of the 1980s. He earns this gruesome distinction by a kind of ruthlessness and sadism that seem to belong in the pages of a horror comic.

The murders – of at least twenty-five people – came to light in the summer of 1985. On the afternoon of Sunday 2 June an assistant at a hardware store, South City Lumber, in San Francisco, observed a slight, bespectacled youth walking out of the store with a $75 vice for which he had not paid, and called a policeman. The man – who was obviously Asiatic – was putting the vice in the boot of a car, and when the policeman approached he immediately ran away. An older, bearded man, explained that his companion thought he had already paid for it. The policeman pointed at a hold-all in the car boot. 'What's in there?' 'I don't know. It belongs to him . . .' The bearded man opened the hold-all, and revealed a .22 automatic pistol with a silencer. Since this was against the law in California, the policeman told the man that he would have to accompany him to headquarters.

261

There the man offered his driving licence for identification; it was in the name of Robin Scott Stapley. The policeman said he would have to do a computer check, and that the suspect would then have to post bond before he could be released. The man asked if he could have a glass of water, and when one was provided put a plastic capsule into his mouth, swallowed and drank it down; seconds later, he slumped forward. His interrogators at first assumed he had suffered a heart attack; but in hospital it was discovered that he had taken a cyanide capsule. Belying cyanide's reputation as an 'instant killer', the man took four days to die.

Meanwhile, the computer check had revealed that he was not Robin Stapley; the latter was a twenty-six-year-old who had been missing for months. A further check revealed that, soon after Stapley had been reported missing, his pick-up truck and trailer had been involved in a minor accident in San Francisco. The slight, Chinese youth who had been driving said he took full responsibility for the accident, and that there was no need to report it, but the driver whose goods vehicle had been grazed had to report it under his company's rules. The pick-up truck then proved to belong to the missing Robin Stapley. By this time, the Chinese youth and the truck had vanished.

The car the two men had been driving proved to be registered in the name of Paul Cosner. Cosner had also been reported missing. He had told his girlfriend that he had sold the car to a 'weird-looking man' who would pay cash, and had driven off to deliver it; no-one had seen him since. When forensic experts examined the car, they discovered two bullet holes, two spent bullets, and some bloodstains.

In the pockets of the man who had died from cyanide poisoning police found bills made out to 'Charles Gunnar', with an address near Wisleyville, in Calaveras County, 150 miles north-east of San Francisco. The sheriff there, Claude Ballard, was able to tell the investigators that Gunnar owned a small ranch, and that he lived with a young Chinese named

Charles Ng (pronounced Ing). In fact, Ballard had already been checking on the two men. They had been advertising various things for sale, such as television sets, videos and articles of furniture, and Ballard had suspected they might be stolen. However, checks on serial numbers had come to nothing. What was more ominous was that Gunnar had offered for sale furniture belonging to a young couple, Lonnie Bond and Brenda O'Connor, explaining that they had moved to Los Angeles and had given him the furniture to pay a debt. No one had heard from them since. At a nearby camp site, another couple had simply vanished, leaving behind their tent and a coffee pot boiling on the stove.

By now, a check on the dead man's fingerprints had revealed that he had a criminal record – for burglary and grand larceny in Mendocino County – and had jumped bail there. His real name was Leonard Lake.

The ranch house, in Blue Mountain Road, proved to be a two-bedroom bungalow set in three acres of land. The sight of the master bedroom increased the forebodings of the detectives; hooks in the ceiling and walls, and chains and shackles found in a box, suggested that it might be some kind of torture chamber. A wardrobe proved to contain many women's undergarments and some filmy nightgowns. On the hillside at the back of the house there were burnt bones that looked ominously human. In a cinderblock bunker cut into the hillside they discovered more hooks and chains, and walls covered with pictures of girls posing in their lingerie. What was disturbing about this was that the backdrop of many of these showed a forest scene mural that covered one of the walls; they had obviously been taken in the same room. The expression on some of the faces suggested that the girls were not enjoying it.

The grimmest piece of evidence was a filing cabinet full of videotapes. The police slipped one of these – labelled 'M Ladies, Kathy/Brenda' – into the recorder, and found themselves looking at a frightened girl handcuffed to a chair, with a young Chinese – Charles Ng – holding a knife beside her. Then a large, balding man with a beard enters the frame, takes off the handcuffs, shackles her ankles, and orders her to undress. She does so reluctantly, hesitating before removing her knickers. The bearded man tells her: 'You'll wash for us, clean for us, fuck for us.' After this, she is made to go into the shower with the Chinese. A later scene showed her strapped naked to a bed, while the bearded man tells her that her boyfriend Mike is dead.

Two five-hundred-page journals – in Lake's handwriting – left no doubt what had been happening. His obsessive fantasy was to have women as sex slaves – and he was willing to torture and kill to temporarily create his fantasy in reality.

One couple – Brenda O'Connor, her boyfriend Lonnie Bond, and their two-year-old baby – had been invited to the house for dinner; the man and baby had been killed, and Brenda O'Connor had been handcuffed in the chair, while Ng cut off her clothes. On the video she asks: 'Why do you guys do this?', and he tells her: 'We don't like you. Do you want me to put it in writing?'

'Don't cut my bra off .'

'Nothing is yours now.'

'Give my baby back to me. I'll do anything you want.'

'You're going to do anything we want anyway.' Lake's journal commented: 'The perfect woman is totally controlled. A woman who does exactly what she is told to do and nothing else. There is no sexual problem with a submissive woman. There are no frustrations – only pleasure and contentment.'

Other videos showed the girls being raped and murdered; there were also snapshots of dead bodies, and bags of human bones that seemed to have been boiled clean of flesh.

By now police had dug up four bodies from a trench at the back of the house, two of them black. Ng had been seen driving to the ranch with two black men, yet was known to hate Blacks and Hispanics. He had also taken various transients to work at the 'ranch'; now it began to look as if some of them may never have left. Another person who had disappeared was Lake's younger brother Donald, who had failed to return after a visit to his brother in an earlier 'survivalist compound' in Humboldt County.

Two months before Lake's arrest, a San Francisco couple, Harvey and Deborah Dubs, together with their sixteen-month-old son, had vanished from their San Francisco home, and the detective who had looked into their disappearance had been told that a young Chinese-looking man had been seen moving their furniture out of their apartment; by coincidence, the same officer was now working on the Lake case.

Ng was now one of the most wanted men in America, but had not been seen since his disappearance. A few days later, a San Francisco gun dealer who had been repairing an automatic pistol belonging to Ng notified the police that Ng had telephoned him from Chicago asking if he could send him the gun by post. When the gun dealer had explained that it would be illegal to send handguns across state lines, Ng had sworn at him and hung up.

On Saturday 6 July 1985, five weeks after Lake's capture, a security guard in a department store in Calgary, Alberta, saw a young Chinese slipping food under his jacket. When challenged, the thief drew a pistol, and as they grappled he fired, wounding the guard in the hand. The man ran away at top speed, but was intercepted by other guards. It became obvious that he had some training in Japanese martial arts, but he was eventually overpowered. Identification documents revealed that he was Charles Ng. A Canadian court sentenced Ng to four-and-a-half years in prison for armed robbery, but resisted the demand that he should then be extradited to California, on the grounds that California still had a death penalty.

FBI agents flew to Calgary to question him. Ng's story was that he knew about Lake's murders, but had taken no part in them. Ng gruesomely described how Lake had killed car dealer Paul Cosner, whose car he was driving when arrested, and also how Lake had killed two employees of a removal company, one of whom was burnt to death.

FBI agents looking into Ng's background learned that he was the son of a wealthy Hong Kong family. Born in 1961, Ng had been educated at a private school in north Yorkshire, from which he had been expelled for theft. Although Ng was never short of money, he was a lifelong kleptomaniac. He had lived for a while in Preston, Lancashire, then his parents sent him to San Francisco to complete his education. At the age of eighteen, Ng had been involved in a hit-and-run accident, and to escape a jail sentence, he joined the marines. At Kaneoke Air Base on Oahu in Hawaii, he was arrested for thefts of weapons amounting to more than $11,000. He escaped and made his way back to San Francisco, where he met Lake, and became his close companion; they were later arrested on burglary charges in Mendocino County, where Ng was identified as an army deserter.

Convicted on the Hawaii arms theft charges, he spent some time in the Federal Prison at Fort Leavenworth, Kansas. When paroled, he found a job as a warehouseman in San Francisco, and took an apartment there. But he spent much of his time at Lake's 'ranch' at Wisleyville. Comments by Ng's attorney made it clear that Ng liked to think of himself as an anti-social 'outsider'; he boasted of placing cyanide in the salt cellars at the Hawaii air base, dropping heat tabs into mail boxes, and of 'assassinating' a man in California.

Leonard Lake, born in 1946 in San Francisco, had an even more disturbing history. He had been in the marines in Vietnam, as a technician, but was discharged on the grounds of his evident psychiatric problems. Joel Norris's investigation into Lake's background revealed a classic picture of a child rejected by both parents at an early age, and raised by his grandmother, a strict disciplinarian. Both his father and mother came from a family of alcoholics. The grandfather, also an alcoholic, was a violent type who subjected the child to a kind of military discipline. His younger brother Donald, his mother's favourite, was an epileptic who had experienced a serious head injury; Donald practised sadistic cruelty to animals and had tried to rape both his sisters. Leonard protected the sisters 'in return for sexual favours'

From an early age Leonard had displayed the kind of sexual obsession that seems to characterise serial killers. He took nude photographs of his sisters and cousins (allegedly encouraged to do so by his alcoholic mother).

After returning from Vietnam, Lake had, in his own way, settled down. He married and secretly started to make sadomasochistic porno movies – starring himself. Discovery of the latter led to the dissolution of the former. A second marriage did not survive long either; his wife divorced him after being forced to co-star in one too many of Lake's creations. Being thus abandoned by two women must have badly bruised the ego of a man who believed women existed only to fulfil male demands.

As well as a smouldering sexual resentment, Lake shared another characteristic of many serial killers: he lived in a world of fantasy – boasting, for example, of daring exploits in Vietnam when, in fact, he had never seen combat.

He was also skilful in hiding his abnormality, teaching grade school, working as a volunteer fire-fighter, and donating time to a company that provided free insulation in old people's homes. Like the boy-killer John Gacy, he seemed an exemplary citizen; but his outlook was deeply pessimistic. He believed that World War III would break out at any moment, and this is why he had built the bunker – stocked with tinned food – at the ranch. Like other 'survivalists', he often dressed in combat fatigues, and talked of living off the land. As time went on his behaviour had become increasingly odd. In his original 'survivalist compound' in Mother Lode, Humboldt County, the police found maps of the area with crosses marking 'buried treasure' – actually the dead bodies of his victims.

It was at Mother Lode that he had murdered his best friend

from the marines, Charles Gunnar, and assumed his identity. After being forced to flee from that compound because of burglary charges, he had moved on to Wisleyville.

As noted above, Lake's second marriage, to Cricket Balazs, had broken up, but she had continued to act as a fence for stolen credit cards and other items. Lake seems to have loved her – at least he said so in a last note, scrawled painfully as he was dying – but he nevertheless clung to the paranoid notion that women were responsible for all his problems.

In his journal, Lake describes himself 'with death in my pocket and fantasy in my soul'. He daydreamed of a more heroic and violent era – Vikings and Norse sagas – and of having chained girls as sex slaves (the 'cells' in his bunker were built for them). According to Norris, the later journals show increasing disillusionment. 'His dreams of success had eluded him; he admitted to himself that his boasts about heroic deeds in Vietnam were all delusions, and the increasing number of victims he was burying in the trench behind his bunker only added to his unhappiness. By the time he was arrested in San Francisco, Lake had reached the final stage of the serial murderer syndrome: he realised that he had come to a dead end with nothing but his own misery to show for it.'

What happened, we can see, is that Lake went one step further than most sadistic fantasists: instead of merely daydreaming about treating people as soulless sex objects, he translated his fantasies into reality. He murdered men simply for fun, bigotry or just because their continued existence was inconvenient to him. This latter reason seems to have been why he casually murdered babies; an act of brutality that places him beyond even most other serial killers.

But these murders of men and children were usually just on his path to his true goal – the capture of women that he could then try to turn into sex slaves. But when extreme fantasy is brought into contact with reality, it is bound to melt away. Our sense of our own humanity depends on feeling ourselves to be members of society, and on having at least a few close relationships with other human beings. To kill men – including his own brother and his best friend – and to rape and torture women, was bound to cause a sense of revolt in the part of him that still had a capacity for human warmth.

In fact Lake might be seen as having systematically raped his own humanity – deliberately dehumanising himself in order to chase a fantasy that was always just beyond his grasp. After all, it must be remembered that Lake never kept any 'sex slave' for very long. All his female victims eventually proved inadequate to fulfilling the demands of his overheated imagination and were then killed. And in dedicating his life to such extreme fantasy, he ended up destroying much of himself just as he destroyed his victims.

Certainly, even if he had not been arrested, Lake might well have killed himself anyway. If he had chosen to bluff it out in the San Francisco police station, sticking to his story that he was Robin Stapley, he might well have walked out a free man. Yet his journals reveal that he was being eaten away by the darkness that he had made the centre of his life. The time to end a meaningless existence had arrived, and Lake became his own executioner.

And Charles Ng? He remained in Canada after his sentence for armed robbery was served. Under international law, states like Canada which do not have the death penalty do not usually extradite people to countries that might pass such a sentence. But nobody seemed too grief-stricken when, in 1998, Ng was extradited to California. He was convicted of eleven murders – six men, three women and two babies. These figures alone seem to suggest his role: he was the junior partner in the killing. Both Lake and Ng seem to have been mainly obsessed with the female victims – yet it was Lake who usually got to murder the women. Of the twenty-five suspected victims, Ng was the one who was usually given the job of killing the less interesting men and babies.

At time of writing, Ng remains on death row, still fighting to escape his own execution.

Jack Unterweger

Jack Unterweger, poet, dramatist and serial killer, qualifies as one of the strangest criminals of the twentieth century.

From the point of view of law enforcement, his case began on 14 September 1990, when the naked body of a shop assistant, Blanka Bockova, was found on the banks of the Vltava River, near Prague. She had been beaten and strangled with stockings. Although lying on her back with legs apart, a tampon was still in place, and there were no traces of semen. She had been out drinking with friends in Wenceslas Square the previous evening, but had decided not to leave with them at 11.45 p.m. The police were baffled; there were simply no leads.

On New Year's Eve 1991, in a forest near Graz, Austria, nearly 300 miles south of Prague, another woman was found strangled with her pantyhose. She was Heidemarie Hammerer, a prostitute who had vanished from Graz on 26 October 1990. Although fully clothed, there were signs that she had been undressed and then re-dressed after she was dead. Bruises on her wrist suggested she had been tied with rope or handcuffed. Again, no semen was present. Some red fibres found on her clothes were preserved as forensic evidence, as were minute particles of leather, probably from a jacket.

Five days later, a badly decomposed woman was found in a forest north of Graz. She had been stabbed and strangled – again, probably with her pantyhose. She was identified as Brunhilde Masser, another prostitute.

There was another disappearance from Graz on 7 March 1991, a prostitute named Elfriende Schrempf. Her decomposed body was found eight months later, on 5 October, in a forest near Graz. And still the police had no clue to this multiple killer of prostitutes.

When four more prostitutes, Silvia Zagler, Sabine Moitzi, Regina Prem and Karin Eroglu disappeared in Vienna during the next month, it looked as if the killer had changed his location. Although the police claimed there was no established connection between the crimes, the press began to speak of a serial killer. They called him 'the Vienna Courier'.

And at this point, investigators found a vital lead. Ex-policeman August Schenner, retired for five years from the Vienna force, was reminded of the MO of a murderer he had met seventeen years earlier, in 1974. His name was Jack Unterweger, and he was now a famous writer and media personality.

The case dated back to the time when Unterweger was 23. Two women had been strangled. The first, Margaret Schaefer, 18, was a friend of Barbara Scholz, a prostitute, who had turned him in. She told how they had robbed Schaefer's house, then taken her to the woods, where Unterweger had strangled her with her bra after she refused oral sex. He had left her naked and covered with leaves – just as in most of the more recent killings.

The second 1970s victim, a prostitute named Marcia Horveth, had been strangled with her stockings and dumped in a lake. Unterweger was not charged with this murder, because he had already confessed to the first and had been sentenced to life. Nevertheless he had pleaded guilty to the murder of Horveth, claiming that as he was making love to her, he had seen the face of his mother before him. This, apparently, was his reason to kill her. A psychologist diagnosed him a sexually sadistic psychopath with narcissistic tendencies.

Unterweger, a good-looking youth, was the son of a prostitute and an American GI. He was also an illiterate. This was not so surprising because, at 23, he had already been in prison fifteen times for offences like pimping, rape and car theft. Such a life had naturally cut into his school time. But now in prison for life, he set about learning to read and write. He took to literacy so well that he was soon editing the prison newspaper, had started a literary review, and wrotten his autobiography, a book called *Purgatory* (*'Fegefeur'*), which claimed that he was totally rehabilitated, and had killed the prostitutes because he hated his mother.

The book made him an overnight literary celebrity and influential people began to lobby for his release. He was paroled on 23 May 1990, after sixteen years. And he was now a celebrity, who quickly became rich when his book was made into a movie. Since then he had written plays, given readings of his poetry, and been a regular guest on TV talk shows. He habitually wore a white suit and drove expensive cars. Moreover, as a magazine writer, he had even interviewed the police about the 'Vienna Courier', and been critical of their failure to catch him. Could this charming, brilliant new literary celebrity be a serial killer?

As they reviewed the evidence, the Vienna police – and especially a detective called Ernst Geiger, decided the answer had to be yes.

To begin with, when they checked his credit card receipts, to establish his whereabouts at the times of crimes, they learncd that Unterweger was in Graz in October, when Brunhilde Masser was killed. And he was there again in March when Elfriede Schrempf vanished. He was also in Bregenz, where Heidemarie Hammerer was taken, in December and, moreover, resembled the last person with whom she was seen. Unterweger had been in Prague the previous September, and when the police contacted their counterparts in Prague, they learned about the murder of Blanca Bockover. All this seemed beyond mere coincidence. After months of secretly investigating the celebrity, investigators finally decided that it was time to show their hand.

They interviewed Unterweger on 2 October 1991. He denied everything. Moreover, he renewed criticism of the police for their failure to catch the Vienna Courier. Support for him among Viennese intellectuals and his society friends remained strong. (But how could they admit that their enthusiasm for his writing had unleashed a killer on Vienna? Was it not more likely, as Unterweger told them, that the authorities were persecuting this ex-criminal who had now become their scourge?)

Undeterred, investigator Ernst Geiger went on with his search. Prostitutes who had been with Unterweger testified that he liked to handcuff them during sex – which was consistent with some of the marks on the wrists of the Vienna Courier's victims. Police tracked down the BMW that Unterweger had bought on his release from prison, and found in it a dark hair with skin on the root. It was tiny, but using the PCR technique to make multiple copies of DNA, they were able to identify it as belonging to victim Blanca Bockover.

A search of Unterweger's apartment revealed a red scarf whose fibres matched those found on Bockover, as well as a leather jacket, and receipts from California, where Unterweger had gone to research a magazine article on prostitution in Hollywood. It seemed that Unterweger had gone to the LAPD and introduced himself as a European writer researching red light areas. He traveled with police in patrol cars, and was treated as a distinguished guest.

A check with the Los Angeles Police Department revealed that there had been three murders of prostitutes in the five weeks Unterweger was there, while the 'Courier's' activities in Vienna ceased. All three women – Irene Rodriguez, Shannon Exley and Sherri Long – had been strangled with their bras and left out in the open.

It was time to arrest the suspect. In February 1992 a judge signed a warrant. But when the police arrived at his apartment, Unterweger was gone. They learned from his friends that he had gone on holiday with his latest girlfriend, 18-year-old Bianca Mrak, whom he had picked up in a restaurant, and with whom he had been living since the previous December.

It seemed they had gone to Switzerland, and then, when friends tipped him off by telephone that there was a warrant out for him, to New York.

Before leaving Europe, Unterweger had telephoned Vienna newspapers to insist that the police were trying to frame him. He also made an offer: if the officer in charge of the case would drop the warrant for his arrest, he would return voluntarily to 'clear his name'. He had alibis, he said, for all the murders – on one occasion he had been giving a reading of his work.

Unterweger and Bianca moved to Miami, Florida, and rented a beach apartment. But they were running short of money, and Bianca took a job as a topless dancer. Bianca's mother also kept them supplied with money transfers from Europe.

When the police learned about this, they called on the mother, and prevailed on her to inform them the next time her daughter made contact. And when Bianca asked her mother to telegraph more cash to the Western Union office in Miami, two agents were waiting for them. The alert Unterweger spotted them and fled, urging Bianca to go in another direction. But he was caught after running through a restaurant, causing havoc, and out at the back, where an agent with a gun arrested him. When told he was wanted for making a false customs declaration in New York – he had failed to admit his prison record – he looked relieved. But when they added that he was also wanted in Vienna for murder, he began to sob.

Learning that he was also wanted in California, where his semen had been found in one of the victims, Unterweger decided to resist extradition to Europe and opt for trial in Los Angeles. Then he was told that California – unlike Austia – had a death penalty. So he immediately changed his mind.

Back in Vienna, the final outcome was inevitable. The

strength of the evidence against him was overwhelming. As the trial – which began in April 1994 – dragged on for two-and-a-half months – his support among journalists and former admirers began to ebb away. He failed to produce any of the unshakeable alibis he had promised. On 28 June 1994, the jury found him guilty, and he was sentenced to life imprisonment.

US agent Gregg McCrary, who had been actively involved since 1992 as a psychological profiler, advised the Vienna police to keep a suicide watch on Unterweger, since he had frequently boasted that he would never spend another day in prison. They failed to heed his warning. A few hours after being sentenced to life imprisonment, and perhaps with a feeling of grim irony, Jack Unterweger hanged himself in his cell with the cord from his prison jumpsuit.

Andrew Cunanan

In 1994 the Hollywood director Oliver Stone released the movie *Natural Born Killers* – a deliberately shocking story of a young couple that travel around America brutally killing strangers for fun. A satire on the casual attitude towards violence and murder in the media, Stone clearly meant the movie to be controversial, but perhaps he got more than he bargained for.

The very media he was satirizing became almost hysterical over the film, with television and newspaper pundits wailing that it could inspire weak-minded people (not themselves, of course) to become serial killers. On the whole this seems an unlikely possibility; as we've seen in this book, the path to becoming a serial killer usually involves being abused as an adolescent, followed by years of sadistic sexual fantasies – a movie would have to be rather intense to re-create such a downward spiral in those who watched it. But within three years the US was traumatized by a series of killings that seemed as random and heartless as any of those depicted in the Stone movie.

The case started, some believe, when twenty-eight-year-old male prostitute, Andrew Cunanan, began to suspect he had contracted AIDS. He went for a blood test in early 1997, but could not bring himself to collect the results. After that date his friends began to notice that the usually humorous and effervescent Cunanan seemed increasingly depressed –

perhaps because he assumed that he indeed had the fatal disease. Another cause of depression in Cunanan was his jealous fear that two of his former boyfriends, Jeffrey Trail (a former navy officer) and David Madson (a Minneapolis architect) were seeing each other behind his back. In an attempt to soothe his ex-lover's suspicions, Madson invited Cunanan to fly from his home in San Diego to Minneapolis to meet with himself and Trail to talk matters over. The meeting, on 27 April 1997 in Madson's apartment, proved stormy and ended with Cunanan grabbing a meat mallet from a kitchen drawer and beating Jeff Trail's skull in.

It is a mystery just why David Madson – a respected and successful professional – then helped Cunanan to roll the corpse in a rug, and then went on the run with the killer, but he did. The mystery will remain unsolved because Cunanan shot Madson dead and left him in a roadside ditch several days later. Ironically, the revolver Cunanan used had belonged to Jeff Trail.

At this point Andrew Cunanan seems to have decided to live the life of a carefree outlaw, and never made any particular effort to cover his tracks – even leaving photographs of himself in Madson's Cherokee Jeep when he abandoned it in Danville, Illinois, a week after the murder of Jeff Trail.

As he left no diaries, or similar indication to his mental workings, it is a matter of conjecture why Cunanan became a serial killer. However, his next killing almost certainly stemmed from a sick urge to re-enact a scene from one of the sadomasochistic pornographic videos he loved to watch (and had at least once 'acted' in).

After abandoning Madson's Jeep, he walked a few blocks and approached seventy-two-year-old Chicago-based property developer Lee Miglin. Drawing his revolver, Cunanan forced Miglin into the garage of Miglin's home and bound and gagged the old man with duct tape. Then, apparently re-creating a scene from a video called *Target for Torture*, he beat and kicked Miglin, stabbed him several times in the chest with a pair of pruning shears, then slowly sawed the old man's throat open with a hacksaw. Cunanan then crushed the corpse to a pulp with Miglin's own car – driving over it backwards and forwards several times. Then, after stealing some ornamental gold coins from the house, Cunanan simply drove off.

Evidence that movies like *Natural Born Killers* and *Target for Torture* can turn people into serial killers? It would seem more likely that the sort of person who will eventually become a serial killer is highly likely to want to watch sado-masochistic movies. But sadists with no access to such material still become serial killers – so blaming the movies for serial crime is as oversimplistic as blaming wars on Hollywood, because the politicians who declare wars sometimes watch war movies.

The Miglin murder, taking place as it did in a separate state from the first two killings, allowed the FBI to become involved in the case. They realized that they had a very unstable serial killer on the loose (Cunanan had killed the requisite three people to earn this categorization). The federal authorities issued a nationwide police alert and placed Cunanan at the top of the Ten Most Wanted list. Yet he avoided all attempts to catch him, either through incredible luck or, more likely, grotesque police bungling. Cunanan certainly wasn't making much effort to avoid detection, driving Miglin's stolen, blood-spattered Lexus all the way to New Jersey before dumping it to get a new vehicle.

To do this he murdered forty-five-year-old William Reece – a harmless grounds-keeper at the Finn's Point Cemetery, near Pennsville. It seems that Cunanan arrived at the cemetery, abandoned the Lexus and then approached Reece and asked for an aspirin and a glass of water (both were found spilled next to the body). Following him into the ground keeper's lodge, Cunanan shot Reece dead and stole his Chevy pick-up truck. Then he drove to Florida.

It seems certain that Cunanan pre-planned his next killing –

that of the high-flying fashion designer Gianni Versace. At fifty, Versace was at the top of his profession and counted international idols like Princess Diana among his closest friends. When it was later discovered that, some years before, Versace had met Cunanan at a San Francisco party, some wondered if the homosexual fashion designer and the gay toyboy had been lovers, but there is no evidence to back this conjecture. For whatever reason Andrew Cunanan had decided to kill Versace, it doesn't seem to have been a crime of passion.

For two months Cunanan wandered about Miami quite openly, keeping an eye on Versace's favourite clubs and restaurants.The fact that the Miami police failed to pick Cunanan up in this time is a matter of considerable embarrassment to the department, especially as it was quickly realized – as soon as Reece's abandoned Chevy was found – that the killer might be at large in the city.

On the morning of 15 July 1997, Cunanan finally caught sight of Gianni Versace outside his Miami mansion. As the designer went to open the gate, Cunanan stepped up behind him and shot him twice in the head, killing him instantly.

This was to be Cunanan's last murder. He went into hiding as hundreds of law officers and FBI agents flooded the city to hunt for him. Eventually, eight days after the Versace killing, he was discovered hiding in a luxury houseboat by the caretaker. Before the police could capture him, however, Cunanan shot himself in the temple with Jeff Trail's revolver. Some experts believe that Cunanan went on his killing spree because he thought he was dying of AIDS. While it remains uncertain just what it takes to turn a person *into* a serial killer, it is clear that fear of retribution is the main break that *stops* many borderline sadists from becoming habitual killers. Perhaps, with that brake removed – thinking he had nothing left to lose – Andrew Cunanan gave in to his dark temptations. Ironically, although it has never been officially confirmed, it is rumoured that the AIDS test carried out during Cunanan's autopsy proved negative. If true, he might have never become a serial killer if he had had the courage to collect the results of his blood test earlier in the year.

Dr Harold Shipman

In September 1998 police arrested Manchester general practitioner (GP) Harold Frederick Shipman, on suspicion of murder. At the time, even investigators found it hard to convince themselves that this pleasant-mannered man, with a practice of over 3,000 patients, could be a killer. But as the evidence mounted, they began to suspect that he was actually the most ruthless serial killer in British legal history.

It is clear from what we know about his life and background that Shipman was not one of those people who impress others with their vitality and charisma. On the contrary, he seemed a rather quiet and colourless little man. Born in Nottingham in 1946, he struggled out of his dull working-class background because he wanted to live up to the expectations of his mother, Vera, for 'Fred' was her favourite, and she deeply believed in him. When she died of cancer when he was seventeen, he felt he had to justify her belief in him, and in spite of an initial failure, got into Leeds University Medical School, where he was a less than brilliant student.

His problem was always a certain lack of self-belief. At medical school he remained a loner, without close friends and without even that indispensable appendage of the randy medical student, a girlfriend.

Then came the event that transformed his life. On the bus that took him to medical school every morning, he noticed a plump, quiet girl among the teenagers. Primrose Oxtoby was a 'plain Jane', who was completely under the thumb of her parents. They were so strait-laced that they would not even allow her to attend a youth club – and Primrose would never have dreamed of trying to assert herself. She was three years his junior, and when he realized that she regarded him with wide-eyed admiration, he was hooked. Because she adored him, this quiet, shy virgin became an addiction. Unfortunately, soon after she surrendered her virginity, she discovered she was pregnant. They married in 1966, but her parents were so shocked that they disowned her. Shipman later admitted her pregnancy was 'a mistake'. But it was a mistake he had to live with. The daydreams of a great career in medicine were over. Primrose was not even a very good housekeeper – police who later came to search their house were shocked by the dirt and general untidiness. There were three years in which he was a junior houseman in Pontefract General Infirmary. It was dull, grinding work, and by now there was a second baby. His first professional appointment, in March 1974, was in the small town of Todmorden, in the Pennines. And it was there he became a drug addict. He claimed later that he began taking pethidine, a morphine derivative, because of a back injury.

Whether the excuse was true or not, Shipman certainly found that pethidine made life seem brighter and more bearable. He obtained the drug by forging prescriptions, and overprescribing it for patients who needed it and keeping the extra. One year later, Dr John Dacre, a senior partner in the practice, checked the prescriptions and asked Shipman what was happening. Shipman confessed, and begged for a second chance. This was denied him, and at his trial for forging prescriptions in February 1976, he was temporarily suspended and fined £658. Primrose had to return to live with her disdainful family.

And it was probably after his drug habit had been exposed that he turned into a killer. At least one man in Todmorden, the husband of Eva Lyons – who was dying of cancer – believed that Shipman injected his elderly wife with an overdose of morphine as a mercy killing. Soon thereafter, eight more elderly patients were found dead after Shipman had been to see them.

It was a year later, in 1977, that Shipman became a member of the Donnybrook House practice in Hyde, in Greater Manchester, an area made notorious by former resident Ian Brady.

By this time he had developed the characteristics of a male whose attempts to express his dominance have always been frustrated: touchiness and swollen self-esteem. He enjoyed bullying, and taking it out on those over whom he had authority. He was brutal to a young female drugs representative, out on her first assignment, and browbeat her until she was in tears. When a receptionist forgot his coffee, he went white with rage. When his wife rang him to say that they were hungry and waiting to eat dinner he snapped: 'You'll wait until I get there.'

Oddly enough, his patients felt that he was the ideal doctor – caring, patient and endlessly helpful. But then, a man of Shipman's immense self-centredness and ruthlessness would be a good doctor, for it was important to be liked and admired. But for those who had nothing to contribute to his self-esteem, he could scarcely bring himself to be polite.

Shipman came under suspicion after the sudden death of an elderly patient, Kathleen Grundy, on 24 June, 1998. Mrs Grundy had apparently left a will in which her considerable fortune – over £300,000 – was left to her doctor, Harold Shipman. But the will was carelessly typed, and two witnesses who had also signed it would later explain that they had done so as a favour to Dr Shipman, who had folded the paper so they could not see what they were signing. Mrs Grundy's daughter, Angela Woodruff, reported her suspicions to the police. Detective Inspector Stan Egerton noted that this looked like a case of attempted fraud. But could it be more than that? The death rate among Shipman's patients, especially elderly women, was remarkably high, but there seemed to be no other cases in which Shipman had actually benefited from the death of one of them, at least not in their wills. (But when he was finally arrested, police found a large quantity of jewellery – around £10,000 worth – which was fairly obviously taken from dead patients.) In fact, the above-average death rate had been noted by one of Shipman's colleagues, Dr Linda Reynolds. In 1997, she had realized that Shipman seemed to have been present at the deaths of an unusually high number of patients – three times as many as might have been expected – and reported her suspicions to the local coroner. This all came to nothing because there seemed to be no reason why a popular GP should kill his patients.

Mrs Grundy's body was now exhumed, and the post-mortem showed that she had died of an overdose of morphine. (This is easy to detect because it remains in the system for a long time after death.) After that, another fourteen exhumations of Shipman's patients revealed the same thing. Moreover, it was clear that these fifteen were only a small proportion of the victims. When he was questioned on suspicion of fifteen murders, Shipman angrily denied any wrong-doing, sure that he had covered his trail so carefully that he was safe. But the investigators soon discovered that he had made extensive changes in his patients' records to make them seem more ill than they actually were. He was almost certainly unaware that the computer registered automatically the date and time of every one of these changes.

On 7 October 1998, Shipman was full of self-confidence when he was interviewed by the police and confronted with evidence of his crimes. But when a woman detective constable began to question him about changes he had made in the patients' records, pointing out that many of them had been made within minutes of the death of the patient, he began to falter and flounder. That evening he broke down and sobbed. Yet there was no confession. From that moment onwards, he simply refused to co-operate during interviews, often sitting with his back to the interviewer and refusing to speak.

In most cases of serial murder, there is a clear sexual element. Where Shipman was concerned, however, the only hint of a possible sexual hang-up can be found in the case of seventeen-year-old Lorraine Leighton, who went to see him about a lump in her breast. In her case Shipman abandoned the kindly, sympathetic manner that endeared him to so many patients, and made such rude comments about the size of her breasts that she fled the surgery in tears.

One thing that seems clear is that Shipman felt no guilt about killing his patients. After his imprisonment, someone said something that implied a comparison with Myra Hindley, and Shipman snapped: 'She is a criminal. I am not a criminal.' He was given fifteen life sentences for murdering fifteen of his elderly patients by injecting them with lethal doses of diamorphine (medical heroin). Yet a government report later concluded he possibly murdered between 215 and 260 people over the twenty-three-year period of his general practice.

Statistically speaking, Shipman had 236 more in-home patient deaths than would normally be expected for an average doctor working in the areas that he did. Unfortunately, as Shipman was found hanged in his cell on the morning of 13 January 2004, and disinterment and effective forensic autopsies on so many bodies is practically impossible, we will probably never know just how many people Harold Shipman murdered. Why he became a murderer is also difficult to comprehend. Unlike most serial killers, there seems to have been no sexual or sadistic element to Shipman's murders: he killed most of his victims in their own homes, convincing them that he was giving them a normal, harmless drugs injection, soothing them before administering the fatal dose with his most gentle bedside manner and, as often as not, a nice cup of tea. But these were definitely not mercy killings: although all his known victims were elderly, few were actually seriously ill or even in particular discomfort.

287

As Shipman is now dead, apparently leaving no confession or diaries, we can only guess at why he killed. One possibly important fact may be that Shipman, at the age of seventeen, had watched his mother die of lung cancer. He would hurry home from college to comfort and chat with her, but it was only a daily injection of morphine, given by her GP, that visibly eased her pain.

Was Shipman masochistically re-enacting his mother's own death each time he injected a lethal dose of diamorphine into an elderly patient? Given his character, it seems more likely that he simply enjoyed the godlike power of handing out death. To him his victims, like everyone else in his life, lived and died for the sole purpose of feeding his bloated ego.

John Muhammad,
the 'Washington Sniper'

On 2 October 2002 James D. Spring, a program analyst at the National Oceanic and Atmospheric Administration, was crossing a car park in the Weaton district of Washington DC. There was the crack of a gunshot and Spring fell to the ground; he had been shot dead by a single, high-velocity rifle bullet. It was immediately plain to investigators that this was no ordinary murder – even in crime-ridden DC, police rarely see murders by sniper fire. The high-velocity rifle is a specialist weapon, not the sort of gun used in gang drive-by shootings: whoever had killed James Spring had done so expertly with a single shot, suggesting either military or paramilitary training. Given the events of 11 September, just over a year before, some officers feared that the murder had been a terrorist incident.

Over the following twenty-four-hours – between 3 and 4 October – five more DC residents were killed by long-range sniper shots. James Buchanan, aged thirty-nine, was killed while cutting the grass at a car dealership in the White Flint area. Prenkumar Walekar, a fifty-four-year-old taxi driver, was killed as he filled up with petrol at a station in the Aspen Hill area. Sarah Ramos, a thirty-four-year-old mother, was killed while reading a magazine on a bench outside a post office in the Silver Spring district. Lori Ann Lewis-Rivera, twenty-five, was killed as she vacuumed her van at a petrol station in Kensington district. The last fatality that grim day was a retired seventy-two-year-old carpenter, Pascal Charlot, who was killed while standing at a bus stop in the inner city – however, he was not the last victim. A forty-three-year-old woman was also shot while crossing a parking lot in Fredericksburg – a town forty miles south of Washington DC – but fortunately she survived. The assassin clearly liked to move about and wasted no time. One harassed police officer grimly commented that his local county homicide rate 'just went up 25 per cent today'. This concentration of murders in such a short period suggested either a terrorist operation or a so-called 'spree killer'. At this stage few police officers thought it likely that they had a serial killer on their hands. The difference between a spree killer and a serial killer is not just one of time, but of motive. Spree killers murder lots of people then, after a few hours, generally turn the gun on themselves. Serial killers are hunters, taking a victim at a time, cautiously, usually over a period of years, not hours. The difference seems to be that serial killers are essentially sadistic perverts (disinclined to risk their liberty, let alone kill themselves) while spree killers are often social misfits who become homicidally violent after suffering a massive nervous break-down. Leaving aside the actual killing, the difference in motivation between a serial killer and a spree killer is as wide as the difference between that of a rapist and a suicide. Panic spread across Washington DC as soon as the story hit the broadcast news: a sniper was stalking the capital and nobody was safe. Some people refused to leave their homes and many didn't dare use self-service petrol stations as these seemed one of the killer's favourite hunting areas. Suddenly DC residents had a horrible taste of what life had been like in Sarajevo during the 1990s Yugoslav civil war. After a few days' pause, the killing began again. A thirteen-year-old boy was shot in the stomach as he got off his school bus in the Maryland suburbs of Washington DC. Surgeons struggled to save his life, but he died of massive internal injuries. The following day the killer returned to the scene of the boy's murder and left a tarot card with the words 'Dear Mr Policeman. I am God' written on it.

On 9 October the sniper once again moved away from the suburbs of Washington DC, killing civil engineer Dean Harold Meyers, fifty-three, at a petrol station in the Virginia town of Manassas. Two days later Kenneth H. Bridges, fifty-three, was shot dead at a petrol station near the town of Fredericksburg. On 14 October the sniper killed Linda Franklin, aged forty-seven, who was shot dead as she and her husband loaded their car outside a shop at the Seven Corners Shopping Center on one of northern Virginia's busiest inter-sections. Ironically, Linda Franklin was an FBI analyst.

On 19 October the sniper attacked what was to be his last victim. A thirty-seven-year-old man was shot once in the stomach as he left a restaurant in the town of Ashland, seventy miles south of Washington. He suffered severe damage to his internal organs, but survived.

Suspicion that the sniper might be an Islamic terrorist seemed partly scotched by the bizarre tarot card note left at a crime scene: no true Moslem would claim to be 'God', not even in jest. More evidence to this effect came in the form of a letter found at the Ashland crime scene. The writer again referred to himself as God, and accused the police of incompetence – adding that it was their fault that five people had had to die. Presumably this indicated that he had expected to be caught after the first two days of his killing spree. The letter demanded a ten-million-dollar ransom to stop the killings and added chillingly: 'Your children are not safe anywhere or at any time.' So the sniper was apparently a murderous extortionist, not an Islamic terrorist.

By this stage the police were, understandably, becoming desperate. In an attempt to pacify the sniper they even complied with a bizarre demand he had made. A police spokesman read the statement 'we've caught the sniper like a duck in a noose' on national television. This was a cryptic reference to a folk tale in which an overconfident rabbit tried

291

to catch a duck, but ended up noosed itself. The sniper evidently wanted the authorities to feel that they were his playthings as much as his murder victims were.

Then, on 24 October, the police caught him . . . or rather, them. There turned out to be two perpetrators working together: John Allen Muhammad, aged forty-one, and John Lee Malvo, aged seventeen, the older Afro-American, the younger Afro-Jamaican. A member of the public had noticed a car parked for a long time in a road stop on the Virginia Interstate Route 70 and had become suspicious. The police were informed and investigated as a matter of routine – having little thought that they were about to catch the Washington Sniper. Muhammad and Malvo were fast asleep in the car, but fortunately the officers did not simply move them on. Closer inspection of the vehicle showed that it had been modified to allow a man to lie inside it and aim a rifle while remaining unseen.

Muhammad, who seems to have done all the actual killing, turned out to have been an ex-US Army soldier who had served in the 1992 Gulf War and had subsequently converted to Islam. Lee Malvo was a Jamaican who lived with Muhammad and evidently regarded the older man as a father figure (nobody has ever suggested there was a sexual relationship between the pair). Both were convicted of murder, extortion and terrorism charges in 2003. Muhammad was sentenced to death and Malvo to life imprisonment without chance of parole.

Why the pair became killers remains something of a mystery. Malvo claims to have been brainwashed by Muhammad, but why Muhammad led the boy on a murder spree remains hard to pinpoint. He was not a militant Islamist, he had no extremist political views, and friends and former colleagues claimed he was always a gentle, quiet man. It seems more likely he was simply a serial killer – a man who had become addicted to murder. Support for this explanation came when it was suggested that the Washington DC killings had not been his first. Investigating police believed that Muhammad was responsible for several as yet unsolved murders.

Zodiac

Between 20 December 1968 and 11 October 1969, an unknown serial killer, who signed his letters to the police 'Zodiac', committed five known murders and seriously wounded two more victims.

On the chilly, moonlit night of 20 December 1968, a station wagon with two teenage lovers was parked in the Vallejo hills overlooking San Francisco. Neither David Farraday nor his girlfriend Bettilou Jensen paid any attention to the white car that drew up and parked about ten feet away. They were jerked out of their absorption by the sound of an exploding gun; as shattered glass from the rear window sprayed into the car, and another bullet ploughed into the bodywork, the girl flung open the passenger door and scrambled out. The boy was following her when the gunman leaned in through the driver's window and shot him in the head. David Farraday slumped across the seat. As the girl ran away, screaming, the man ran after her and fired five times. Bettilou Jensen collapsed before she'd run thirty feet. The gunman then calmly climbed back into his car and drove away. Five minutes later, another car drove past the open space by the pumping station where the two teenagers lay. Its woman driver saw Bettilou sprawled on the ground, but she did not stop. Instead she accelerated on towards the next town – Benica – and when she saw the flashing blue light of a police car coming towards her, she frantically blinked her own lights to attract its attention.

When, three minutes later, the two officers arrived at the pumping station, they found that David Farraday was still alive, but Bettilou was dead. David Farraday died shortly after his arrival in hospital.The case was baffling. The boy's wallet was intact; the girl had not been sexually assaulted. An investigation into the background of the teenage lovers ruled out the theory that some irate rival had shot them; they were ordinary students whose lives were an open book.

On 4 July 1969, the unknown psychopath went hunting again. In a car park only two miles from the place where the teenagers were shot, a twenty-two-year-old waitress named Darlene Ferrin was sitting in a car with her boyfriend, Mike Mageau. Neither paid much attention when, not long before midnight, a white car pulled alongside them; there were several other cars in the park. The car drove away after a few minutes then returned and parked on the other side. Suddenly, a powerful light shone in on them. Assuming it was a police spotlight, Mike Mageau reached for his driver's licence. There was an explosion of gunfire and Darlene collapsed. Moments later, a bullet tore into Mike Mageau's neck. The man turned and walked back to his own car, paused to fire another four shots at them; then drove off so fast he left a smell of burning rubber.

A few minutes later, the switchboard operator at the Vallejo police headquarters received a call; a man's voice told her that he wanted to report a murder on Columbus Parkway. 'You'll find the kids in a brown car. They're shot with a 9 mm Luger: I also killed those kids last year. Goodbye.' When the police arrived at Blue Rock Park, they discovered that the caller had been mistaken in one particular: it was not a double murder. Mike Mageau was still alive, although the bullet had passed through his tongue, preventing him from speaking.

This time at least there were a couple of leads. Four months earlier, Darlene Ferrin's babysitter had been curious about a white car parked outside her apartment. When she asked Darlene about it, the waitress replied: 'He's checking up on me again. He doesn't want anyone to know what I saw him do. I saw him murder someone.' She was able to offer a description of the man – round face, with brown wavy hair, probably middle-aged. When Mike Mageau recovered enough to talk, he described the killer as round-faced with wavy brown hair.

A month later, on 1 August 1969, three local newspapers received hand-printed letters which began: 'Dear Editor, this is the murderer of the two teenagers last Christmas at Lake Herman & the girl on 4th of July . . .' It went on to give details of the ammunition which left no doubt that the writer was the killer. Each letter also contained a third of a sheet of paper with a message in cipher – the writer claimed it gave his name. Each letter contained a different third. He asked that it should be printed on the front page of the newspapers, and threatened that if this was not done, he would go on a killing rampage 'killing lone people in the night'. The letters were signed with the symbol of a cross inside a circle: it looked ominously like a gunsight.

All three letters were published – at least in part and the text of the cryptograms were published in full. Code experts at the Mare Island Naval Yard tried to crack it – without success. But one man – a schoolteacher from Salinas named Dale Harden – had the inspired idea of looking for groups of signs that might fit the word 'kill'.

In ten hours Harden and his wife had decoded the letter. In it the Zodiac said that he preferred killing people to animals because it was so much more fun. He also bragged that he had already killed five people in the San Francisco Bay area. The writer went on to say that when he was reborn in paradise, his victims would then attend him as his slaves. As a result of the publication of the letter, the police received more than 1,000 tips; none of these led anywhere.

But another letter to a newspaper began with the words: 'Dear Editor, this is Zodiac speaking . . .' And went on to offer more facts about the Darlene Ferrin murder that left no doubt he was the killer.

Two months later, on 27 September 1969, a young couple went for a picnic on the shores of Lake Berryessa, thirteen miles north of Vallejo. They were Bryan Hartnell, twenty, and Cecelia Ann Shepard, twenty-two, and both were students at nearby Pacific Union College, a Seventh Day Adventist Institution. They had been lying on a blanket in the warm September sunlight, kissing; then they had eaten their picnic.

At about 4.30, both noticed a man across the clearing; he seemed stockily built and had brown hair. The man vanished into a grove of trees. Minutes later, he emerged again, wearing some kind of mask, and carrying a gun. As he came closer, they saw he had a white symbol on the front of the material that hung down from the hood – a circle with a cross inside it. 'I want your money and your car keys,' said the soft voice inside the hood. Hartnell said he was welcome to the seventy-six cents he had. The man began to talk in a rambling way, explaining that he was an escaped convict. He finally explained that he had to tie them up and produced a length of clothes line; he ordered Cecelia to tie up Hartnell. Then the hooded man tied up Cecelia. They talked for several more minutes, then the man announced: 'I'm going to have to stab you people.' 'Please stab me first,' said Hartnell, 'I couldn't bear to see her stabbed.' 'I'll do just that,' said the man calmly. He dropped to his knees and plunged a hunting knife seven times into Hartnell's back. Sick and dizzy with pain, Hartnell then watched him attack Cecelia.

After the first stab, the killer seemed to go berserk. He stabbed her five times in the chest, then turned her over and stabbed her five more times in the back. When she finally lay still, the man walked over to their car, drew something on the door with a felt-tipped pen, then walked away. A fisherman who had heard their screams found them soon after. They were both alive when the Napa police arrived. The police had been alerted by an anonymous telephone call. A man with a gruff voice had told them: 'I want to report a double murder', and gave the precise location of the 'bodies'. He left the phone dangling.

Cecelia Shepard died two days later without recovering from her coma. But Bryan Hartnell recovered slowly and was able to describe their attacker. The police had already guessed his identity. The sign on the door of their car was a circle with a cross in it.

This time, at least, the police seemed to have a promising clue. The dangling telephone had been located within six blocks of the Napa Police Department, and it held three fingerprints. But a check with records was disappointing: they were not on file.

Two weeks later, on Saturday, 11 October 1969, a fourteen-year-old girl looking out of a window at the intersection of Washington and Cherry Streets, San Francisco, realized she was watching a crime in progress. A stocky man was sitting in the front of a cab across the street, searching the driver. Then the man got out, leaving the driver slumped across the seat, and began wiping the door with a cloth. Then he turned and calmly walked off northwards.

The girl had called her brothers over to see what was happening. As the man walked off, they rang the police department. Unfortunately, the operator who logged the call just before 10 p.m. made one mistake: she described the assailant as a Negro male adult – NMA. The police patrolman who actually passed the stocky man a few minutes later, and asked him if he'd seen anything unusual, allowed him to go.

The police who arrived at the crime scene found the taxi driver, twenty-nine-year-old Paul Stine, dead from a gunshot wound in the head. The motive seemed to have been robbery. Three days later, the *San Francisco Chronicle* received another Zodiac letter. 'I am the murderer of the taxi driver by Washington Street and Maple Street last night, to prove this here is a bloodstained piece of his shirt. I am the same man who did in the people in the North Bay area.' The letter went on to jeer at the police for failing to catch him, and concluded: 'Schoolchildren make nice targets. I think I shall wipe out a school bus some morning. Just shoot out the tyres then pick off all the kiddies as they come bouncing out.' It was signed with a cross in a circle.

The bloodstained piece of cloth proved to be from Paul Stine's shirt tail. The bullet that killed Stine was reported to be from the same .22 that had killed David Farraday and Bettilou Jensen; in fact, it was a .38.

Despite the threats, the murder of Paul Stine was Zodiac's last officially recorded crime. Yet his taste for publicity seemed to be unsated. At 2 a.m. on 22 October, eleven days after the murder of Paul Stine, an operator of the Oakland Police Department heard a gruff voice telling her: 'This is Zodiac speaking . . .' He went on: 'I want to get in touch with F. Lee Bailey . . . If you can't come up with Bailey I'll settle for Mel Belli . . . I want one or the other to appear on the channel seven talk show. I'll make contact by telephone.' The men he referred to were America's two most famous criminal lawyers.

The only one of the two who was available at short notice was Melvin Belli. He agreed to appear on the Jim Dunbar TV talk show at 6.30 that morning. By that time, the news had spread and people all over the bay area were up early to watch it.

At 7.20, a young-sounding caller told Belli that he was Zodiac, but said that he preferred to be called Sam. 'I'm sick. I have headaches.' Bryan Hartnell and the two telephone operators who had actually talked with Zodiac shook their heads; this voice was too young. The caller was eventually traced to the Napa State Hospital and proved to be a mental patient.

Zodiac, meanwhile, kept up his correspondence. In one letter he claimed that he had now killed seven people, two more than Zodiac was known to have killed. And at Christmas, Melvin Belli received a card that began: 'Dear Melvin, this is Zodiac speaking. I wish you a merry Christmas. The one thing I ask of you is this, please help me . . . I'm afraid I will lose control and take my ninth and possibly tenth victim.' Another piece of Paul Stine's blood-stained shirt was enclosed for identification. Handwriting experts who studied the letter confirmed that the writer's mental state seemed to be deteriorating.

Zodiac's correspondence continued. On 24 July 1970, he wrote a letter in which he spoke of 'the Woemen and her baby that I gave a rather interesting ride for a couple of howers one evening a few months back that ended in my burning her car where I found them'. The 'Woemen' that he was referring to was Kathleen Johns, of Vallejo. On the evening of 17 March 1970, a white Chevrolet had pulled alongside her car, and the driver shouted that her rear wheel was wobbling. When she finally pulled in, a 'clean-shaven and neatly dressed man' offered to tighten her rear wheel. But when he had 'fixed' it, and she set off again the rear wheel had spun off. The stranger offered her a ride to a nearby service station. When the man drove straight past it, she realized she was in trouble. 'You know I'm going to kill you?' he said in an oddly calm voice.

Fortunately, she kept her head. When the man accidentally drove onto a freeway ramp, she jumped out and ran, her baby in her arms. As she hid in an irrigation ditch, the man searched for her with a torch. At this point, an approaching truck caught the man in its headlights, and he ran for his car and drove off at top speed. An hour later, as she told her story in a police station, Kathleen Johns looked up at a wanted poster and recognized Zodiac in the composite portrait as her abductor.

When her car was found, it had been burned out; Zodiac had returned and set it alight.

Kathleen Johns had been able to observe Zodiac at close quarters for a longer time than anyone else. Yet even with this new lead, police found themselves unable to trace him. Since that time, the police have received a number of Zodiac letters, a few of which have been authenticated, threatening more murders. But most policemen in the bay area take the view that Zodiac is dead, or that he is in prison outside the state for another crime. But what seems far more probable is that

301

Zodiac decided to quit before his incredible run of luck came to an end.

But the story of Zodiac is by no means at an end. Its latest chapter is perhaps the most bizarre so far. In December 1980, Gareth Penn, a California writer with an interest in cryptography, was told by his father – who worked in the Attorney-General's Office in Sacramento – about a Zodiac letter that had not been publicized. In this one, which included a cypher of thirty-two characters, he suggested that 'something interesting' would be found if the authorities were to place a radian on Mount Diablo, a prominent landmark in the San Francisco bay area. A month later, another Zodiac letter said: 'PS: the Mount Diablo Code concerns radians & # along the radians.' It struck Gareth Penn that, for a man whose letters often suggested that he was little more than a moron, Zodiac must be fairly intelligent to talk about radians. A radian is an angle which is frequently used by engineers.

The simplest way to explain it is as follows: picture a circle, whose radius is made of a piece of black sticking tape. Now take this black sticking tape, and stick it on the outside of the circle. Now it covers an arc whose length is exactly the same as that of the radius. Now draw two lines from the ends of this arc to the centre of the circle. The angle in the centre of the circle – which is 57 degrees, 17 minutes and 44 seconds – is a radian.

Penn was curious about this suggestion. So he went out and bought himself a piece of clear acetate and a marking pen. On the acetate, he drew the angle of a radian. He then laid the acetate on a map of the San Francisco bay area, with the point of the radian on Mount Diablo. He then rotated it slowly, to see what would happen. When the upper arm of the radian passed through the site where Darlene Ferrin and Michael Mageau had been shot, he felt 'as if a ton of bricks had fallen' on him. For the lower arm of the radian passed neatly through the spot on the Presidio Heights where the last victim, taxi driver Paul Stine, had been shot.

He suddenly realized why the last victim was so completely different from the other six. Zodiac had *wanted* to kill someone at that particular spot in the Presidio (an area of parkland given over to the military): because it would fall on the lower line of his radian. In other words, Zodiac was killing with some purely geometrical plan in mind. In a book called *Times 17*, in which he describes these experiences, Penn writes: 'I don't believe in psychic phenomena, but I suspect that there are subjective experiences which give the impression of ESP. I had one that evening. All of a sudden, there was no sound. Other people were talking in the next room, but I couldn't hear them. The children stopped making noise with their new Christmas toys. The clock stopped ticking. The blackness of the night outside the windows congealed into a sluggish liquid that seemed to ooze through the glass, slowly filling up the room; it was frigid; the cold was not uncomfortable – it was just there. I was transported into someone else's head, someone whose evil I could sense the way I could sense the coldness of the black ooze that filled the room. I was looking out through his eyes, but I didn't know where I was or what I was seeing. All I knew was that I felt utterly dirty. I was disgusted and fascinated at the same time. What an incredible feeling he must have had, to have this knowledge all to himself all these years! Can you imagine what it must feel like to be the sole knower of such a secret?

'It wasn't just that he was a murderer. It was that he had made an orderly, intellectual design appear to be the product of lunacy, and no one had recognized it for what it was – that was his biggest secret. He had had it all to himself until now, and I was sharing it with him. I had the eeriest feeling, one which I still have six years later, of being one of only two people on this planet.'

Naturally, his first action was to go to the police. Captain Ken Narlow, the only original Zodiac investigator still on the job, was certainly interested in this discovery, and so was the *San Francisco Chronicle*. Penn asked the *Chronicle* to make quite sure that they did not mention his name if they used this information. He didn't want his family to become a target for the Zodiac killer.

He told the *Chronicle* reporter something he had noticed and that the reporter said he had noticed too: all the places where Zodiac had murdered people were connected with water. The first two victims had been parked near a water pumping works. The next two had been murdered near Blue Rocks Springs. The next two had been stabbed close to a lake. And the taxi driver's cab had been left parked next to a fire hydrant.

Penn discovered an interesting thing about this last murder. The murder weapon had been a .38. In his trip-book, Paul Stine had made a note saying that he was to take his passenger to the corner of Maple and Washington. In fact, the cab was found a block away, by the fire hydrant, at Cherry and Washington. In the letter in which he admitted murdering Paul Stine, Zodiac had stated that the place was Maple and Washington – as Stine had written.

Penn went to the scene, to see if he could understand the contradiction. Then he realized that the block between Maple and Cherry on Washington Street is the 3800 block – that is to say, every house number in that block begins with 38. Zodiac had shot Paul Stine with a .38. Yet he had asked him to stop his taxi a block further on – by a fire hydrant. Again, Zodiac was playing his peculiar and obsessive mathematical game.

In that case, what was the significance of water in the 'cipher'? Was it possible that Zodiac's name was Waters, or Goldwasser, or Dellacqua?

There was another, even simpler possibility. The formula for water is H_2O. The simple way to write this would obviously be HOH. Could this be the initials of the murderer? A new lead was suggested by one of his friends. The construction of gigantic geometrical figures on the landscape, like the Nazca lines in Peru, or the Cerne Giant in England, is known as Earthform Art. Zodiac's gigantic radian

304

with its apex at Mount Diablo suggested that Zodiac himself might be interested in Earthform Art. This seemed to be confirmed by the fact that one of his communications was on a postcard whose stamp showed a view of the earth from space taken by Apollo 9.

In the Napa library, Penn consulted a biographical directory of artists. What he was looking for was a sculptor whose initials were HOH. He went through the Hs first, looking for someone with a name like Habakkuk Oliver Henderson. He found only one name listed that fitted the initials. And it advised him to look under another name in the dictionary.

Now at this point it must be explained that Gareth Penn actually names the person he is speaking about. And in his book, *Times 17,* he goes on to accuse that person of being Zodiac. His book was privately printed in 1987 and is certainly known to the man whom we shall call HOH. In writing about him in this way, Penn was almost inviting a suit for libel and defamation of character. Yet the person he names has ignored the book – so that now, under the Statute of Limitations, it is no longer possible for him to take legal action. For obvious reasons, I shall continue to refer to his suspect simply as HOH.

Penn turned to the cross reference elsewhere in the dictionary. What he found was an account of a Jewish sculptress who was born in 1907, and was therefore in any case too old to be the Zodiac killer, but the entry mentioned that she had married in 1938, and had one son – whose initials were HOH.

Now admittedly, all this sounds so absurd that it is difficult to take it seriously – rather like the cranks who attempt to prove that the plays of Shakespeare were written by Francis Bacon by digging out complicated ciphers from the Shakespeare plays and poems. It will be up to the reader to decide whether Gareth Penn is a wild crank, whose obsession with cryptography has led him to accuse an innocent man. But first, we need to tell the rest of the story. What Penn demonstrates very convincingly is that Zodiac has a mind very like his own – obsessed by cryptographs. (Gareth Penn is a member of MENSA, an organization whose members – in terms of IQ – are among the top 2 per cent of the population.) The result is that much of his long book is concerned with numbers and codes. To discuss even half of these would be quite impossible. What follows is simply intended as a brief sample, to give the reader a taste of Penn's method of argument.

Penn quickly noticed that Zodiac seemed to be obsessed by the word 'time'. He also noticed that on the map which had accompanied the Mount Diablo letter, Zodiac had written a series of numbers corresponding to those on a clock face. On the letter to Melvin Belli, there was a message: 'Mail early in the day', together with a clock face. At the scene of his first crime – of which we shall speak in a moment – Zodiac left behind a man's Timex watch stopped at 12.22. In his letters he harped on the word 'time'. One extract read: 'When we were away from the library walking, I said it was about time. She asked me: "About time for what?" I said it was about time for her to die.' In a letter to the *Examiner* Zodiac talked of his killings as 'good times'. Then he asked if the police were having a 'good time' with his cipher. His favourite correspondent was the *Chronicle* – meaning a record of time. A letter that came to be called 'The Confession' was addressed to the *'Daily Enterprise,* Riverside, Calif, Attn: crime'. Noting that the name of the paper is not the *Daily Enterprise* but the *Riverside Press-Enterprise* and that the newspaper has no crime department, Penn observes that the address contains precisely thirty-eight letters. The first sentence of his early cryptogram letter is: 'I like killing people because it is so much fun.' Again thirty-eight letters. Zodiac had, of course, killed the taxi driver with a .38.

The letter to Melvin Belli was addressed to '228 MTGY' – an abbreviation for Montgomery. But Belli did not live at 228, but at 722. Penn observes that the number 722 and 228 have something in common – both are exact multiples of 38. Penn found himself wondering how someone who wanted to express ideas – or names – in numbers would translate letters into figures. One obvious way would simply be to number the letters of the alphabet, so that A was one, B was two, and so on. Another way would be morse code. And the obvious way of writing morse code would be to use Os for the dots and Is for the dashes. Penn tried writing the word 'time' in this code, and then calculated that, as a binary number (binary code, of course, uses only Os and Is) it added up to 38. One of the few letters that had a return address simply had the letters 'R.P.' in morse code. Again, these add up to 38.

When Gareth Penn succeeded in getting hold of a biographical summary of his suspect HOH, he discovered that he had been at a well-known east coast university. He had majored in architecture, and his extra-curricular activities included editorship of a magazine whose title included the number 38. (He also proved to be a member of the Harvard Rifle Team.)

Zodiac also seemed to attach some importance to the number 17. A letter to the *Los Angeles Times* ends with the figure '17+'. One of his letters to the *Chronicle* has a code 'Fk. I'm crackproof'. F is the sixth letter of the alphabet and K is the eleventh, and together they add up to 17. But what does 'times' and '17' mean? Penn wrote out the phrase 'times 17' in morse code – using Os and Is. The figure he obtained was 9745. In American chronology, this could be read as 7 September 1945. He suddenly recalled that HOH's mother had been born in Poland on 7 September 1907. On 7 September 1945, she had celebrated her thirty-eighth birthday. Penn came to the conclusion that 'times 17' is a disguised form of her thirty-eighth birthday. These two figures would seem to explain Zodiac's curious obsession with 17 and 38.

The total number of stab wounds inflicted on Bryan Hartnell and Cecelia Shepard add up to 17. This murder differs from the others in many respects. This is the only murder in which Zodiac wore a hood over his head, with his sign, the cross in the circle, inscribed on it. The day of this murder was the twenty-sixth birthday of Penn's suspect HOH. At that date, his age in days was precisely 9745 – the date at which his mother was thirty-eight. Although the police and the *Chronicle* soon lost interest in Penn's Zodiac researches – no doubt feeling that all this was little more than a game with numbers – many other people were interested.

Penn admits that he had one major problem. His suspect still lived on the east coast, in the city where he had been to university. The east coast is 3,000 miles away from the west coast of America. So it seemed highly unlikely that the San Francisco Zodiac killer lived on the east coast. Penn admits: 'If it turned out that he didn't look like the Zodiac, write like the Zodiac, or have a history of travel to California during the Zodiac episode, then it was high time for me to stick my head in a bucket of cold water.'

And at this point the *San Francisco Chronicle* revealed Penn's identity. A reporter named Bill Wallace described the discovery of the radian design on the map, and said that it had been advanced by Gareth Penn, a resident of Napa County.

Penn angrily rang the *Chronicle,* and was told that he was paranoid to be so worried. Apart from that, he was not able to get any kind of apology – or even explanation – out of the *Chronicle*.

Five days later, Penn was sitting up late, reading. At exactly half past one in the morning, the phone rang. When he picked it up, there was merely a dialling tone. Moments later, the phone rang again. Again, just a dialling tone. 'I didn't need to speak to the caller to know who it was,' Penn records. In fact, Penn had been rash enough to drop some postcards – hinting at his discoveries – to his suspect's address on the east coast. They would be franked with the Napa County postmark. Now his suspect knew exactly who he was. Soon after, he was told that his suspect had complained to the FBI about the postcards. Penn was summoned to the FBI office in San Francisco. The official told him that they had received a complaint about 'what might be construed as extortionate communications'. Had Penn ever demanded money from his suspect?

Penn explained his reasons for believing that HOH was the Zodiac killer. The official told him that they did not believe this could be so, because they had psychological profiles that said so. HOH had a PhD, had taught for seven years at another major educational institution, and was now a Cabinet-level official in the government. He was married – and psychological profiles said that serial killers did not marry. (Penn was later able to list a number of serial killers who were married.)

Penn and the FBI parted on good terms. Penn sent them his material on his suspect, but heard no more. On 22 June 1981, his phone rang again at exactly 1.30 p.m. The caller asked: 'Is Jim there?' Penn said no, he must have the wrong number. At three in the morning, Penn looked out of his window, and saw that the whole eastern side of the mountains around the Napa Valley were in flames. Subsequently, aeroplanes came and discharged water onto the fire. At exactly 1.30 p.m., his phone rang again, and again the voice asked: 'Is Jim there?' When Penn said he had the wrong number, the caller said: 'Oh,' and hung up. Later, it was discovered that the fire had been started deliberately by an unknown arsonist, who had planted a string of bombs. There were nine altogether, containing timers. The timers had been set to go off at 1.30 p.m. Understandably, Penn felt that whoever had set the bombs to go off at 1.30 was also the individual who had been calling him up so persistently at exactly 1.30. All this still left the major objection: Penn's suspect lived on the east coast, and the Zodiac murders took place on the west coast. He persuaded a friend to call up his suspect's ex-wife, on the pretext of doing a credit check. He managed to learn from her that her husband had been commuting regularly to California in late 1969 – the period of the Zodiac murders. Immediately after this phone call, HOH himself rang the friend back, said that he did not have to go to his wife to get details about his career, and offered to send him

309

a CV which would fill in the details of his life. In fact, when this résumé arrived, it claimed that the job that took him to California ended in 1968. Penn was able to disprove this by getting hold of some papers written by his suspect as late as 1970 in which he claimed that he was still working for this firm.

One of the Zodiac postcards of 1971 was an artist's drawing of a condominium project on the east shore of Lake Tahoe, Nevada – within easy reach of California. Penn now learned that his suspect had been working on this project at the time of the postcard.

Penn's collaborator managed to get hold of photographs of the suspect, and some handwriting samples. The handwriting was strikingly similar to that of Zodiac – in *Times 17* Penn prints several pages, comparing the two. Similarities are certainly striking. And the picture of the suspect was also strikingly similar to the composite picture of the Zodiac drawn from the descriptions of those who had seen him face to face.

Penn is convinced that Zodiac committed two more murders, apart from those with which he credited himself. On 30 October 1966, a girl called Cheri Jo Bates drove up to the Riverside City College library, and parked her VW Beetle outside. When she came out, it would not start. A man approached her and offered her a lift. She accepted. On the pretext of walking her to where his car was parked, he lured her three blocks away into an alley where he struggled briefly with her, pinned her to the ground, and cut her throat from ear to ear. He left a Timex watch, set at 12.22 at the side of the body.The wristband was broken, so it looked as if it had come off accidentally during the struggle. A month later, he sent the letter now labelled 'The Confession' to the *Press-Enterprise* that said: 'Miss Bates was stupid. She went to the slaughter like a lamb.' Five months later, another letter was sent in triplicate to the same newspaper, the police and the girl's father. It read: 'Bates had to die. There will be more.' The

310

copy addressed to Cheri Jo Bates's father was signed 'Z'. But the Z was made to look a little like the Arabic numeral 3.

Penn turned the name 'Bates' into morse code, and found that it added up to 1072. Then he turned the word 'death' into morse code – it also added up to 1072. This seemed to be what the writer meant by 'Bates had to die'. Her name was death. A more recent cipher letter, of thirty-two characters, and ending with the Greek letter omega, has led Penn to believe that Zodiac was also responsible for the murder of a twenty-six-year-old Harvard graduate student called Joan Webster, who disappeared from Boston's Logan Airport terminal on 28 November 1981. Penn believes that the Greek letter omega –the last of the alphabet – is intended as an indication that this is the last of the Zodiac murders.

Times 17 is a bewildering and baffling book, yet it is argued with clarity that leaves no doubt that Gareth Penn is a sane and balanced individual whose experiences have convinced him that he has discovered the identity of Zodiac. The main objection to the book is that it involves so much analysis of numbers and ciphers that the average reader will find it totally confusing. Ronald Knox once satirized the 'Shakespeare cipher' enthusiasts in an essay in which, by analysing Tennyson's 'In Memoriam' he was able to prove, by rearranging the letters in some of its most famous lines, that it was actually written by Queen Victoria. So the sceptical reader will certainly be inclined to feel that it is possible to prove almost anything in this way. On the other hand, it seems fairly clear that Penn was not simply imagining it all. It seems clear that, whether his suspect is the Zodiac killer or not, he certainly entered into the spirit of the thing, and began playing a game of intellectual hide and seek with his tormentor. Only one thing is certain: that when Penn writes, 'I can guarantee that you will find this book to tell one of the strangest stories that you have ever read,' he is telling no more than the unvarnished truth.

Recent developments in this story are as baffling as the

story itself. In 1987, Gareth Penn concluded *Times 17* with this paragraph: 'In publishing the book which you have just read, I have exposed myself to civil and criminal prosecution, to the possibility of assassination, to harassment, to ridicule and scorn. I have stuck to my guns for six years, and now I am throwing down the glove. I appoint you, gentle reader, to be my jury. You have seen the evidence. You have patiently and indulgently listened to my interpretation of that evidence for whatever it is worth. I leave it to you to decide whether the effort, the expense, and the risk were worth it.' He is undoubtedly correct in saying that he has exposed himself to civil and criminal prosecution. Anyone who is publicly accused of being a mass murderer has the right to demand damages. Yet his suspect, HOH, has flatly refused to sue, in spite of being invited to do so several times. In May 1987, a month after *Times 17* was published, Gareth Penn received an invitation from Jerome Maltz, owner of General Broadcasting System in Los Angeles, to appear on no less than seven talk shows. On 29 May Penn appeared on a three-hour talk show hosted by Anthony Hilder. Hilder had the interesting idea of persuading HOH to appear on the talk show in his capacity as an expert on a running dispute involving the City Council. After twenty minutes, Hilder said that he had one last question: was HOH aware of the recent publication of a book by Gareth Penn in which he was accused of having murdered seven innocent people? HOH declined the invitation to debate with Gareth Penn on the air, but he did answer the question as to why he was not suing Penn for libel. He said that he consulted with his lawyers and was told that he could not sue, because he could not prove that he had been damaged. Penn knew enough about the law to know that if a libel takes the form of an accusation of committing a crime, no proof of damage is required.

HOH later called up Jerome Maltz, owner of the station, to complain about the underhand way in which he had been induced to appear on the show. Again, he was asked why he was not suing Gareth Penn. He replied that a lawsuit would be useless, and that an injunction would be unenforceable. Penn took the trouble to consult a number of lawyers. Without exception, he was told that if HOH were to file suit, he could immediately obtain an injunction requiring him not only to cease publishing the book, but to purchase back every copy that had been sold. 'In other words, he could inflict major economic damage on me for nothing more than the cost of his filing fee.' Moreover, if Penn sold a single copy of the book after the injunction had been obtained, he could go to prison.

In a letter to Maltz, HOH explained that one of his fears is that grief-stricken relatives of the Zodiac victims might seek him out for revenge. Penn has commented that the most efficient way of protecting oneself against this kind of thing is to prove the allegation wrong. After all, all that HOH would have to do would be to prove that he was on the east coast for just one of about thirty dates in which Zodiac was clearly on the west coast.

Even stranger, HOH ended his letter by urging Maltz not to 'rush into a retraction'. In short, having been accused on the radio of being a multiple killer, HOH asked Maltz not to make amends.

Two months later, a reporter on the *Boston Herald* called HOH's lawyer to ask for an interview. The lawyer said that he had advised his client not to give interviews. The reporter then called HOH at his summer home. HOH's reply was: 'People write books about bacteria, too, but nobody interviews the bacteria.' He then went on to explain to the reporter that he was not suing Penn because he could not prove that he had been damaged. In fact, the subject of a libel does not have to prove that he has been damaged. If he is accused of a crime, then he has automatically been damaged.

HOH also commented that a lawsuit would be too costly and that the filing fee alone would bankrupt him. In fact, the fee would be well within the range of a tenured academic with two homes.

Pressed further by the reporter, HOH commented: 'Oh, I suppose I could afford to sue him. But I don't have the time, and time is the most valuable thing I've got.' Penn comments that after reading *Times 17,* most readers would find that statement highly significant. On 29 October 1987, the *Boston Herald* published a two-page article headlined 'Author targets lecturer in Zodiac case'. The article included a picture of HOH as he was in 1971, and the artist's impression of Zodiac.

The result was two programmes on radio in Boston, including interviews with Gareth Penn. Still HOH declined to take any kind of action.

In April 1990, the Statute of Limitations for a lawsuit expired in California. A week later, the remains of the Boston student Joan Webster were found in Hamilton. Again, a local paper contacted HOH, raising Penn's allegation that HOH had killed Joan Webster and asking why he was not suing. Once again, HOH explained that he could not prove that he had been libelled.

Two years later, the Statute of Limitations in Massachusetts – where HOH lived and taught – also expired.

Penn concludes his update on *Times 17* by raising the question of why HOH continues to refuse to sue him. His conclusion is that, if anything, HOH is pleased to have been identified as Zodiac. An enormous number of serial killers have written letters to the police – they obviously feel some need to speak about their 'achievement'. But the problem of being an unknown serial killer is that public recognition would also mean being arrested and going to prison. There is a sense then in which, according to Penn, HOH has the best of both worlds. He has been publicly identified as Zodiac, yet he's still at liberty.